Better Homes and Gardens®
Annual Recipes 2012

SKILLET CORN
GRIDDLE CAKES

From the editor

Whether you're looking for a quick weeknight dinner or the perfect menu for a special celebration, you'll find it in the pages of this book.

Although the details of our daily lives may differ, most of us live according to a general rhythm: Weekdays are busy with work, school, lessons, sports, and meetings. On weekends, there may be much of the same, but maybe we have a little extra time at home. In the middle of all of this busyness, we want to live well. We want to feed our families delicious and nutritious food—on a budget—and we want to take time now and then to invite friends over to celebrate a holiday, special occasion, or the specialness of a particular season.

At *Better Homes and Gardens®*, we are well acquainted with this rhythm. We plan the food section of the magazine each month according to it. It is how you live, and it's our job to help you make your life simpler and more enjoyable—and to help you become a better cook. That's why we put all of the recipes and how-to tips from an entire year of the magazine into one volume—so you can simply reach for this book to find the right recipe for the right situation. It's organized by month to make it that much easier.

For those hectic weeknights, look to the Everyday Easy feature. In March, for instance, there is a variety of warming soups and stews to choose from, including Smoky Cheese and Potato Soup (page 73), Southwestern Meatball Chili, and Fast Shrimp Bisque (both on page 71)—all done in less than 30 minutes from start to finish.

For the wallet watchers out there (and who isn't one, really?), there is the Delicious on a Dollar feature. These main dishes, hearty brunch dishes—even appetizers to take to a party—will please palates and help you pinch pennies too.

And for weekends when you can take some time to putter in the kitchen—either for entertaining or simply just to enjoy a wonderful home-cooked meal with your family—there are inspiring recipes from our own Test Kitchen and from a wealth of chefs and expert cooks whose talent we tapped. In February, we feature the fabulous pizzas of bread expert Peter Reinhart; in May, cake decorating expert Karen Tack (of *Hello, Cupcake!* fame) shares her best tricks and techniques for making incredible party cakes; and in July, we conjure up an all-out celebration of American summer with fun new takes on burgers, hot dogs, and cold and creamy milk shakes. (How about a Barbecue Potato Chip Crunch Dog and a Peach Pie Shake?)

No matter the meal or season, we endeavor above all to help you hone your cooking skills so that your time in the kitchen—and what you create there—is fun and fabulous. From our kitchen to yours—enjoy!

Gayle

Gayle Goodson Butler, Editor in Chief
Better Homes and Gardens® magazine

Better Homes and Gardens.
Annual Recipes 2012

Test Kitchen

Our seal assures you that every recipe in *Better Homes and Gardens. Annual Recipes 2012* has been tested in the Better Homes and Gardens. Test Kitchen. This means that each recipe is practical and reliable, and meets our high standards of taste appeal. We guarantee your satisfaction with this book for as long as you own it.

All of us at Meredith Consumer Marketing are dedicated to providing you with information and ideas to enhance your home. We welcome your comments and suggestions. Write to us at: Meredith Consumer Marketing, 1716 Locust St., Des Moines, IA 50309-3023.

Pictured on front cover:
Pistachio-Honey Cake with Berries and Cream, page 79

MEREDITH CONSUMER MARKETING
Vice President, Consumer Marketing: Janet Donnelly
Consumer Product Marketing Director: Heather Sorensen
Consumer Product Marketing Manager: Wendy Merical
Business Director: Ron Clingman
Senior Production Manager: Al Rodruck

WATERBURY PUBLICATIONS, INC.
Editorial Director: Lisa Kingsley
Associate Editor: Tricia Bergman
Creative Director: Ken Carlson
Associate Design Director: Doug Samuelson
Contributing Copy Editors: Terri Fredrickson, Gretchen Kauffman
Contributing Indexer: Elizabeth T. Parson

BETTER HOMES AND GARDENS. MAGAZINE
Editor in Chief: Gayle Goodson Butler
Creative Director: Michael D. Belknap
Senior Deputy Editor: Nancy Wall Hopkins
Editorial Assistant: Renee Irey

MEREDITH NATIONAL MEDIA GROUP
President: Tom Harty

MEREDITH CORPORATION
Chairman and Chief Executive Officer: Stephen M. Lacy

In Memoriam: E.T. Meredith III (1933–2003)

FOOD IS BEST ENJOYED IN SEASON—locally raised if possible—and that's the underlying theme of this year's *Better Homes and Gardens® Annual Recipes*. And from backyard grillouts to big-city restaurants, fresh food enjoyed simply with family and friends is hotter than ever. Need new ideas for asparagus—the surest sign of spring? Or perhaps how-to lessons for creating a cake that's as pretty as it is luscious? If the grill is an extension of your kitchen, this book shows you how vegetables can earn their stripes. Plus time-honored holiday recipes give you everything you need to create a memorable occasion. Whether you're a seasoned pro or a newbie in the kitchen, this book is filled with inspiration, deliciously doable recipes, and practical how-tos.

Look for:

Our Monthly Feature Each chapter highlights recipes befitting the season. Whether it's eating well with the help of Ellie Krieger in January, indulging in warm and gooey chocolate desserts straight from the oven in February, or summer entertaining with a new take on classic all-American burgers, dogs, and shakes, this is THE chapter for delving into a single food topic—like springtime asparagus in March or nature's sweet gift of honey in April. And learn how to create cakes that are a treat for the eyes as well as the taste buds with innovative decorating tricks that turn ordinary ingredients into festive flourishes.

Home Cooking Celebrated cookbook authors and chefs share their passion and expertise with recipes designed to ignite a spark in your cooking repertoire. Scott Peacock gets fresh with sweet corn, Peter Reinhart crafts the perfect pizza, and Jamie Purviance provides expert direction on how to add a savory accent to steak, pasta, and cheese using your backyard grill.

Delicious on a Dollar Recipes that serve up savings without sacrificing flavor is what this feature is all about. You'll find appetizers that match flavor with flair, savory main dishes that feed a hungry family, and desserts that satisfy everyone's sweet tooth—all without breaking the bank.

Everyday Easy After a long day, getting a fresh, home-cooked meal on the table in 30 minutes or less can be a challenge. Everyday Easy recipes use just a handful of ingredients and simple preparation, so you know making a great-tasting meal is doable even on the busiest days.

Hot off the Grill The thrill of the grill has captured the attention of many home cooks and chefs across the country. These tasty recipes feature flavors and techniques to inspire you to think of your grill as another tool in your kitchen arsenal.

Prize Tested Recipes® *Better Homes and Gardens*® readers share their recipes in a monthly contest, and we publish the winners for you to enjoy.

Recipe Icons Helpful recipe icons indicate whether a recipe is Fast (30 minutes or less), Kid Friendly, or Low Fat (see nutrition guidelines on page 335).

OVERNIGHT PULL-APART
CINNAMON LOAF

contents
2012

34

129

137

MINESTRONE
SOUP

PROSCIUTTO-
ARUGULA PANINI

january

A NEW YEAR Please everyone at the table—including yourself—with recipes that are healthy and full of flavor.

17

22

23

BUTTERNUT SQUASH
RISOTTO

A Healthy Touch

"Eating well is the cornerstone of a good life," says nutritionist, cookbook author, and TV personality Ellie Krieger. When she makes dinner for her husband and daughter, she relies on recipes that are filled with nutritious ingredients and flexible enough to make the whole family happy. "It's important to me that everyone sits down to the same meal," she says.

KID FRIENDLY | **LOW FAT**

Butternut Squash Risotto

"This dish is pure luxury, made with the simplest ingredients," Ellie says. "Its decadent creaminess comes from the natural starch of the Arborio rice and the butternut squash puree."

PREP 15 min. COOK 40 min.

- 5 cups low-sodium chicken broth or low-sodium vegetable broth
- 1 Tbsp. olive oil
- 1 medium onion, finely chopped
- 1½ cups Arborio rice
- ½ cup dry white wine
- 1 10-oz. pkg. frozen butternut squash puree, thawed (1⅓ cups)*
- 2 Tbsp. chopped fresh sage
- ½ cup finely shredded Parmesan cheese (2 oz.)
- ½ tsp. salt, plus more to taste Freshly ground black pepper to taste

1. In a medium saucepan heat broth until hot but not boiling. Reduce heat to low; cover to keep warm.

2. In a large saucepan heat oil over medium heat. Add onion. Cook and stir for 6 to 8 minutes until softened but not browned. Add rice; cook and stir for 1 minute. Add wine and simmer about 2 minutes, stirring constantly until it is absorbed.

3. Add ½ cup of the hot broth. Simmer over medium heat, stirring frequently, until it is absorbed. Repeat with the remaining broth, ½ cup at a time, allowing each addition to absorb before adding more, about 30 minutes total. When all the broth is incorporated and the rice is tender and creamy, add the squash, sage, all but 2 Tbsp. of the cheese, the salt, and pepper. Season with additional salt to taste. Garnish with reserved cheese. Serve immediately. Makes 4 servings.

*To make butternut squash puree, wash and halve lengthwise a 1½-lb. butternut squash. Remove seeds. Place, cut sides down, in a baking dish with 2 Tbsp. water. Microwave, covered with vented plastic wrap, for 7 to 10 minutes or until tender, rearranging once. Let stand, covered, 5 minutes. Scoop flesh out of skins; mash until smooth. Measure 1⅓ cups. Reserve remaining squash for another use.

EACH SERVING *415 cal, 7 g fat, 10 mg chol, 784 mg sodium, 70 g carb, 3 g fiber, 11 g pro.*
Make it vegetarian: Use the vegetable broth option as directed.

ITALIAN NIGHT "This is healthy Mediterranean eating at its best and most accessible—the whole meal is good for you, simply prepared, and enjoyed as a family."

FAST

Green Salad with White Beans, Apples, and Walnuts

This hearty salad has walnuts and white beans for protein and gets a crunchy bite from Granny Smith apples, making it a great main dish or side salad.

START TO FINISH **30 min.**

½	cup walnut pieces
3	Tbsp. extra virgin olive oil
1	Tbsp. plus 1 tsp. apple cider vinegar
1	tsp. chopped fresh thyme leaves (¼ tsp. dried)
½	tsp. Dijon mustard
1	medium clove garlic, finely minced Freshly ground black pepper, to taste
1	14-oz. can low-sodium white beans, such as cannellini, drained and rinsed
1	bunch chicory (about ½ lb.) or other hearty lettuce, thinly sliced
½	medium Granny Smith apple, diced

1. In a dry skillet over medium-high heat toast walnuts 2 minutes, stirring frequently, until fragrant; cool. For dressing, in a bowl whisk together oil, vinegar, thyme, mustard, garlic, ¼ tsp. salt, and pepper.
2. In a bowl toss the beans with 1 tsp. of the dressing. In a large bowl combine the chicory with the toasted walnuts, diced apple, dressed beans, and remaining dressing. Toss to coat. Makes 4 (1½-cup) servings.
EACH SERVING *293 cal, 21 g fat, 0 mg chol, 215 mg sodium, 22 g carb, 8 g fiber, 8 g pro.*

KID FRIENDLY | **FAST**

Garlic Breadsticks

"One of my first jobs helping Mom in the kitchen was to slather the Italian bread with butter and sprinkle it with garlic powder," Ellie says. "You can make it even better by mixing a touch of butter with olive oil and using fresh garlic."

PREP **15 min.** BAKE **18 min.**
OVEN **350°F**

2	Tbsp. olive oil
1	Tbsp. unsalted butter
3	cloves garlic, minced
½	tsp. salt
1	12-oz. loaf whole grain Italian bread
¼	cup finely chopped fresh parsley leaves

1. Preheat oven to 350°F. In a small saucepan combine oil, butter, garlic, and salt. Heat over medium-low heat until butter is melted; remove from heat.

2. Cut the bread in half lengthwise, then cut each half crosswise into 3 pieces. Then cut each piece into four ½-inch-thick sticks. Brush the breadsticks with the garlic-infused mixture, sprinkle with parsley, and place on a baking sheet. Bake until the edges are golden brown, about 18 to 20 minutes. Makes 6 servings.
EACH SERVING *200 cal, 9 g fat, 5 mg chol, 436 mg sodium, 26 g carb, 2 g fiber, 4 g pro.*

FOR ITALIAN NIGHT
Start with a healthful salad and look for easy ways to boost nutrition beyond the typical ingredients. Add thinly sliced red cabbage for crunch, color, and vitamin C. Beans and nuts are delicious and filling proteins that can stand in for high-calorie meat and cheese. Another option is to add crunchy apples in place of croutons. For pasta dishes, cook extra vegetables or beans in with the pasta and opt for tomato- or vegetable-base sauces instead of cream-base ones.

GARLIC BREADSTICKS

GREEN SALAD WITH
WHITE BEANS, APPLES,
AND WALNUTS

MINESTRONE
SOUP

PROSCIUTTO-
ARUGULA
PANINI

SOUP NIGHT "I boost the nutrition with colorful vegetables, whole grains, and beans, and I keep the panini portions small and packed with arugula."

KID FRIENDLY **LOW FAT**

Minestrone Soup

"This mouthwatering meal in a bowl is a case that shows you don't need to lean on salt for flavor when you use lots of herbs—basil, oregano, and parsley—and aromatics such as garlic and onion," Ellie says.

PREP 20 min. COOK 32 min.

1   large onion, diced
2   Tbsp. olive oil
4   cloves garlic, minced
2   ribs celery, diced (½ cup)
1   large carrot, peeled and diced
1   medium zucchini (about 8 oz.),
     diced
1   tsp. dried oregano
1   tsp. dried basil
1   tsp. salt
½   tsp. freshly ground black pepper
6   cups low-sodium vegetable broth or
     low-sodium chicken broth (48 oz.)
1   28-oz. can no-salt-added diced
     tomatoes
1   14-oz. can no-salt-added crushed
     tomatoes
1   15-oz. can low-sodium cannellini
     beans, drained and rinsed
½   cup whole grain elbow pasta
⅓   cup finely shredded Parmesan
     cheese
2   Tbsp. chopped fresh parsley leaves

1. In large soup pot over medium-high heat cook and stir onion in hot oil 4 minutes or until translucent. Add garlic; cook for 30 seconds. Add celery and carrot. Cook and stir 5 minutes until vegetables begin to soften. Add zucchini, oregano, basil, salt, and pepper. Cook for 2 minutes, stirring frequently.

2. Add the broth and the diced and crushed tomatoes. Bring to boiling. Reduce heat to medium-low. Simmer, uncovered, for 10 minutes. Add the beans and pasta. Cook 10 to 15 minutes more or until pasta and vegetables are tender. Top servings with cheese and parsley. Makes 6 servings.

EACH SERVING *236 cal, 7 g fat, 3 mg chol, 719 mg sodium, 36 g carb, 9 g fiber, 10 g pro.*
Make it vegetarian: Use the vegetable broth option as directed.
For hearty appetites: Serve with Prosciutto-Arugula Panini.
Make it gluten-free: Use gluten-free broth and substitute ½ cup of uncooked rice for the pasta. Cook 5 minutes longer or until rice is tender.

LOW FAT **FAST**

Prosciutto-Arugula Panini

Removing some of the soft center bread helps the sandwich to come out of the grill pan or panini press thin and crisp.

PREP 10 min. COOK 12 min.

1   12-oz. whole wheat baguette or
     Italian bread (about 18 inches long)
3   Tbsp. prepared basil pesto
8   thin slices prosciutto (3 oz.)
1   cup lightly packed arugula leaves,
     chopped
½   cup shredded part-skim mozzarella
     cheese
     Olive oil spray

1. Cut bread in half horizontally, then cut each half crosswise in 6 equal portions. Scoop out the soft center of bread; freeze for making bread crumbs or discard. Spread cut sides of bread with pesto. Divide prosciutto, arugula, and mozzarella among 6 of the bread pieces. Replace tops of bread. Lightly coat top and bottom with olive oil spray.

2. Heat a nonstick grill pan or panini press over medium-high heat. Cook 3 sandwiches at a time in hot pan, weighting sandwiches with a press or heavy skillet. Cook about 3 minutes per side until cheese is melted and bread is toasted. Cut in half to serve. Makes 6 servings.

EACH SERVING *232 cal, 9 g fat, 18 mg chol, 736 mg sodium, 26 g carb, 2 g fiber, 11 g pro.*
Make it vegetarian: Omit prosciutto from recipe.

FOR SOUP NIGHT
Broth- or tomato-base soups will have fewer calories than milk- or cream-base ones. Bulk up soup with vegetables and low-sodium canned beans, and you'll have plenty to eat without many calories or much sodium. Add brown rice or whole wheat pasta for a serving of whole grains. And a little of a flavorful topping, such as Parmesan cheese, goes a long way.

OPEN-FACE PHILLY
CHEESESTEAK
SANDWICHES

SANDWICH NIGHT "Sandwiches are crowd-pleasers—the heartier, the better. By serving them open-face with a light cheese sauce and lean meat, you can cut calories down to a third of the typical sandwich."

KID FRIENDLY

Open-Face Philly Cheesesteak Sandwiches

"When you bite into this sandwich, you'll be thinking how insanely good it is—not about health," Ellie says. "But it's moderate in saturated fat, has the goodness of whole grain, and is an excellent source of 18 essential nutrients. The trick is to use lean meat."

PREP 20 min. COOK 16 min.

½   cup cold low-fat (1 percent) milk
1   Tbsp. all-purpose flour
2   oz. extra-sharp cheddar cheese, finely shredded (½ cup, packed)
2   Tbsp. olive oil
1   lb. boneless top loin beef steak, very thinly sliced*
     Freshly ground black pepper
1   large onion, sliced in very thin wedges
1   green sweet pepper, thinly sliced
1   red sweet pepper, thinly sliced
2   whole grain Italian rolls (each about 6 inches long and 4 oz.), halved lengthwise

1. For cheese sauce, in a small saucepan whisk together milk and flour to blend. Heat and stir over medium-high heat to bring to a simmer. Reduce heat to medium-low. Cook 2 minutes, stirring frequently until thickened. Stir in cheese and ¼ tsp. salt until cheese is melted. Simmer about 2 minutes, stirring frequently, until sauce is velvety and thick. Remove from heat. Cover surface with foil to keep warm and to prevent a skin from forming on top.

2. In a large nonstick skillet heat 1 Tbsp. of the oil over medium-high heat. Sprinkle beef with ¼ tsp. each of salt and black pepper. Add to skillet and cook for 4 to 5 minutes, just until browned and cooked through. Transfer to a plate; cover with foil to keep warm.

3. In same skillet cook onion and sweet peppers in 1 Tbsp. hot oil over medium-high heat for 12 to 14 minutes, until edges are browned and onion is tender. Season with ¼ tsp. each salt and black pepper.

4. Lightly toast split rolls. Evenly divide the onion-pepper mixture, meat, and cheese sauce among roll halves. Makes 4 servings.

*To make slicing beef easy, freeze for 45 to 60 minutes before slicing.

EACH SERVING 472 cal, 20 g fat, 77 mg chol, 879 mg sodium, 39 g carb, 6 g fiber, 37 g pro.

Make it vegetarian: Use 1 large sliced portobello mushroom per sandwich in place of the beef. Sauté as directed for the beef.

FOR SANDWICH NIGHT

The main thing to keep in mind is portion control—especially when it comes to meat, cheese, and bread. One easy way to cut calories and sodium is to go for open-face sandwiches. Keep meat portions in check by sautéing mushrooms and other vegetables with beef or chicken. But don't keep anything off limits. Enjoy a BLT with real bacon from time to time; just keep it to two slices of bacon per sandwich.

STIR-FRY NIGHT "I love the rhythm of making a classic stir-fry—and it's so easy to load in more vegetables. You get everything ready, and in 15 minutes it's on the table."

KID FRIENDLY

Sesame Chicken with Broccoli Stir-Fry

"There is magic to the sweet-tart, spicy-salty balance of Chinese sauces like this one," Ellie says. "Here it is poured over chicken, sprinkled with a generous helping of toasted sesame seeds, and served with crisp steamed broccoli. It's delicious and really good for you."

PREP 25 min.   MARINATE 20 min.
COOK 15 min.

5   Tbsp. reduced-sodium soy sauce
2   tsp. toasted sesame oil
5   tsp. honey
1¼ lb. skinless boneless chicken breasts, cut in 1-inch chunks
2   Tbsp. canola oil
2   green onions, white parts thinly sliced and green tops reserved
1   Tbsp. grated fresh ginger
3   cloves garlic, minced
1½ cups low-sodium chicken broth
4   tsp. cornstarch
1   Tbsp. rice vinegar
1   tsp. chili paste
1   small head broccoli, cut in florets, steamed until crisp-tender, 4 to 5 minutes
3   Tbsp. toasted sesame seeds
     Hot cooked brown rice (optional)

1. In a medium bowl whisk together 3 Tbsp. of the soy sauce, 1 tsp. sesame oil, and 2 tsp. honey. Add cut-up chicken, toss to coat, then marinate for 20 minutes. Remove chicken from marinade with a slotted spoon. Discard marinade.
2. In a large nonstick skillet or wok heat 2 tsp. of canola oil over medium-high heat. Cook half the chicken at a time for 6 minutes until browned and cooked through, turning once or twice. Transfer to a large serving plate. Heat 2 tsp. canola oil to cook remaining chicken. Transfer to serving plate.
3. In the same skillet heat the remaining 2 tsp. of the canola oil over medium-high heat. Add the white parts of onions, ginger, and garlic. Cook and stir for 1 to 2 minutes until fragrant. For sesame sauce, in a small bowl whisk together broth, remaining soy sauce, remaining honey, the cornstarch, vinegar, and chili paste until cornstarch and honey are incorporated. Add sauce to skillet. Cook and stir for 2 to 3 minutes until thickened and darkened in color. Stir in remaining 1 tsp. sesame oil.
4. To serve, pour sauce over chicken. Surround chicken with steamed broccoli. Sprinkle with sesame seeds and green onion tops. Serve with brown rice if desired. Makes 4 servings.
EACH SERVING *365 cal, 14 g fat, 82 mg chol, 882 mg sodium, 21 g carb, 4 g fiber, 39 g pro.*
Make it vegetarian: Use 1½ cups vegetable broth in place of the chicken broth and extra-firm tofu instead of chicken.

FOR STIR-FRY NIGHT
When you crave Chinese food, the first step in making it more healthful is to cook it yourself. Because many Chinese foods are stir-fries, use only a little of a healthy oil—such as canola oil. Then measure to know for sure how much you're using. Serve the stir-fry with steamed vegetables and brown rice for a balanced dish with a whole grain boost.

SESAME CHICKEN
WITH BROCCOLI
STIR-FRY

**CRISPY BEEF AND
BEAN TACOS**

"I want to keep meals a joyful time, a time when we are all together. Everyone's involved, especially my daughter. Sometimes she even shops with me and helps pick out the vegetables for dinner. If children help in the kitchen, they are more likely to try different foods and make healthier meal choices."

KID FRIENDLY

Crispy Beef and Bean Tacos

These are Ellie's healthful take on this popular food. "It's no wonder taco night has become a beloved all-American tradition," Ellie says. "It's fun, interactive, easy, and delicious. Making a few tweaks to the typical meat filling and making baked crispy corn shells makes them extra healthful too."

MAKES 4 servings PREP 20 min.
BAKE 7 min. COOK 12 min.

Crispy Shells
8   6-in. corn tortillas
1   tsp. olive oil
¼   tsp. salt

Beef and Bean Filling
½   lb. lean ground beef (90% lean or higher)
1   cup reduced-sodium black beans, drained and rinsed
2   cloves garlic, minced
2   tsp. chili powder
½   tsp. dried oregano
¼   tsp. salt
⅛   tsp. cayenne pepper
¼   cup water

Toppings
1   medium tomato, seeded and diced
¼   cup chopped red onion
½   cup shredded cheddar cheese
2   cups shredded romaine lettuce
¼   cup fresh cilantro leaves

1. For the Crispy Shells, position the oven rack in center of oven. Preheat oven to 375°F. Wrap tortillas in damp paper towels. Microwave on high about 40 seconds until warm and softened. Lightly brush both sides of tortillas with oil; sprinkle with salt. Slide oven rack out slightly. Carefully drape each tortilla over two bars of oven rack, forming shells with flat bottoms (sides will drape farther as they bake). Bake about 7 minutes until crispy. Using tongs, transfer warm shells to a plate. (Or allow shells to cool completely on oven rack, then wrap in foil to use later. Shells may be made up to 1 day ahead.)

2. For the Beef and Bean Filling, in a large nonstick skillet over medium-high heat cook beef for 8 minutes, stirring occasionally and breaking up meat with a wooden spoon, until no longer pink. Add beans and garlic. Cook and stir for 2 minutes. Add chili powder, oregano, salt, cayenne pepper, and the water. Cook and stir for 2 minutes until heated through.

3. To serve, divide filling among shells. Serve toppings in separate bowls. Makes 4 servings.

PER SERVING *335 cal, 13 g fat, 52 mg chol, 36 g carb, 577 mg sodium, 8 g fiber, 21 g pro.*

In Ellie's latest book, *Comfort Food Fix* (Wiley, $30), she shares healthy spins on comfort food classics, giving side-by-side nutritional comparisons of the typical dish and her made-over version. "You don't have to choose between your favorite foods and your well-being," she says. In the book she includes easy changes to make big differences, such as thickening soups or sauces with flour instead of cream and adding extra beans and vegetables to a dish to boost the portion while keeping calories and fat in check.

Stuffed Mushrooms

Baked and filled, these easy, savory caps are ready to party.

1. Ham, sweet potato, green sweet pepper, garlic

2. Roast beef (sliced), asparagus, blue cheese

3. Apple slices, bacon (crisp-cooked), smoked cheddar

4. Hard-cooked eggs, cherry tomatoes, spinach

5. Cream cheese, raspberry preserves, jalapeño peppers

6. Shrimp, Boursin cheese, mayo, thyme leaves

7. Hummus, sun-dried tomatoes, olives

8. Sausage, pizza sauce, mozzarella cheese, parsley

9. Smoked turkey, cranberry relish, fresh sage

10. Chicken (shredded), carrot strips, green onion, fresh ginger, wasabi

Place cleaned and stemmed caps, stem sides down, on baking pan. Lightly coat with cooking spray. Bake at 425°F for 5 minutes. Drain, stem sides down, on paper towels; fill.

Delicious on a Dollar

Think meat is out of reach when you're on a budget?
These pork chops prove careful shopping pays off.

Brown Sugar Pork Chops with Onions

Loin and rib chops cook alike and taste similar, so choose whichever fits your budget better. Either cut will be delicious with this onion sauce spooned over and fresh steamed green beans served on the side.

PREP 15 min. COOK 10 min.

- 2   tsp. vegetable oil
- 4   boneless pork rib or loin chops, ½ to ¾ inch thick
- ¼   tsp. ground black pepper
- 1   medium onion, halved lengthwise and thinly sliced
- ¼   cup orange juice
- 2   Tbsp. packed brown sugar
- ¼   tsp. crushed red pepper (optional)

1. In a large skillet heat oil over medium heat. Sprinkle chops with black pepper. Cook chops in hot oil for 6 to 8 minutes, until brown on outside and slightly pink in center, turning once halfway through cooking time. Remove chops from skillet; cover and keep warm.
2. For sauce, in same skillet cook onion over medium heat for 3 minutes or until tender. Push onion aside. Remove skillet from heat; add orange juice and brown sugar. Return to heat. Cook and stir for 1 minute or until sugar is dissolved. Stir onions into sauce.
3. Spoon sauce over chops; sprinkle with crushed red pepper if desired. Serve with steamed green beans. Makes 4 servings.

EACH SERVING *304 cal, 18 g fat, 68 mg chol, 51 mg sodium, 11 g carb, 1 g fiber, 23 g pro.*

BROWN SUGAR PORK CHOPS WITH ONIONS

CHOCOLATE-FILLED
RED VELVET CUPCAKES

february

WARM AND GOOEY Whether they're rich and creamy chocolate desserts or perfectly crafted pizzas, these recipes satisfy sweet and savory tastes alike.

33

42

44

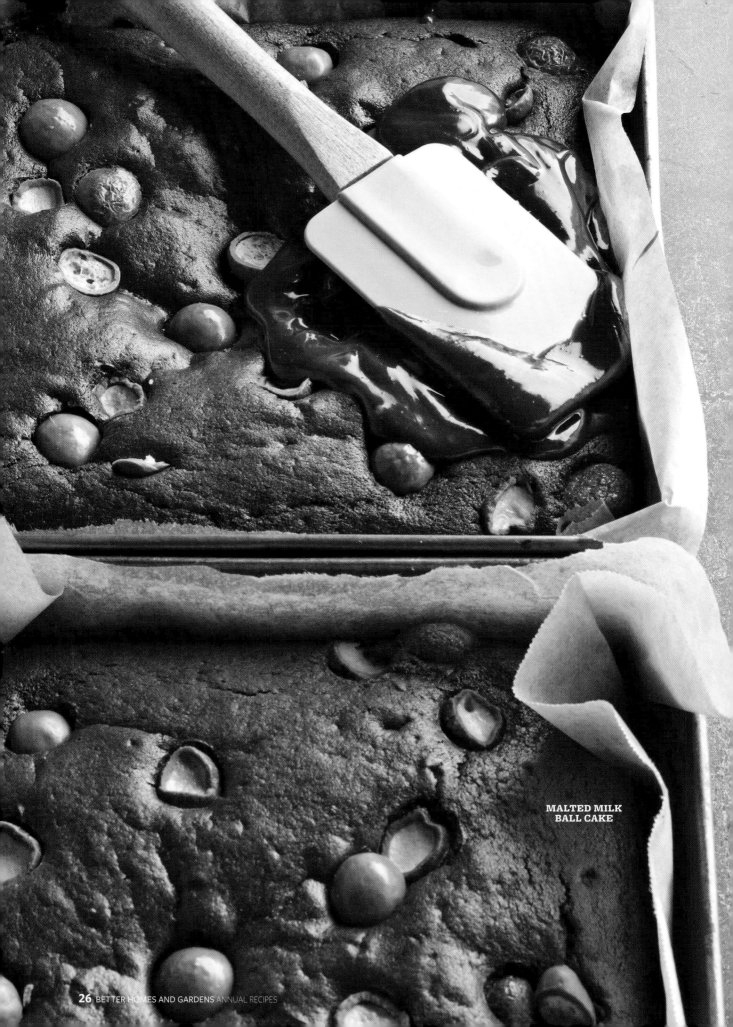

MALTED MILK
BALL CAKE

Hot! Chocolate!

Serve these seven easy, heart-meltingly good desserts straight from the oven—at their warm and gooey best.

KID FRIENDLY

Malted Milk Ball Cake

It's hip to be square, but this scrumptious cake can also be made in two 9×1½-inch round baking pans. Serve as weeknight snack cakes or layer the two cakes for Sunday dinner dessert.

PREP **30 min.** BAKE **25 min.**
OVEN **350°F**

2	cups all-purpose flour
½	cup unsweetened cocoa powder
1	tsp. baking powder
½	tsp. baking soda
⅔	cup butter, softened
1¾	cups sugar
3	eggs
4	oz. unsweetened chocolate, melted and cooled
2	tsp. vanilla
1½	cups milk
1	cup malted milk balls, coarsely chopped
1	recipe Chocolate Malt Frosting

1. Line two 9×9×2-inch baking pans with parchment paper. Grease pans; set aside.
2. In medium bowl stir together flour, cocoa powder, baking powder, baking soda, and ½ tsp. salt; set aside.

3. Preheat oven to 350°F. In a large mixing bowl beat butter with electric mixer on medium-high for 30 seconds. Add sugar; beat until combined. Add eggs, 1 at a time, beating 30 seconds after each. Beat in chocolate and vanilla. Alternately add flour mixture and milk, beating on low speed until thoroughly combined.
4. Divide batter between prepared pans; spread evenly. Bake for 10 to 15 minutes. Sprinkle with malted milk balls, pressing in slightly if needed (see tip, right). Continue baking 10 to 15 minutes more (25 minutes total). Cool in pans on wire rack for 10 minutes. Remove cakes from pans. Transfer cakes to wire racks to cool. Spread with warm Chocolate Malt Frosting. Serve warm. Makes two cakes, each 12 to 16 servings.
Chocolate Malt Frosting In a microwave-safe bowl whisk together 2 cups whipping cream and ⅓ cup malt powder. Microwave on 50 percent power (medium) for 2 minutes or until bubbly. Place two 11.5-oz. pkgs. milk chocolate pieces in a medium bowl. Pour hot cream over chocolate pieces. Let stand 5 minutes; stir until smooth. Pour and spread warm frosting on cakes. Makes 1⅔ cups frosting.
EACH SERVING WITH FROSTING *319 cal, 17 g fat, 51 mg chol, 195 mg sodium, 40 g carb, 2 g fiber, 5 g pro.*

HOW-TO: MALTED MILK BALL CAKE
Here's how to keep the yummy crunch and shape of the chopped milk balls: Partially bake the batter until almost set, then remove from the oven. Gently press the milk ball pieces into the cake, then return to the oven for the remaining baking time.

Bring on the drizzles and the drips. Here's to cascading fudge sauce, gooey centers, and melting messy joy!

UPSIDE-DOWN BANANA SPLIT PIE WITH EASY FUDGE SAUCE

Upside-Down Banana Split Pie

For extra chocolate flavor, grate a chocolate bar over the top before serving.

PREP 30 min. BAKE 13 min./25 min.
COOL 1 hr. OVEN 450°F / 325°F

2	cups all-purpose flour
2	Tbsp. unsweetened cocoa powder
⅓	cup shortening
⅓	cup butter
6	to 7 Tbsp. cold water
4	oz. semisweet chocolate chips
¾	cup sugar
¼	cup cornstarch
3	cups milk
4	oz. unsweetened chocolate, chopped
5	egg yolks, beaten
1	Tbsp. butter
2	tsp. vanilla
	Sweetened whipped cream
	Sliced bananas, maraschino cherries
1	recipe Easy Fudge Sauce

1. For pastry crust, in large bowl stir together flour, cocoa, and ¼ tsp. salt. Using pastry blender, cut in shortening and ⅓ cup butter until pieces are pea size. Sprinkle 1 Tbsp. of the water into mixture; toss with fork. Push moistened dough to side of bowl. Repeat, using 1 Tbsp. water at a time, until all dough is moistened.
2. Preheat oven to 450°F. Divide dough in half; form each in a ball. Cover and refrigerate 1 ball. On lightly floured surface, flatten remaining ball. Roll from center to edges to a 12-inch circle. Transfer to 9-inch pie plate. Gently fit into plate, avoiding stretching. Trim edges. Line with double layer of foil.
3. Bake pastry 8 minutes. Remove foil; bake 5 minutes more until dry. Sprinkle with chocolate chips. Cool completely on wire rack. Reduce oven to 325°F.
4. For chocolate filling, in 2-quart saucepan stir together sugar and cornstarch. Stir in milk and unsweetened chocolate. Cook and stir over medium heat until thickened and bubbly. Cook and stir 2 minutes more.
5. Slowly stir 1 cup hot chocolate mixture into beaten yolks. Pour chocolate-egg mixture into hot filling in pan. Bring just to boiling; reduce heat. Cook and stir 2 minutes. Remove from heat. Stir in butter and vanilla. Cool 10 minutes.

6. Meanwhile, on lightly floured surface, flatten remaining dough. Roll from center to edges to a 12-inch circle. Pour warm filling into baked pastry shell. Place unbaked pastry over filling, pressing edges to seal. Trim pastry to edge of pie plate.
7. Gently prick top of pastry with a fork. Bake 25 minutes until crust is firm and dry. Cool 1 hour on wire rack.
8. To serve, invert serving plate on pie. Turn pie upside down. Remove pie plate. Just before serving top with sweetened whipped cream, bananas, cherries, and some of the Easy Fudge Sauce. Or, to serve just a few slices, top each slice with the whipped cream and toppings. Cover and store remaining pie (without toppings) in the refrigerator up to 2 days. Individual slices can be reheated in the microwave for 10 to 15 seconds. Makes 12 servings.
EACH SERVING *454 cal, 25 g fat, 105 mg chol, 165 mg sodium, 54 g carb, 4 g fiber, 8 g pro.*

Easy Fudge Sauce

Serve this sauce with Upside-Down Banana Split Pie and Hot Chocolate-Stout Float, page 33. Flavor the sauce with vanilla or, for darker chocolate taste, use instant coffee or espresso powder.

START TO FINISH 10 min.

1	cup packed brown sugar
½	cup unsweetened cocoa powder
½	cup butter
½	cup milk or half-and-half
2	tsp. vanilla or instant coffee crystals or espresso powder

1. In small bowl mix together brown sugar and cocoa powder; set aside.
2. In heavy saucepan melt butter with milk. Cook and stir over medium heat for 5 to 6 minutes, just until mixture bubbles around edge of pan. Add sugar-cocoa mixture. Cook, stirring constantly, 1 to 2 minutes, until sugar is dissolved and mixture is smooth and thickened.
3. Remove from heat; stir in vanilla or coffee crystals. Serve at once. Store, covered, in refrigerator up to 1 week. Reheat in microwave, stirring every 15 seconds until warm. Makes 1½ cups (12 servings).
EACH SERVING *154 cal, 8 g fat, 21 mg chol, 78 mg sodium, 21 g carb, 1 g fiber, 1 g pro.*

HOW-TO: DOUBLE PIE CRUST
To place the top crust for the Upside-Down Banana Split Pie, roll the chilled pastry to a 12-inch circle. Transfer the dough to the top of the pie by wrapping the dough around the rolling pin. Carefully lay over pie filling, avoiding stretching the dough. Trim the edge even with the pie plate using a small knife. Press the top and bottom crust edges together to seal.

KID FRIENDLY

Chocolate-Filled Red Velvet Cupcakes

Nestled in each of these cupcakes is a chocolate truffle. As the cupcakes bake, the chocolate centers melt into a saucy filling.

PREP **25 min.** FREEZE **1 hr.**
BAKE **15 min.** COOL **10 min.**
OVEN **375°F**

1   cup milk chocolate pieces
¼   cup whipping cream
¼   cup plus 1 Tbsp. butter
1   egg
1   cup all-purpose flour
2   tsp. unsweetened cocoa powder
¾   cup sugar
2   tsp. red food coloring
½   tsp. vanilla
½   cup buttermilk
½   tsp. baking soda
½   tsp. vinegar
      Raspberry preserves (optional)

1. For filling, in small saucepan combine chocolate pieces, cream, and the 1 Tbsp. butter. Stir over low heat until chocolate is melted. Transfer to small bowl; cool for 15 minutes, stirring occasionally. Cover and freeze about 1 hour, until fudgelike consistency. Divide filling into 12 portions. Working quickly with hands, roll each portion in a ball. Place in freezer.
2. Meanwhile, let ¼ cup butter and egg stand at room temperature 30 minutes. Preheat oven to 375°F. Line 12 (2½-inch) muffin cups with paper bake cups. In small bowl stir together flour, cocoa powder, and ¼ tsp. salt; set aside.
3. In medium mixing bowl beat the ¼ cup softened butter with mixer on medium to high for 30 seconds. Gradually add sugar; beat on medium until combined. Beat on medium 2 minutes more, scraping side of bowl occasionally. Beat in egg, food coloring, and vanilla. Alternately add flour mixture and buttermilk, beating on low after each addition just until combined. In small bowl combine baking soda and vinegar; stir into batter.
4. Divide half the batter among prepared cups. Place a ball of filling on batter in center of each cup. Spoon remaining batter into cups.
5. Bake 15 to 18 minutes or until tops spring back when lightly touched. Remove from oven. Cool 10 minutes. Serve warm topped with raspberry preserves if desired. Makes 12 servings.
EACH SERVING *289 cal, 11 g fat, 39 mg chol, 180 mg sodium, 44 g carb, 1 g fiber, 3 g pro.*

HOW-TO: MELTED TRUFFLE CENTERS
To make the ooey-gooey centers in the Chocolate-Filled Red Velvet Cupcakes, spoon half the batter into the muffin cups. Place one of the chilled balls of chocolate filling in each muffin cup, in the center away from edges. Spoon remaining batter over the filling and bake as directed.

CHOCOLATE-FILLED
RED VELVET CUPCAKES

CHOCOLATE-RASPBERRY
GRILLERS WITH
WARM CHOCOLATE GRAVY

Chocolate-Raspberry Grillers

START TO FINISH 18 min.

8 ½-inch slices challah or Hawaiian sweet bread
2 Tbsp. butter, melted
4 to 6 oz. semisweet chocolate, finely chopped
1 cup raspberries
1 recipe Warm Chocolate Gravy

1. Heat a large heavy nonstick skillet over medium-low heat. Meanwhile, brush one side of each bread slice with the melted butter. Place half the bread slices, butter sides down, on a plate. Sprinkle with chocolate and raspberries to within ¼ inch of crusts. Top with remaining bread, buttered sides up. Place sandwiches, two at a time, in pan. Weight with a heavy skillet.
2. Grill sandwiches over medium-low heat for 6 to 8 minutes or until chocolate is melted and bread is golden brown, turning once. Grill remaining sandwiches. Cut in half to serve. Pass Warm Chocolate Gravy for dipping. Makes 8 (half-sandwich) servings.

EACH SERVING 217 cal, 8 g fat, 10 mg chol, 180 mg sodium, 33 g carb, 3 g fiber, 4 g pro.

Warm Chocolate Gravy

Serve this thick yet light chocolate sauce alongside Chocolate-Raspberry Grillers, above. Or try it over French toast.
START TO FINISH 10 min.

¼ cup sugar
2 Tbsp. unsweetened cocoa powder
1 Tbsp. all-purpose flour
1 Tbsp. butter
1¼ cups milk

In small bowl stir together sugar, cocoa powder, and flour. In medium saucepan melt butter. Thoroughly stir in sugar mixture until no lumps remain. Gradually add milk, stirring constantly. Cook and stir over medium heat until thickened and bubbly; cook and stir 1 minute more. Serve with Chocolate-Raspberry Grillers. Makes 1¼ cups (10 two-tablespoon servings).

EACH SERVING 51 cal, 2 g fat, 1 mg chol, 26 mg sodium, 8 g carb, 0 g fiber, 1 g pro.

HOT CHOCOLATE-STOUT FLOAT

EASY FUDGE SAUCE

Hot Chocolate-Stout Float

Chocolate stout is a type of beer that has a dark chocolaty flavor; some brands are even brewed with a small amount of chocolate. They vary in taste ranging from sweet to bitter. Adjust the amount of chocolate sauce to taste.
START TO FINISH 15 min.

½ cup Easy Fudge Sauce, page 29
1 12- to 16-oz. bottle chocolate stout beer or stout beer
1 quart vanilla bean ice cream
   Edible rose petals (optional)

1. In small saucepan heat Easy Fudge Sauce and ¼ cup of the beer until warm and combined.
2. Place 2 scoops of ice cream in each of 6 soda glasses. Spoon 2 Tbsp. warm fudge sauce into each. Pour some remaining beer over ice cream. Top with rose petals if desired. Serve at once with long spoons. Makes 6 servings.

EACH SERVING 329 cal, 16 g fat, 48 mg chol, 99 mg sodium, 37 g carb, 0 g fiber, 3 g pro.

PEANUT BUTTER, JELLY, AND BROWNIE COOKIES

Gooey Chocolate Pudding Cakes

Dip into these pudding cakes and find a layer of thick chocolate sauce. To make one large cake, pour the batter into a 1-quart casserole dish and increase baking time to 35 to 40 minutes.

PREP **20 min.** BAKE **20 min.**
OVEN **350°F**

½   cup all-purpose flour
¼   cup sugar
¾   tsp. baking powder
⅓   cup milk
1   Tbsp. oil
1   tsp. vanilla
¼   cup chocolate-hazelnut spread (Nutella)
⅓   cup semisweet chocolate pieces
½   cup sugar
¼   cup unsweetened cocoa powder
¾   cup boiling water
    Coffee-flavor or vanilla ice cream (optional)
    Sliced strawberries (optional)
    Unsweetened cocoa powder (optional)

1. Preheat oven to 350°F. In medium bowl combine flour, the ¼ cup sugar, baking powder, and ¼ tsp. salt. Add milk, oil, and vanilla. Whisk until smooth. Stir in chocolate-hazelnut spread and chocolate pieces.
2. Divide batter evenly among six 5- to 8-oz. oven-safe bowls or ramekins. Place in 15×10×1-inch baking pan. Set aside. In same bowl stir together the ½ cup sugar and cocoa. Gradually stir in the boiling water. Pour evenly over batter in dishes.
3. Bake, uncovered, 20 minutes or until wooden toothpick inserted into cake portion comes out clean. Serve warm with ice cream and strawberries. Sprinkle additional cocoa powder if desired. Makes 6 servings.

EACH SERVING *272 cal, 9 g fat, 1 mg chol, 178 mg sodium, 49 g carb, 2 g fiber, 3 g pro.*

Peanut Butter, Jelly, and Brownie Cookies

Store leftover brownies in a covered container up to 3 days.

PREP **25 min.** FREEZE **30 min.**
BAKE **30 min.** OVEN **350°F**

1   16.5-oz. pkg. refrigerated peanut butter cookie dough
¾   cup butter
3   oz. unsweetened chocolate, coarsely chopped
1⅓ cups sugar
2   tsp. vanilla
3   eggs
1   cup all-purpose flour
2   Tbsp. unsweetened cocoa powder
⅓   cup cherry or strawberry jam, jelly, or preserves

1. With your hands on lightly floured baking sheet or flat freezer-safe dish, slightly flatten cookie dough roll to an 8×2½-inch rectangle. Freeze 30 minutes. Slice dough in half lengthwise. Cut each half into 16 slices. Using a fork dipped in sugar, make a crisscross pattern on each cookie. Bake according to package directions or until golden brown. Cool on wire racks.

2. Meanwhile, in medium saucepan stir butter and chocolate over low heat just until melted. Remove from heat. Using a wooden spoon, stir in sugar and vanilla. Cool 5 minutes.
3. Preheat oven to 350°F. Line bottom and sides of 8×8×2-inch baking pan with heavy foil. Grease foil, then set aside.
4. Add eggs one at a time to butter mixture, beating after each just until combined. Stir in flour and cocoa powder. Evenly spread batter in prepared pan. Bake 30 to 35 minutes or until a wooden toothpick inserted near center comes out clean.
5. While brownie is still warm and soft, scoop up a spoonful of the brownie and mash onto the flat side of a cookie. Top with 1 tsp. jam and a second cookie, flat side down. Repeat with remaining cookies, brownies, and jam. Place sandwich cookies on a cookie sheet; return to 350°F oven for 4 minutes or until warm. Serve immediately. Makes 16 cookies.

EACH COOKIE *223 cal, 11 g fat, 27 mg chol, 149 mg sodium, 28 g carb, 1 g fiber, 3 g pro.*

GOOEY CHOCOLATE
PUDDING CAKES

**WARM CHOCOLATE-SWIRL
VANILLA RICE PUDDING**

Warm Chocolate-Swirl Vanilla Rice Pudding

PREP 25 min. BAKE 45 min.
OVEN 325°F

3   eggs, lightly beaten
2   cups half-and-half, light cream, or whole milk
½   cup milk
½   cup sugar
1   tsp. vanilla or ½ tsp. almond extract
1   cup cooked white rice, cooled
1   cup sugar
3   tbsp. unsweetened cocoa powder
1   1 oz. square semisweet or bittersweet chocolate, finely chopped
⅛   tsp. salt
⅓   cup water
1   tbsp. molasses
½   tsp. vanilla
    Lingonberry sauce (optional)
    Sweetened Whipped Cream (optional)

1. Preheat oven to 325°F. For rice pudding, in a large mixing bowl beat together the eggs, half-and-half, milk, the ½ cup sugar, and vanilla with a rotary beater or wire whisk. Stir in rice. Pour into a 1½- or 2-quart oval baking dish. Place dish in a roasting pan set on a rack. Carefully pour 1 inch of boiling water into the baking pan. Bake, uncovered, for 45 to 50 minutes until a knife inserted near center comes out clean.

2. Meanwhile, for the chocolate sauce, in a small saucepan stir together the 1 cup sugar, cocoa powder, chopped chocolate, and salt. Stir in the water. Cook and stir over medium heat until chocolate is dissolved and the sauce comes to a simmer. Remove from heat. Stir in molasses and the ½ tsp. vanilla. Transfer sauce to a serving bowl; cover with plastic wrap.

3. As soon as rice pudding is removed from oven, stir and swirl in some of the chocolate sauce. Serve rice pudding warm with lingonberry sauce and Sweetened Whipped Cream if desired. Pass remaining chocolate sauce. Makes 8 servings.

EACH SERVING *315 cal, 11 g fat, 93 mg chol, 98 mg sodium, 50 g carb, 1 g fiber, 6 g pro.*

Sweetened Whipped Cream In a chilled large mixing bowl combine 1 cup whipping cream, 2 tbsp. sugar, and ½ tsp. vanilla, Beat with an electric mixer on medium speed until soft peaks form. Makes about 2 cups.

CHOOSE YOUR CHOCOLATE

"The great thing about chocolate is that there is a bar for everyone," senior deputy food editor Nancy Wall Hopkins says. "From sweet milk chocolate to the darkest bittersweet, you can enjoy a range of flavors. Swap in your favorite in any recipe that calls for pieces, opting for a sweeter or darker chocolate—or even a chopped chile-spiked chocolate bar." So that the desserts are not too intense, choose chocolate that is no more than 72 percent cacao.

Home Cooking

PERFECT PIZZA AT HOME Transform everyday ingredients—flour, canned tomatoes, and dry herbs—into artisan-style pizza with the help of cookbook author and pizza pro Peter Reinhart.

THE DOUGH "The quality of the pizza is determined by the crust. A pizza with a great crust can have anything on it and still be memorable."

KID FRIENDLY | LOW FAT

All-Purpose Pizza Dough

PREP 20 min. STAND 30 min.
CHILL overnight or up to 3 days

5   cups unbleached bread flour
1   Tbsp. sugar (or honey)
1½   tsp. table salt (or 2½ tsp. coarse
     kosher salt)
1   tsp. instant yeast, also called bread-
     machine or fast-rising yeast
2   Tbsp. olive oil
1¾   cups plus 1 Tbsp. water, room
     temperature
     Nonstick cooking spray or olive oil

1. In the bowl of an electric mixer fitted with dough hook or in a large bowl using a large spoon, combine all ingredients except cooking spray. Mix on slow speed or by hand, about 3 minutes, until ingredients are combined and all the flour is wet. Dough will be soft and gluten won't be fully developed at this point.
2. If using an electric mixer, increase the speed to medium and continue mixing for an additional 2 minutes. If working by hand, keep mixing with the spoon; you may also turn dough out onto counter and knead. Mix long enough to create a smooth, supple dough, about 3 minutes. If dough seems very stiff, incorporate more water, a teaspoon at a time, as you mix; if the dough is wet and sticky, sprinkle in more flour as you mix. Dough should be tacky but not sticky. Lightly grease a bowl with olive oil or nonstick cooking spray. Form dough into smooth ball and place in bowl, turning to coat the surface with oil. Cover bowl with plastic wrap but do not let wrap touch dough. Let dough stand at room temperature 30 minutes, then refrigerate overnight or up to 3 days (dough will continue to rise in bowl until it goes dormant from the cold).
3. Two hours before you plan to make the pizzas, mist a baking sheet or cookie sheet with nonstick cooking spray or rub lightly with olive oil. Cut dough into 4 equal pieces and form each piece into a smooth, round ball. Place dough on prepared pan, mist lightly with nonstick cooking spray, and cover lightly with plastic wrap. While dough proofs prepare toppings and preheat oven. Stretch as directed at right before baking. Use dough to prepare pizzas. Makes 4 crusts.
EACH SERVING (HALF OF A PIZZA WITHOUT TOPPINGS) *351 cal, 5 g fat, 0 g chol, 440 mg sodium, 63 g carb, 2 g fiber, 10 g pro.*

KID FRIENDLY | LOW FAT

Multigrain Pizza Dough with Honey

PREP 20 min. STAND 30 min.
CHILL overnight or up to 3 days

4   cups unbleached bread flour
¾   cup whole wheat flour
¼   cup rye flour (or cornmeal
     or additional whole wheat flour)
1½   Tbsp. honey
1½   tsp. table salt (or 2½ tsp. coarse
     kosher salt)
1½   tsp. instant yeast, also called bread-
     machine or fast-rising yeast
2   Tbsp. olive oil
2   cups water, room temperature

1. To prepare, follow directions for All-Purpose Pizza Dough, left. Use dough to prepare pizzas on pages 42 and 43. Makes 4 crusts.
EACH SERVING (HALF OF A PIZZA WITHOUT TOPPINGS) *340 cal, 5 g fat, 0 g chol, 440 mg sodium, 64 g carb, 3 g fiber, 10 g pro.*

THUMBS UP
To shape dough, use your hands to form it into a disk, then drape it over the backs of your hands and use your thumbs to turn the dough and gently stretch it into a circle. Shape all your dough at once and set it on a counter. The dough might contract slightly as it stands; tug it back into shape just before topping.

THE SAUCE "Many people don't realize how easy it is to make your own and how good it is. Resist the urge to use too much; the sauce should just kiss the dough."

KID FRIENDLY | LOW FAT | FAST

All-Purpose Pizza Sauce

"For an 8- to 10-inch pizza, use just ¼ cup of sauce," Peter says. "When you want bolder flavor, the variations at the end of the recipe are the ones that have been a hit with my friends."

PREP 5 min.

1 28-oz. can crushed tomatoes
1½ tsp. red wine vinegar
½ tsp. granulated garlic or garlic powder
½ tsp. dried basil
¼ tsp. dried oregano
¼ tsp. dried thyme
¼ tsp. ground black pepper
¼ to ½ tsp. salt
¼ to ½ cup water

In a medium bowl whisk together all ingredients except the salt and the water. Taste sauce and whisk in the ¼ cup water and enough salt to taste. If necessary, add more water to thin. "If the sauce is thick at this stage it will be pasty on the pizza," Peter says. "It should easily spread over the dough." Taste again and adjust the salt, if needed. Makes 3 cups.

Spicy Puttanesca Sauce Add ½ cup chopped Kalamata olives or black olives, 1 Tbsp. capers, and ½ tsp. crushed red pepper.

Garlic-Robusto Sauce Add 2 to 3 Tbsp. of the garlic oil from the recipe for Caramelized Garlic (page 41) and ½ tsp. crushed red pepper.

EACH SERVING (2 TBSP.) ALL-PURPOSE SAUCE *11 cal, 0 g fat, 0 mg chol, 68 mg sodium, 3 g carb, 1 g fiber, 1 g pro.*

Multipurpose Herb Oil

Italians call pizza made without tomato sauce pizza bianco, which means white pizza—it's anything but bland, however. Brush this hearty mixture over your dough before topping. It's also delicious drizzled over tomatoes, clams, or shrimp on top of the pizza.

PREP 10 min. STAND 30 min.

1 cup olive oil
1 Tbsp. granulated garlic (or 1½ tsp. garlic powder)
1 Tbsp. dried basil

1 Tbsp. dried parsley
1 tsp. dried oregano
1 tsp. dried or fresh rosemary, crumbled
1 tsp. dried crushed red pepper (optional)
½ tsp. Spanish paprika, mild or hot
½ tsp. dried thyme
1 to 1½ tsp. salt, or to taste
¼ tsp. ground black pepper

Whisk all the ingredients together for about 15 seconds, long enough to evenly distribute them. Taste a small amount before the salt and herbs settle to the bottom. Adjust the seasonings to taste (primarily the salt). "Remember that most of the spices and herbs will tend to settle after a few minutes," Peter says, "so always whisk or stir the mixture before using." Let herbs steep in oil for at least 30 minutes at room temperature before using. Store, tightly covered, in a cool dark place up to two weeks. Makes 1 cup.

EACH (1 TBSP.) SERVING *121 cal, 14 g fat, 0 mg chol, 146 mg sodium, 0 g carb, 0 g fiber, 0 g pro..*

TOMATO CHOICES

"The best brand of tomatoes for pizza sauce is the one you already love. They all work well," Peter says. "This sauce doesn't need cooking because the tomatoes are cooked when they're canned and the sauce cooks in the oven."

THE TOPPINGS "The only limit is your imagination, but using a lesser amount of excellent ingredients is preferable to using a lot of mediocre ingredients," Peter says. "More is not always better; better is better."

Treat the cheese right.

For the best flavor, grate your cheese the same day you make the pizzas; it will taste fresher. Use enough to cover the pizza but not overpower other flavors. That translates to about ½ cup shredded per pizza. Traditional cheese favorites include mozzarella, Jack, cheddar, Swiss, Gouda, provolone, and Fontina. You can also substitute ¼ cup of a soft cheese, such as feta, chèvre, or a blue cheese. Try an American blue such as Maytag or BelGioioso, or use Stilton, Gorgonzola, or Roquefort. Whichever cheese you use, sprinkle or crumble onto the sauce just before baking.

Choose a meat.

For many people, it's just not pizza without pepperoni or chunks of sausage. Peter recommends about ¼ cup sliced or chopped meat per pizza. "Genoa salami is especially good, cut into matchstick-size pieces," Peter says. You can also use pepperoni, bacon crumbles, Canadian bacon, ham, or cooked sausage. Seafood can also make a distinctive contribution. Try shelled baby clams, mussels, scallops, calamari, or shrimp. Before using, marinate them for 15 minutes in Multipurpose Herb Oil (page 40).

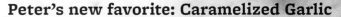

Peter's new favorite: Caramelized Garlic

"I love garlic on pizza, but this technique makes the flavor much richer—it has totally revolutionized the way I use garlic," Peter says. "It makes every pizza better, regardless of what else is on top." Place a cup of peeled garlic cloves (that's 3 to 4 bulbs) in a small saucepan with enough olive oil to cover the garlic—about a cup. "Simmer over medium heat for about 20 minutes, or until they become a rich dark golden brown on the outside—they should develop what looks like a crust," Peter says. "It will be tempting to take them off when they become light brown, but keep cooking them until they reach a dark, rich brown color. Stir occasionally to keep the garlic from sticking to the bottom of the pan and burning." Remove from heat but leave the garlic in the oil for 15 minutes, then remove with slotted spoon and transfer to plate lined with paper towels. Transfer remaining oil to a jar with a tightly fitting lid. Store garlic and oil, tightly covered, separately in the refrigerator up to 2 weeks.

TO BAKE PIZZAS

About 45 minutes before baking, arrange a rack one-third of the way up from bottom of the oven. Place pizza stone or invert heavy baking sheet on rack. Preheat oven to 500°F. Prepare pizzas as directed in recipe; you'll bake one at a time. Using the peel or cookie sheet, slide topped pizza onto the hot baking stone or baking sheet and bake 5 to 7 minutes until toppings are bubbling, cheese is turning golden, and edges of the pizza are golden brown. Rotate pizzas halfway through for even baking. Let stand 5 minutes before slicing.

Marinated Artichoke Pizza

PREP 20 min.   COOK 20 min.
BAKE 5 to 7 min.   OVEN 500°F

1   recipe Multigrain or All-Purpose pizza dough, page 39
2   large onions, sliced into strips
2   Tbsp. sugar
1   Tbsp. balsamic vinegar
1   4-oz. jar marinated artichoke hearts, drained and sliced into strips
1   16-oz. jar fire-roasted red peppers, drained and sliced into strips
1¼ to 1½ cups purchased salsa fresca, drained
1   cup sliced black olives

1. Remove dough from refrigerator 2 hours before you plan to make pizzas. Preheat oven as directed, left. In a large skillet heat 2 Tbsp. olive oil over medium heat. Add onions; cook and stir until onions are limp and translucent, about 10 minutes. Stir in sugar and balsamic vinegar; cook until juices bubble. Transfer onions to a strainer set over a bowl. Drain 3 minutes; return juices to skillet; cook over medium heat 5 minutes until consistency of honey. Remove from heat, return onions to skillet, stir to coat; set aside.

2. To assemble, stretch each dough portion into circle as directed on page 39; transfer one circle onto pizza peel (a pizza-size spatula) or rimless cookie sheet dusted with flour. Top in following order using one-fourth of each topping per pizza: onion mixture, artichokes, peppers, salsa, and olives.

3. Bake as directed, left. While one pizza is baking, repeat with remaining dough and toppings. Makes 8 servings.

EACH SERVING (HALF OF A PIZZA)
521 cal, 16 g fat, 0 mg chol, 811 mg sodium, 78 g carb, 4 g fiber, 12 g pro.

Mushroom-Garlic Pizza

PREP 20 min.   COOK 20 min.

BAKE 5 to 7 min.   OVEN 500°F

1   recipe All-Purpose or Multigrain pizza dough, page 39
1   recipe Caramelized Garlic, page 41
1½ cups sliced fresh shiitake mushrooms
1½ cups sliced cremini or button mushrooms
2   cups shredded Gruyère or provolone cheese
4   tsp. Multipurpose Herb Oil, page 40
¼   cup fresh Italian (flat-leaf) parsley, chopped

1. Remove chilled dough from refrigerator 2 hours before you plan to make pizzas. Preheat oven as directed on page 42. In a 12-inch skillet over medium-high heat, preheat 2 Tbsp. oil from Caramelized Garlic recipe. Add mushrooms; cook and stir 4 to 5 minutes, or just until they begin to glisten. Remove from heat. Season to taste with salt and pepper; set aside to cool.

2. To assemble pizzas, stretch each dough portion into circle as directed on page 39; transfer one circle onto pizza peel or rimless cookie sheet dusted with flour. Top each pizza with ½ cup of the grated cheese, one-fourth of the sautéed mushrooms (about ½ cup), and 6 to 8 cloves of Caramelized Garlic.

3. Bake pizza as directed on page 42. While one pizza is baking, repeat with remaining dough and toppings. Just before serving, drizzle each pizza with 1 tsp. Multipurpose Herb Oil and sprinkle with chopped parsley. Makes 8 servings (4 pizzas).

EACH SERVING (HALF OF A PIZZA) *494 cal, 16 g fat, 31 mg chol, 611 mg sodium, 66 g carb, 3 g fiber, 20 g pro.*

Peter's Pizza Margherita

Remove the chilled dough from the refrigerator 2 hours before you plan to make pizzas. Prepare and preheat oven as directed. Stretch dough into 8- to 10-inch rounds as directed on page 39. Top each pizza with ¼ cup All-Purpose Pizza Sauce, page 40, ½ cup shredded mozzarella cheese, 1 Tbsp. grated Parmesan cheese, and several basil leaves brushed with olive oil. Bake as directed on page 42.

> "Homemade pizzas are lighter, puffier; more like ones you find at artisan pizza restaurants," Peter says.

MEET PETER REINHART
He's the award-winning author of eight cookbooks, including *Peter Reinhart's Artisan Breads Every Day* (Ten Speed Press, 2009). Peter is also a baking instructor at Johnson and Wales University.

Delicious on a Dollar

Enjoy noodle casserole featuring chicken and an easy sauce made from scratch.

Chicken-Noodle Casserole

PREP 15 min. COOK 33 min.
BAKE 30 min. OVEN 375°F

4	stalks celery, chopped
1	medium onion, chopped
1	Tbsp. vegetable oil
2	lbs. chicken legs and/or thighs
½	tsp. ground black pepper
1	tsp. dried thyme, crushed
½	tsp. salt
1	slice bread
1	12-oz. pkg. jumbo or extra-large egg noodles
1	8-oz. container sour cream dip, cheddar French onion or French onion flavor
2	Tbsp. all-purpose flour
	Nonstick cooking spray
2	Tbsp. fresh parsley

1. Preheat oven to 375°F. In a Dutch oven cook two-thirds each of the celery and onion in hot oil over medium heat for 3 minutes. Add chicken, pepper, thyme, and salt; cook for 2 minutes. Add 6 cups of water. Bring to boiling; reduce heat. Simmer, covered, 20 to 25 minutes, until chicken is no longer pink.

2. Meanwhile, for topping, tear bread in small pieces. Finely chop remaining celery and onion. In a small bowl toss together bread, celery, and onion; set aside.

3. With a slotted spoon transfer chicken to cutting board. Add noodles to simmering broth; boil gently 7 to 8 minutes just until tender, stirring occasionally. With slotted spoon transfer noodles, celery, and onion to 3-quart baking dish.

4. For sauce, in a bowl whisk together sour cream dip and flour. Gradually whisk in 1 cup of the hot broth until smooth. Add to broth in Dutch oven; cook and stir until boiling.

5. Meanwhile, discard skin and bones from chicken. Chop chicken, then add to noodles in dish. Gently stir in sauce. Sprinkle with topping, then lightly coat with nonstick cooking spray.

6. Bake, uncovered, for 30 to 35 minutes until heated through and topping begins to brown. Top with parsley just before serving. Makes 8 servings.

EACH SERVING *400 cal, 13 g fat, 147 mg chol, 417 mg sodium, 38 g carb, 2 g fiber, 30 g pro.*

CHICKEN-NOODLE
CASSEROLE

**GRILLED
ASPARAGUS SOUP
WITH CHILI
CROUTONS**

march

SPRING GREEN Grab a bite of spring with asparagus—the vegetable that easily goes from baked to steamed to battered and fried. And become sausage savvy with the help of Chef Scott Peacock.

69

73

74

Spring Green

Tasty asparagus spears are the surest sign of spring. Grab a bundle or two and try these eight fresh ways to use them—from light salads to crispy fritters.

ROASTED ASPARAGUS-ORANGE SALAD

Avocado and Asparagus Egg Sandwiches

The avocado-asparagus spread can double as a dip to serve with vegetable sticks or corn chips. If desired, serve the sandwiches open-face with a knife and fork.

START TO FINISH 25 min.

1 avocado, halved, seeded, peeled, and chopped
1 tsp. lime juice
½ lb. green, white, and/or purple asparagus, trimmed
2 Tbsp. butter
4 eggs
8 slices white, wheat, or brioche bread, toasted
8 slices crisp-cooked bacon

1. In a small bowl mash avocado with lime juice; set aside.
2. Place asparagus in single layer in shallow baking pan. Cover with about 2 cups of boiling water. Let stand for 10 to 12 minutes, until bright green and crisp-tender. Drain. Finely chop three of the asparagus spears and stir into mashed avocado; set aside remaining spears.
3. Meanwhile, in large skillet melt butter over medium heat. Break eggs into skillet. Lightly sprinkle with salt and pepper. Reduce heat to medium-low. Cook eggs for 6 minutes, until whites are completely set and yolks begin to thicken. If desired, turn eggs to fully cook yolks.
4. Spread avocado-asparagus mixture on four slices of bread. Sprinkle with salt. Layer bacon, egg, asparagus spears, and remaining bread. Makes 4 sandwiches.
EACH SANDWICH 410 cal, 24 g fat, 219 mg chol, 896 mg sodium, 31 g carb, 5 g fiber, 18 g pro.

AVOCADO AND ASPARAGUS EGG SANDWICHES

Asparagus brings a fresh taste to every meal. Its delicate flavor works as well with a rich, creamy sauce as it does in a light, citrusy dressing.

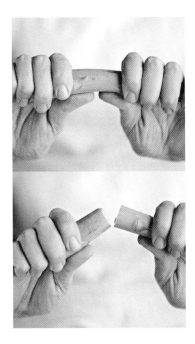

SNAP TO TRIM

Asparagus will snap easily where the woody base meets the tender upper stalk. Loosely grip the asparagus and bend until it snaps. You can snap spears one at a time or, for a shortcut, snap one spear and then line it up with the rest of the asparagus. Trim the remaining spears where the first one snapped. Store the woody ends in a freezer bag; use them to make soup stock.

KID FRIENDLY

Ham-and-Asparagus-Stuffed Chicken

Fresh deviled ham spread is whirled together in a food processor and paired with asparagus for a springy combination. The spread can be made up to two days ahead.

PREP **30 min.** COOK **20 min.**

1	cup diced cooked ham, rind removed
2	Tbsp. mayonnaise
1	Tbsp. finely chopped onion
1	Tbsp. snipped fresh tarragon or parsley
1	tsp. Worcestershire sauce
1	tsp. cider vinegar
1	tsp. Dijon-style or whole-grain mustard
⅛	tsp. cayenne pepper
4	large skinless, boneless chicken breast halves (about 2 lb.)
8	oz. green, white, and/or purple asparagus, trimmed
1	Tbsp. olive oil

1. For deviled ham, in a food processor combine ham, mayonnaise, onion, tarragon, Worcestershire, vinegar, mustard, cayenne, and a few grinds of black pepper. Cover and process until ham is very finely chopped and almost smooth, scraping processor bowl as needed. Set aside deviled ham while butterflying chicken breasts or cover and refrigerate up to 2 days.
2. To butterfly chicken breasts, place each breast half on a flat surface or cutting board. With palm on chicken and fingers away from knife blade, cut through one side of the chicken to within ¾ inch of the opposite side. Open to lie flat. Pound chicken with flat side of meat mallet to ¼-inch thickness.
3. To fill chicken, spread ¼ cup of the deviled ham on half of each chicken piece. Top with 3 to 5 asparagus spears. Fold remaining half over stuffing. Tie closed with 100-percent-cotton kitchen string. Sprinkle chicken with salt and pepper.
4. In 12-inch skillet heat oil over medium heat. Cook chicken in hot oil for 10 to 12 minutes per side until browned and no longer pink (170°F). Makes 4 servings.
EACH SERVING *399 cal, 17 g fat, 167 mg chol, 929 mg sodium, 3 g carb, 1 g fiber, 54 g pro.*

**HAM-AND-
ASPARAGUS-
STUFFED CHICKEN**

GARLICKY
ASPARAGUS
FLATBREAD

Garlicky Asparagus Flatbread

This dish makes a yummy appetizer. Or serve it with a salad for a meatless meal.
PREP 20 min. BAKE 16 min.
OVEN 450°F

1   1-lb. loaf frozen pizza dough, thawed
2   Tbsp. butter
2   Tbsp. flour
1   cup milk
½   cup finely shredded Parmesan cheese
6   oz. mozzarella cheese, sliced or grated
1   to 1¼ lb. green, white, and/or purple asparagus, trimmed and cut in 3-inch lengths
1   medium yellow squash, sliced
3   Tbsp. olive oil
5   large cloves garlic, thinly sliced
¼   cup thinly sliced green onions
     Honey (optional)

1. Preheat oven to 450°F. Grease two 15×10×1-inch baking pans; set aside. For flatbreads, cut thawed dough in half. On lightly floured surface roll each half to a 15×10-inch rectangle. (If dough becomes difficult to roll, let rest 5 minutes, then resume rolling.) Press dough into prepared pans, pressing to sides of pans. Prick dough all over with a fork. Bake 6 to 8 minutes or until very lightly browned.
2. Meanwhile, for white sauce, in a small saucepan melt the butter over medium heat; stir in flour. Cook and stir for 2 minutes. Slowly whisk in milk. Cook and stir until thickened and bubbly. Add Parmesan cheese; cook for 1 minute.
3. Spread sauce to within ½ inch of dough edges. Top with mozzarella. Lightly toss asparagus and squash with 1 Tbsp. of the olive oil. Spread on cheese layer. Bake for 10 minutes until browned. Cool slightly.
4. Meanwhile, in small skillet heat remaining 2 Tbsp. oil over medium heat. Cook sliced garlic in oil, stirring frequently, until tender and beginning to brown. Remove from heat. Spoon garlic and oil evenly on flatbreads. Sprinkle with green onions. Pass honey for drizzling if desired. Makes 12 servings.
EACH SERVING *217 cal, 10 g fat, 19 mg chol, 300 mg sodium, 22 g carb, 2 g fiber, 8 g pro.*

Think thin is in? Think again. Fat spears have hearty, crisp centers for extra crunch in each bite. And they're super easy to shave or slice into mealtime action.

ASPARAGUS RIBBONS

Thin asparagus ribbons are easy to make using a sharp vegetable peeler on thick asparagus spears. Trim the asparagus, then lay it flat on a work surface. From the stem end, peel toward the tip. Take care at the tips so they do not snap off. If a few tips do snap, just toss them in with the ribbons.

THICK OR THIN

Each has its fans. Thin asparagus is tender with a slightly crisp center. Thick asparagus has more of a meaty center and therefore more crunch and texture. For thick asparagus spears, peel off the woody outside part—about 2 inches up from the stem end—with a vegetable peeler.

FAST

Fresh Asparagus Ribbon Salad

The tips of the asparagus can be tricky to shave. If desired, cut off the tips to serve whole in the salad along with the ribbons. For nice, crisp ribbons, soak them in cold water while preparing the dressing. The dressing might seem thick when mixing, but it will soak up moisture from the asparagus and thin out when combined.

START TO FINISH **30 min.**

1	lb. thick green, purple, or white asparagus spears (about 14)
2	cloves garlic, peeled
½	tsp. coarse kosher salt
½	cup sour cream
⅓	cup olive oil
3	to 4 Tbsp. lemon juice
½	cup chopped fresh Italian parsley
¼	cup chopped fresh chives
1	Tbsp. milk (optional)
1	head Bibb lettuce, torn (6 cups)
½	English (seedless) cucumber, thinly sliced
3	radishes, very thinly sliced

1. Remove scales from asparagus spears (see "Removing Scales," page 57). Using a vegetable peeler, peel thin "ribbons" from spears (see "Asparagus Ribbons," left). Place ribbons in a medium bowl of ice water; set aside.

2. For dressing, first make a garlic paste. On a cutting board finely chop the garlic, then sprinkle with coarse salt. Holding a large flat chef's knife at a slight angle, blade almost flat with cutting board, mash and rub the salt into the garlic.

3. In a small bowl whisk together the garlic paste, sour cream, olive oil, and lemon juice. Stir in parsley and chives. If desired, thin with milk. Season to taste with black pepper.

4. Drain asparagus ribbons and pat dry (or spin in salad spinner). On a platter arrange lettuce, asparagus ribbons, cucumber slices, and radish slices. Drizzle with dressing. Cover and refrigerate any remaining dressing up to 3 days. Stir dressing well before serving. Makes 6 servings.

EACH SERVING *73 cal, 6 g fat, 3 mg chol, 73 mg sodium, 4 g carb, 2 g fiber, 2 g pro.*

GRILLED ASPARAGUS SOUP WITH CHILI CROUTONS

Grilled Asparagus Soup with Chili Croutons

No time to grill? Follow the directions for quick blanching, right, to cook the asparagus. For the Chili Croutons, toast the bread under the broiler for 1 to 2 minutes per side.

PREP **10 min.** GRILL **4 min.**
COOK **15 min.**

- 2 Tbsp. butter, melted
- 2 to 3 Tbsp. Asian chili sauce, such as Sriracha
- 1 small baguette, sliced diagonally
- 2 lb. green, white, and/or purple asparagus, trimmed
- 2 Tbsp. butter
- 1 small onion, finely chopped
- ¼ tsp. salt
- 3 Tbsp. all-purpose flour
- ½ tsp. ground coriander
- 2 14.5-oz. cans reduced-sodium chicken broth
- ½ cup milk
- 1 Tbsp. lemon juice
  Olive oil (optional)
  Freshly grated nutmeg (optional)
  Additional lemon juice (optional)

1. Preheat grill pan or grill to medium heat. For chili-butter, in large bowl stir together melted butter and chili sauce. Brush one side of each bread slice with some of the chili-butter. Grill bread for 2 minutes or until toasted and crisp, turning once. Set aside.

2. Add asparagus to remaining chili-butter; toss to coat (butter may firm up). Grill spears on grill pan over medium heat or grill rack over direct medium heat; cover. Cook about 2 minutes, turning once. Remove from pan or grill. Set aside one-fourth of the spears. Slice remaining spears in ½-inch rounds; set aside.

3. For soup, in large saucepan melt the 2 Tbsp. butter over medium heat. Cook onion in hot butter for 5 minutes, stirring occasionally, until onion is soft. Add salt. Sprinkle flour on onion; cook and stir for 1 minute. Stir in coriander. Slowly whisk in chicken broth. Add ½-inch asparagus rounds. Bring soup to simmering. Simmer, uncovered, for 10 minutes until thickened, stirring occasionally. Cool slightly.

4. Transfer soup to blender or food processor, working in batches if necessary. Puree soup until smooth. Return to saucepan. Stir in milk and heat through. Cut reserved asparagus spears in 2-inch pieces. Stir asparagus pieces and lemon juice into soup. If desired, drizzle with a little olive oil and serve with freshly grated nutmeg, additional lemon juice, and chili croutons. Makes 4 servings.

EACH SERVING *310 cal, 13 g fat, 33 mg chol, 1,029 mg sodium, 38 g carb, 4 g fiber, 11 g pro.*

REMOVING SCALES
It's optional to remove the dark triangular leaves, or scales, from the asparagus spears, but they can be tough, especially on thick spears. Use a paring knife to peel them off, then discard.

QUICK BLANCHING
The classic blanching method requires boiling, then shocking the asparagus in an ice bath to stop the cooking, resulting in perfectly cooked, yet cold asparagus. To make and serve warm right away without shocking, place asparagus in a single layer in a shallow baking dish. Cover with about 2 cups of boiling salted water. Let stand for 10 to 12 minutes until bright green and crisp-tender. Drain; serve warm.

ASPARAGUS FRITTER STICKS

Roasted Asparagus-Orange Salad

LOW FAT | FAST

For an even simpler roasted asparagus side dish, prepare through Step 1 and serve.

PREP **10 min.** ROAST **15 min.** OVEN **400°F**

2   lb. green, white, and/or purple asparagus, trimmed
1   Tbsp. olive oil
¼   tsp. salt
2   oranges
2   Tbsp. olive oil
1   Tbsp. cider vinegar
1   clove garlic, minced
1   tsp. Dijon-style mustard
½   tsp. fennel seeds, crushed

1. Preheat oven to 400°F. Place asparagus in a 15×10×1-inch baking pan. Drizzle with 1 Tbsp. oil, sprinkle with salt, and toss to coat. Roast, uncovered, for 15 to 20 minutes, until asparagus is crisp-tender, tossing once. Transfer to a serving platter.
2. Meanwhile, for dressing, finely shred enough peel from one orange to equal 1 tsp.; set aside. Juice half an orange. Peel and slice the remaining half and whole orange in rounds. In a jar with tight-fitting lid, combine shredded orange peel, orange juice, 2 Tbsp. olive oil, vinegar, garlic, mustard, and fennel seeds. Cover with lid and shake to combine.
3. Drizzle a little of the dressing on the asparagus; toss to coat. Carefully toss in orange slices. Pass remaining dressing. Makes 8 servings.
EACH SERVING *85 cal, 5 g fat, 0 mg chol, 90 mg sodium, 8 g carb, 3 g fiber, 3 g pro.*

Asparagus Fritter Sticks

KID FRIENDLY | FAST

These crisp sticks are addictive. For easy serving and dipping, place a little dill mustard in tall cups, then stand the spears in the cups.

PREP **10 min.** COOK **3 min.** OVEN **200°F**

1   cup cold water
⅔   cup yellow cornmeal
½   cup all-purpose flour
⅓   cup cornstarch
1   egg, lightly beaten
1   tsp. baking powder
     Vegetable oil for deep-fat frying
1   lb. thick green, white, and/or purple asparagus, trimmed
½   cup Dijon-style mustard
2   Tbsp. snipped fresh dill weed
2   Tbsp. honey

1. For batter, in large bowl whisk together the water, cornmeal, flour, cornstarch, egg, baking powder, and ½ tsp. salt until combined. Batter will be lumpy.
2. In large skillet heat about 1 inch of oil to 350°F. Working with 3 or 4 spears at a time, dip asparagus into batter, letting excess batter drip back into dish. Carefully slide spears into hot oil. Fry 3 to 4 minutes, until golden. Remove with tongs. Drain on paper towels. If desired, after draining, transfer asparagus to baking sheet and place in a 200°F oven to keep warm while frying remaining spears.
3. Meanwhile, for dip, in small bowl combine mustard, dill weed, and honey. Serve with asparagus sticks. Makes 12 servings.
EACH SERVING *132 cal, 9 g fat, 8 mg chol, 298 mg sodium, 11 g carb, 1 g fiber, 2 g pro.*

Asparagus-Tuna Casserole

This casserole is pulled together with a lemony white sauce and creamy provolone cheese.

PREP 20 min. COOK 20 min.
BAKE 25 min. OVEN 375°F

1   cup dried penne pasta
1   lb. tiny new potatoes, cut in ½-inch dice
3   Tbsp. butter
¼   cup chopped onion
2   Tbsp. all-purpose flour
2¼   cups milk
2   tsp. finely shredded lemon peel
4   oz. provolone cheese, shredded
3   4.5-oz. cans tuna packed in roasted garlic olive oil, or desired flavor tuna
½   cup pitted Kalamata olives, halved
1½   lb. green, white, and/or purple asparagus, trimmed, cut in 1-inch pieces
¼   cup soft bread crumbs
¼   cup finely shredded Parmesan cheese

1. Preheat oven to 375°F. In large saucepan cook pasta according to package directions, adding diced potatoes during the last 4 minutes of cooking time. Drain and set aside.

2. Meanwhile, for sauce, in large Dutch oven melt 2 Tbsp. of the butter. Cook onion in butter about 3 minutes, until tender. Stir in flour and a pinch of salt and pepper. Cook and stir 2 minutes more. Whisk in milk all at once. Add lemon peel. Cook and stir until thickened and bubbly. Whisk in provolone cheese until melted. Gently fold pasta, potatoes, tuna, olives, and asparagus into sauce. Pour into a 3-quart rectangular baking dish.

3. For topping, in a small bowl melt the remaining 1 Tbsp. of butter. Stir in bread crumbs and Parmesan. Sprinkle on casserole. Bake, uncovered, for 25 to 30 minutes, until heated through and topping is golden. Makes 6 servings.

EACH SERVING *467 cal, 21 g fat, 50 mg chol, 753 mg sodium, 36 g carb, 5 g fiber, 34 g pro.*

ASPARAGUS-TUNA
CASSEROLE

DRY CURED SAUSAGE Seasoned pork or beef air-cured for weeks or months for distinctive flavor; often studded with peppercorns and flavored with spices: sopressata, pepperoni, salami, and Spanish-style chorizo. Refrigerate up to 3 weeks; freezing not recommended.

SMOKED SAUSAGE Fresh or dried, usually boldly seasoned: Eastern-European-style kielbasa, andouille, and mettwurst. Refrigerate up to 1 week. Refer to label for freezing directions.

FRESH BULK SAUSAGE Pork, beef, poultry, or a meat blend seasoned with garlic, herbs, and spices: Italian, breakfast, country, and Mexican-style chorizo. Refrigerate, tightly wrapped, 1 to 2 days; freeze, tightly wrapped, up to 2 months.

Home Cooking

SAUSAGE SAVVY Contributing chef Scott Peacock shows four delicious ways to cook this meat-lovers' favorite. Sausage comes in countless varieties. Here's a guide to the most basic grocery store options, plus storage tips.

FRESH LINK SAUSAGE
Made with a wide variety of seasonings and meat blends: bratwurst, kielbasa, and Italian sausage. Refrigerate 1 to 2 days; freeze up to 2 months.

SMOKED "Knowing when to add smoked sausage is as important as knowing how much. In this recipe, add sausage during the last 10 minutes of cooking so it flavors the stew without losing taste and texture."

Sausage and White Bean Stew with Kale

This recipe requires planning. The dried beans need to soak overnight before cooking.

SOAK 8 hr. PREP 30 min.
COOK 45 min. STAND 30 min.

1   lb. great Northern beans, picked through,* soaked overnight in water, drained, and rinsed
8   to 9 cups homemade chicken stock, unsalted chicken stock, or reduced-sodium chicken broth
3   Tbsp. plus 1 tsp. extra virgin olive oil
2   cups diced onions (2 medium)
½   cup diced celery (3 stalks)
½   cup peeled and diced carrots (1 to 2 medium)
1½ tsp. finely chopped garlic (about 3 cloves); remove any green shoots inside
¼   tsp. dried thyme, crushed
1   14.5-oz. can whole peeled tomatoes, drained and crushed
    Freshly ground black pepper
1   bunch black kale or regular kale, washed and stemmed (about 8 cups)
1   lb. smoked sausage, such as kielbasa or andouille, cut in ½-inch slices

1. In a heavy nonreactive 4- to 6-quart Dutch oven combine drained and rinsed beans, 8 cups stock, and a generous pinch of kosher salt. Bring to boiling. Reduce heat and simmer, partially covered, 30 to 45 minutes until beans are tender, stirring occasionally and adding stock if level is below top of beans. Beans should move about easily in the stock. Cooking time for beans varies from batch to batch.

2. Meanwhile, in a 12-inch skillet heat the 3 Tbsp. olive oil over medium heat. Cook onions in oil until translucent, stopping before onions are brown. Add celery, carrots, and garlic; sprinkle with a pinch of salt and dried thyme. Stir well. Cook 5 to 7 minutes. Add crushed tomatoes; season with a pinch of salt and a few grinds of black pepper. Cook 5 minutes longer. Add to simmering beans.

3. In a large pot of lightly salted boiling water, cook kale for 5 minutes. Drain; set aside to cool. When cool enough to handle, squeeze any remaining water from kale, then coarsely chop kale.

4. Rinse and wipe out skillet. In skillet cook sausage in 1 tsp. olive oil over medium-high heat about 3 minutes until well browned on each side.

5. When beans are tender, add kale and sausage to beans in Dutch oven. Simmer 10 minutes. Taste for seasoning. Let stand 30 minutes. (Soup flavor improves when allowed to rest 30 minutes or longer before serving. This soup can be made up to 2 days ahead and reheated.) Makes 8 servings.

*To pick through dry beans, spread them on a large rimmed baking pan. Examine beans, discarding shriveled beans and small stones.

EACH SERVING *453 cal, 16 g fat, 40 mg chol, 1,199 mg sodium, 52 g carb, 14 g fiber, 27 g pro.*

DRY CURED "A little bit can go a long way when it's a flavorful, peppery dried sausage like sopressata. Cut the sausage in small pieces. It's not the main event. Think of it as a seasoning, like salt and pepper or parsley."

FAST

Potato Salad with Sausage and Grainy Mustard Dressing

This warm potato salad is also delicious at room temperature or chilled. Just add the parsley and green onions a few minutes before serving.

PREP **15 min.** COOK **15 min.**
STAND **2 min.**

1 lb. small red new potatoes, halved
1 lb. small yellow new potatoes, halved
3 Tbsp. cider vinegar
1 Tbsp. plus ½ tsp. kosher salt
¼ cup coarse-grain mustard
3 Tbsp. cider vinegar
3 Tbsp. sugar
¼ cup peanut or vegetable oil
⅓ cup dry cured sausage, such as sopressata, pepperoni, or salami, cut in ¼- to ½-inch pieces
½ cup torn fresh curly-leaf parsley
2 Tbsp. thinly sliced green onions

1. In a 3- to 4-quart saucepan combine potatoes, 3 Tbsp. cider vinegar, and 1 Tbsp. kosher salt. Add water (about 4 cups) to cover potatoes. Bring to boiling over medium heat. Reduce heat and simmer, uncovered, 15 to 20 minutes, just until potatoes are tender when gently pierced with a fork. Drain well. Let stand for 2 to 3 minutes before adding dressing.
2. For Grainy Mustard Dressing, in a small bowl whisk together mustard, 3 Tbsp. vinegar, sugar, and ½ tsp. kosher salt. In a steady stream, whisk in peanut oil until well blended.
3. Transfer potatoes to a mixing bowl. Add Grainy Mustard Dressing all at once. Mix gently to avoid breaking potatoes. Season with a pinch of kosher salt and a few grinds of black pepper. Gently mix in diced sausage. Add parsley and green onions. Serve warm or at room temperature. Makes 8 (¾-cup) servings.
EACH SERVING *199 cal, 9 g fat, 7 mg chol, 585 mg sodium, 24 g carb, 2 g fiber, 4 g pro.*

EFFICIENT DICING
To chop sausage quickly, safely, and neatly, first cut ¼- to ½-inch slices. Stack a few slices. Then, to prevent finger nicks, curl under fingertips holding the sausage and cut stacked slices in small cubes.

FRESH LINK "The casing on fresh link sausages holds the ingredients intact. If you cook the sausage gently and avoid piercing the casing, you'll get all the juicy flavor on your plate instead of leaving it behind in the pan."

GENTLE POACHING
Precooking sausage in wine or water before the browning step keeps the meat moist when it is cooked all the way through. Precooking also reduces the chance that sausage casings will burst during browning.

Sausage Links with Pineapple

Aleppo pepper is a dried chile from Turkey. Because the seeds have been removed, it has mild, rich heat. Find it at online retailers such as penzeys.com or thespicehouse.com or at cooking specialty stores.

START TO FINISH **46 min.**

1   750-ml bottle white wine or 4 cups water
2   cups water
¼   cup granulated sugar
½   tsp. kosher salt
½   tsp. whole black peppercorns
6   fresh sausage links, such as Italian-style or bratwurst, 1 to 1½ lb.
2   tsp. olive oil
2   tsp. butter
3   Tbsp. fresh pineapple juice reserved from peeling, coring, and slicing pineapple
1   pineapple, peeled and cored, thickly sliced (½ to ¾ inch), then cut in 2-inch pieces
¼   tsp. kosher salt
¼   tsp. Aleppo pepper or a pinch of crushed red pepper
1   Tbsp. packed light brown sugar

1. To poach sausages, in a 4- to 6-quart Dutch oven over medium heat, stir together wine or water, the 2 cups water, sugar, salt, and peppercorns. Bring to boiling. Reduce heat to keep water barely simmering; cook 5 minutes. Add sausage links and cook, partially covered, for 10 minutes. Use a flat spatula to carefully remove sausages without piercing casings; set aside.

2. In a 12-inch nonstick skillet heat olive oil and butter over medium heat. Add poached sausages. Slowly brown on all sides, 8 to 10 minutes. Carefully add pineapple juice to skillet (juices may spatter slightly). Increase heat to high. Cook, rolling sausages in pan, until juice is thickened and sausages are well glazed. Transfer browned and glazed sausages to a warm platter. Add pineapple to pan in a single layer. Sprinkle with salt, Aleppo pepper, and brown sugar. Cook 3 to 4 minutes, turning as needed, until pineapple is hot and caramelized. Serve immediately with warm glazed sausages. Makes 6 servings.

EACH SERVING *469 cal, 27 g fat, 61 mg chol, 820 mg sodium, 25 g carb, 1 g fiber, 11 g pro.*

FRESH BULK "Keep sausage chunks relatively flat, exposing more surface area to the pan. You'll get quicker browning and delicious crust."

FAST

Sausage Dinner Hoagies

START TO FINISH 30 min.   OVEN 425°F

4   thin-crust 6-inch sandwich or hoagie rolls
3   Tbsp. unsalted butter, melted
2   jalapeño peppers,* seeded and minced (about 2 Tbsp.)
⅛   to ¼ tsp. cayenne pepper
1   lime, halved
½   cup mayonnaise
1   Tbsp. olive oil
1   lb. bulk Italian sausage, fresh Italian sausage, or fresh Mexican-style chorizo**
1   cup finely shredded green cabbage
     Kosher salt

1. Preheat oven to 425°F. Using a serrated knife, slice off top ¼ inch of rolls. With fingers, remove most of the bread inside, making "boats" to hold sausage and dressing. (Reserve removed bread for another use, such as making bread crumbs.) Brush insides of rolls and undersides of tops with melted butter. Arrange on an ungreased baking sheet, cut sides up; set aside.
2. For flavored mayonnaise, in a small bowl mix together 4 tsp. of the jalapeños, a pinch of salt, and the cayenne pepper. Add juice from one lime half. Whisk in mayonnaise; set aside.

3. In a 12-inch nonstick skillet heat olive oil over medium-high heat. Loosely pinch off 1 to 1½ in. by ½ in.-thick chunks of sausage (about 24). Cook in hot pan in a single layer with space between. Cook for 10 to 12 minutes until well browned and cooked through, turning once to brown evenly.
4. While sausage is cooking, place buttered bread boats in oven for 5 to 8 minutes until golden brown and crusty.
5. Meanwhile, in a medium bowl combine remaining minced jalapeño and shredded cabbage. Add a pinch of kosher salt and juice from remaining lime half; toss to combine. Spoon a generous tablespoonful of flavored mayonnaise in the bottom of each boat. Divide browned sausage, hot from pan, among boats. Top with shredded cabbage. Generously spread cut sides of roll tops with remaining mayonnaise. Place on sandwiches. Serve immediately. Makes 4 sandwiches.
*When working with fresh chiles, wear rubber or disposable plastic gloves or cover your hands with small plastic bags.
**In some areas, these varieties are sold as links. If so, remove from casing before cooking.
EACH SANDWICH *950 cal, 71 g fat, 119 mg chol, 1,638 mg sodium, 54 g carb, 3 g fiber, 24 g pro.*

FRYING RIGHT
For making sandwiches, large chunks of ground sausage are ideal. To keep the juices sealed in while cooking, place sausage chunks in a hot skillet with space between. Starting with a cold skillet or crowding the sausage results in juices that escape—and steaming rather than browning.

Everyday Easy

Soup's on! Warm the body and nourish the soul with these quick and hearty bowls full of color and tempting flavor.

KID FRIENDLY | LOW FAT | FAST

Minestrone

START TO FINISH 20 min.
BUDGET $1.75

1 28-oz. can diced tomatoes with Italian herbs
1 14- to 15-oz. can garbanzo beans (chickpeas), rinsed and drained
1 cup low-sodium vegetable or reduced-sodium chicken broth
1 medium yellow sweet pepper, chopped
2 tsp. Italian seasoning or 1 tsp. each dried basil and garlic powder
1 cup dry rigatoni or penne pasta
2 to 3 cups baby spinach
   Shaved Parmesan and/or fresh basil (optional)

1. In a Dutch oven combine the tomatoes, 2 cups water, beans, broth, sweet pepper, seasoning, and pasta. Bring to boiling over high heat. Reduce heat to medium. Cook, covered, for 10 minutes, stirring occasionally, just until pasta is barely tender.
2. Stir in spinach. Ladle into individual bowls. Top with Parmesan cheese and/or fresh basil if desired. Makes 4 servings.
EACH SERVING 234 cal, 2 g fat, 0 g chol, 759 mg sodium, 46 g carb, 7 g fiber, 10 g pro.

Southwestern Meatball Chili

START TO FINISH 25 min.
BUDGET $2.68

14 to 16 oz. fully cooked refrigerated or frozen beef meatballs, thawed
1 16-oz. pkg. Santa Fe medley frozen mixed vegetables (corn, black beans, red peppers), thawed
2 cups chopped fresh tomatoes and/or cherry tomatoes
1½ cups water
1 Tbsp. chili powder
3 Tbsp. tomato paste
  Sliced jalapeño peppers, chopped cherry tomatoes, and/or fresh cilantro (optional)

1. In a Dutch oven combine the thawed meatballs, thawed vegetables, tomatoes, the water, chili powder, and tomato paste. Cook, covered, over medium-low heat for 20 minutes, stirring occasionally.

2. Ladle chili into bowls. Top with jalapeño peppers, tomatoes, and/or cilantro if desired. Makes 4 servings.
EACH SERVING 385 cal, 24 g fat, 93 mg chol, 944 mg sodium, 25 g carb, 8 g fiber, 20 g pro.
Perfect Partners Complete the meal with corn muffins—homemade or from the grocery store deli or bakery aisle. Wrap the muffins in foil and warm in a 350°F oven for 15 to 20 minutes while preparing the chili.

Fast Shrimp Bisque

START TO FINISH 25 min.
BUDGET $2.03

2 tsp. Old Bay Seasoning or other seafood seasoning
12 oz. fresh or frozen medium-size shrimp in shells, thawed
2 stalks celery, thinly sliced (1 cup)
1 12-oz. can evaporated milk
1 cup milk
2 Tbsp. all-purpose flour
2 tsp. anchovy paste or 1 or 2 anchovies, finely chopped
  Seafood seasoning (optional)

1. In 4-quart Dutch oven combine 2 cups water, seasoning, shrimp, and celery. Cook, uncovered, over medium-high heat for 5 to 8 minutes or until shrimp shells turn pink and shrimp are opaque. Remove shrimp with slotted spoon or tongs; set aside to cool.

2. In a medium bowl whisk together evaporated milk, milk, flour, and anchovy paste; add to liquid in Dutch oven. Cook, uncovered, over medium heat for 10 minutes, stirring occasionally.

3. Meanwhile, peel the shrimp. Chop about half. Add chopped shrimp to soup. Cook for 1 to 2 minutes or until heated through. Ladle into bowls. Top with remaining shrimp. Pass seafood seasoning if desired. Makes 4 servings.
EACH SERVING 224 cal, 9 g fat, 138 mg chol, 973 mg sodium, 16 g carb, 1 g fiber, 20 g pro.

SUNDAY DINNER
STEW

LOW FAT | FAST

Sunday Dinner Stew

START TO FINISH 28 min.
BUDGET $2.14

1   lb. small new potatoes
3   large carrots, halved lengthwise and
      cut up
1   17-oz. pkg. refrigerated cooked beef
      tips with gravy
1¼   cups water
1   bunch green onions, chopped
      Fresh or dried thyme

1. Rinse potatoes. Halve or quarter large potatoes for fairly uniform size. Place potatoes in large microwave-safe bowl. Cover with vented plastic wrap and microcook on 100 percent power (high) for 5 minutes. Add carrots; cover and cook for 5 to 7 minutes, or until potatoes and carrots are tender.
2. In Dutch oven combine vegetables, undrained beef tips, and the water. Cook over medium-high heat just until bubbly around edges. Add green onions. Cover and cook for 5 minutes more or until heated through. Ladle into bowls. Sprinkle with thyme. Makes 4 servings.
EACH SERVING *302 cal, 9 g fat, 52 mg chol, 686 mg sodium, 36 g carb, 6 g fiber, 22 g pro.*
Versatile Vegetables Substitute 1 pound of sweet potatoes, peeled and cut up, for the new potatoes. Along with the chopped green onions, add a handful of chopped kale. Serve the stew with crusty bread or whole grain crackers.

SMOKY CHEESE AND POTATO SOUP

KID FRIENDLY | FAST

Smoky Cheese and Potato Soup

START TO FINISH 25 min.
BUDGET $2.23

6   oz. smoked cheese (cheddar,
      mozzarella, or Gouda), shredded
1   Tbsp. all-purpose flour
4   oz. ham, finely chopped
1   medium carrot, finely chopped
½   tsp. curry powder
½   tsp. paprika
3   cups whole milk
½   24-oz. pkg. refrigerated garlic
      mashed potatoes
      Canned shoestring potatoes, fresh
      snipped parsley, and/or paprika
      (optional)

1. In a bowl combine cheese and flour; set aside. In a Dutch oven combine the ham, carrot, curry powder, and paprika. Cook and stir over medium heat for 2 minutes. Stir in milk. Cook, uncovered, for 4 to 5 minutes, until milk is hot but not boiling, stirring occasionally. Gradually whisk in mashed potatoes. Cook, stirring frequently, until hot and bubbly. Stir in the cheese and flour mixture. Cook and stir for 2 minutes, just until cheese is melted.
2. Ladle soup into bowls. Top with shoestring potatoes, parsley, and/or paprika if desired. Makes 4 servings.
EACH SERVING *429 cal, 26 g fat, 94 mg chol, 1,059 mg sodium, 22 g carb, 2 g fiber, 25 g pro.*
Vegetarian Option Replace ham with 1 cup cooked cannellini beans. For a change of herbs, swap in chopped chives for the parsley.

Delicious on a Dollar

This one-pan egg dish features crispy browned potatoes, tender carrots, and fresh tomatoes.

KID FRIENDLY
Potato Frittata

Slice potatoes and carrots about ⅛ inch thick to ensure they become tender and golden during cooking.

PREP 25 min. COOK 10 min.
BAKE 18 min. STAND 5 min.
OVEN 375°F

1   lb. Yukon gold or russet potatoes, scrubbed and thinly sliced
2   Tbsp. olive oil
2   large carrots, thinly sliced
12 eggs
½   cup green onions (about 4), chopped
¼   tsp. each salt and ground black pepper
½   cup yellow cherry tomatoes, halved
1   clove garlic, minced
    Fresh snipped parsley and/or cilantro

1. Preheat oven to 375°F. In a 10-inch oven-safe nonstick skillet cook potatoes in hot oil over medium heat for 5 minutes. Add carrots. Cook for 5 minutes more until potatoes and carrots are tender and lightly browned, turning occasionally.
2. In a medium bowl whisk together the eggs, half of the green onions, salt, and pepper. Pour egg mixture over potatoes. Bake, uncovered, about 18 minutes or until frittata appears dry on top. Remove skillet from oven and let stand on a wire rack for 5 minutes. With a spatula loosen edges of frittata from pan. Place a large serving platter over skillet. Using two hands, invert platter and skillet to release frittata onto platter.
3. Meanwhile, in a small bowl toss together remaining green onions, cherry tomatoes, garlic, and parsley. Spoon tomato mixture on frittata. Cut frittata in wedges; serve immediately. Makes 6 servings.

EACH SERVING *258 cal, 14 g fat, 372 mg chol, 267 mg sodium, 18 g carb, 3 g fiber, 15 g pro.*

POTATO FRITTATA

CRISPY HONEY
MUSTARD
PORK CHOPS

april

SPRING BAKING Be deliciously surprised with all you can do with (your) honey. And if you're interested in a spring baking fling, here are the recipes!

91

99

104

PISTACHIO-HONEY CAKE WITH BERRIES AND CREAM

Honey Do!

Give that bear a squeeze for braises, sauces, cakes, and more—then be prepared to be deliciously surprised.

KID FRIENDLY

Pistachio-Honey Cake with Berries and Cream

Matching the flavor star—honey—with pistachios and creamy mascarpone makes this cake a new favorite. To make ahead, cover and refrigerate cake. Add topping right before serving.
PREP **30 min.** BAKE **30 min.**
COOL **5 min.** OVEN **325°F**

1 cup all-purpose flour
½ cup cornmeal
¼ cup pistachio nuts, ground
2 tsp. baking powder
½ tsp. salt
½ cup butter, softened
¾ cup honey
2 eggs
½ cup milk
2 Tbsp. orange juice
½ cup mascarpone cheese, chilled, or cream cheese, softened
1 cup whipping cream, chilled
2 Tbsp. honey
1 pint strawberries, halved or sliced
   Chopped pistachio nuts

1. Preheat oven to 325°F. Butter a 9×1½-inch round cake pan. Line bottom with parchment; set aside.

2. In medium bowl combine flour, cornmeal, ground pistachios, baking powder, and salt; set aside. In large mixing bowl beat butter with mixer on medium to high for 30 seconds. Add ½ cup of the honey; beat 3 minutes until fluffy. Slowly beat in eggs, one at a time. Add three-fourths of the flour mixture; mix just until combined. Mix in milk and remaining flour mixture just until combined. Pour batter into prepared pan.
3. Bake for 30 to 35 minutes until wooden toothpick inserted near center comes out clean. Cool on wire rack 5 minutes. Remove cake from pan.
4. Meanwhile, in small saucepan heat remaining ¼ cup honey and orange juice, whisking to combine. Poke warm cake with a wooden toothpick. Brush on honey-orange juice until absorbed. Cool cake completely.
5. For topping, just before serving, in medium mixing bowl whip mascarpone on medium to high for 30 seconds. Add cream and 2 Tbsp. honey; beat just to soft mounds. Spoon topping on cake, drizzle with additional honey, and top with strawberries and chopped pistachios. Makes 12 servings.
EACH SERVING *371 cal, 22 g fat, 92 mg chol, 279 mg sodium, 41 g carb, 1 g fiber, 6 g pro.*

HONEY HOW-TO
Honey can be tricky (and sticky!) to work with, so here are a couple of tips from Lia:

● Honey varies in thickness and granulation. To make it easy to pour, warm the jar for a few seconds in the microwave or place the container in a bowl of warm water for a few minutes. If the lid is stuck on the jar, place it under warm water to loosen it.

● To measure honey, coat the measuring cup or spoon with nonstick spray. The honey will slide right out.

MEET LIA HUBER
"Honey plays very well beyond the sweet zone," says Lia Huber, the creator of these recipes. "When used in savory dishes, it lends sweetness and helps draw out other flavors, especially aromatic spices like ginger, curry powder, and anise. I also love it in desserts. The flavor of the honey itself really comes through but doesn't overpower everything else."

Lia is the founder of the Nourish Network (nourishnetwork.com), a site that provides sound nutrition advice and recipes, eco-friendly ideas, and general kitchen tips.

Honey is a busy bee in the kitchen. On the sweet side, it absorbs moisture (unlike sugar) for luscious desserts. With just a brush of honey, savory dishes such as chicken and pork take on a striking bronze glaze. So simple—and no one will know your honey did all the work!

KID FRIENDLY | **FAST**

Honey Roast Chicken with Spring Peas and Shallots

This beautiful glazed chicken is served with a light champagne-and-honey sauce. Lemon slices added during the last few minutes balance the sweetness of the honey. This easily becomes a pan stew when you use chicken pieces (see right).

PREP **15 min.** ROAST **1 hr. 20 min.** COOK **13 min.** OVEN **375°F**

1   3½- to 4-lb. whole broiler-fryer chicken
2   Tbsp. butter, melted
½   tsp. each salt and black pepper
¾   cup honey
2   Tbsp. fresh tarragon
1   cup peeled and sliced shallots
1   cup champagne, sparkling wine, or reduced-sodium chicken broth
½   cup chicken broth
1½   cups fresh or frozen peas
1   small lemon, thinly sliced
     Honey (optional)

1. Preheat oven to 375°F. Rinse chicken cavity; pat chicken dry with paper towels. Skewer neck skin to back; tie legs to tail. Place in a shallow roasting pan. Brush with butter; sprinkle with salt and pepper.

2. Roast, uncovered, for 1¼ to 1¾ hours or until drumsticks move easily and chicken is no longer pink (180°F). Brush with half the honey and sprinkle with half the tarragon. Roast 5 minutes longer or until honey forms a golden brown glaze.

3. Remove chicken from pan and tent with foil. Transfer roasting pan to stove top. Add shallots, champagne, broth, remaining honey, and fresh peas (if using). Simmer, uncovered, about 10 minutes until juices thicken slightly and shallots are tender. Add frozen peas (if using) and lemon slices to pan. Simmer 3 to 5 minutes or until heated through. To serve, return chicken to pan, sprinkle with remaining tarragon, and top with additional honey if desired. Makes 6 servings.

Pan Stew Chicken Arrange chicken pieces skin sides up in shallow baking pan. Brush with butter, then sprinkle with salt and pepper. Roast, uncovered, for 35 minutes. Brush with half the honey and sprinkle with half the tarragon. Roast 5 minutes longer until honey forms a golden brown glaze. Continue as directed in Step 3.

EACH SERVING *811 cal, 44 g fat, 209 mg chol, 461 mg sodium, 47 g carb, 3 g fiber, 52 g pro.*

HONEY ROAST
CHICKEN WITH
SPRING PEAS
AND SHALLOTS

HONEY-PEPPER
BACON POPS

FETA, HONEY, AND
DATE SPREAD

Honey-Pepper Bacon Pops

The sticky glaze on these bacon kabobs is a savory-sweet blend of soy, honey, and spices.

PREP 35 min. BAKE 20 min. OVEN 400°F

12 8- to 10-inch wooden skewers
½ cup honey
1 Tbsp. soy sauce
2 tsp. Chinese five-spice powder
1 tsp. freshly ground black pepper
1 16-oz. package thick cut bacon
   Texas toast (optional)
   Comb honey (optional)

1. Soak skewers in water for 30 minutes. Drain just before threading on bacon.
2. Meanwhile, preheat oven to 400°F. For honey-pepper, in small saucepan warm honey to liquid; stir in soy sauce, five-spice powder, and pepper. Set aside.
3. Thread each bacon slice on a skewer; lay kabob on rack of broiler pan. Bake for 15 minutes. Remove from oven. Brush generously with honey-pepper, turning to coat each side. Return to oven. Bake 5 minutes longer or until crisp. Serve with Texas toast and comb honey if desired. Makes 12 servings.
EACH SERVING 233 cal, 16 g fat, 31 mg chol, 873 mg sodium, 12 g carb, 0 g fiber, 13 g pro.

Feta, Honey, and Date Spread

This spread can be made ahead and stored in the fridge up to 3 days. For a flavorful dipper, brush pita wedges with olive oil and sprinkle with salt and thyme before toasting.

START TO FINISH 20 min.

1 cup crumbled feta (4 oz.)
½ cup toasted almonds, coarsely chopped
½ cup pitted dates, chopped
2 Tbsp. fresh marjoram or 1 Tbsp. fresh thyme, chopped
2 Tbsp. coarsely chopped or sliced green olives
2 tsp. finely shredded lemon peel
¼ cup honey
¼ tsp. cayenne pepper
   Toasted pita bread wedges

In a serving bowl gently stir together feta, almonds, dates, marjoram, olives, and lemon peel. In small microwave-safe bowl combine honey and cayenne; warm in microwave 15 seconds. Drizzle over spread; fold gently to combine. Serve with pita bread. Makes 12 servings.
EACH SERVING 168 cal, 7 g fat, 8 mg chol, 286 mg sodium, 24 g carb, 2 g fiber, 4 g pro.

LOW FAT

Sweet Curry Carrots with Chive Yogurt

Roasting brings out the natural sweetness of the carrots, which is enhanced by the honey and curry.

PREP 20 min. **ROAST** 25 min. **OVEN** 425°F

1½ lb. carrots with tops, trimmed (about 10)
1   Tbsp. extra virgin olive oil
3   Tbsp. honey
1   Tbsp. curry powder
⅔   cup plain low-fat Greek yogurt
¼   cup snipped fresh chives

1. Preheat oven to 425°F. Scrub carrots and peel, if desired. Halve any large carrots lengthwise.

2. Line a 15×10×1-inch baking pan with foil. Toss carrots with olive oil. Evenly spread carrots in prepared pan. Sprinkle with ¼ tsp. salt. Roast carrots for 15 minutes. Meanwhile, in small microwave-safe bowl warm honey in microwave for 30 seconds. Whisk in curry powder; set aside.

3. Remove carrots from oven. Drizzle with honey mixture; toss to coat. Roast 10 minutes longer, turning occasionally, until carrots are glazed and tender when pierced with a fork. Transfer to serving platter.

4. For Chive Yogurt, in a bowl combine yogurt, chives, and ¼ tsp. salt. Serve with carrots. Makes 6 to 8 servings.

EACH SERVING *121 cal, 3 g fat, 1 mg chol, 283 mg sodium, 21 g carb, 4 g fiber, 4 g pro.*

SWEET CURRY CARROTS WITH CHIVE YOGURT

HONEY-SOAKED QUINOA SALAD WITH CHERRIES AND CASHEWS

Just a drizzle of honey in a vinaigrette is downright divine. The molten gold enhances aromatics such as ginger in a way no other sweetener can. Add fresh cherries and red onion slivers. Now you have a salad that will start a buzz.

Honey-Soaked Quinoa Salad with Cherries and Cashews

Place the quinoa in a fine-mesh strainer and hold under running water to remove any saponin, the natural coating on the grain, which may taste bitter. Couscous, cooked according to package directions, can be used in place of the quinoa.

PREP 30 min. COOK 10 min.
STAND 10 min.

Honey Vinaigrette
2   Tbsp. grated fresh ginger
¼   cup honey
2   Tbsp. white wine vinegar
2   Tbsp. freshly squeezed lime juice
1   small clove garlic, minced
¼   cup extra virgin olive oil

Quinoa Salad
1   cup water
⅔   cup uncooked quinoa (rinsed)
¼   tsp. salt
½   cup whole cashews, coarsely chopped
½   cup dried apricots, sliced into thin slivers
1   cup fresh dark sweet cherries, pitted and halved, or red seedless grapes, halved
¼   cup thinly sliced red onion
1   small head butter lettuce, torn (4 cups)

1. For Honey Vinaigrette, in small bowl whisk together ginger, honey, vinegar, lime juice, and garlic. Drizzle in olive oil, whisking constantly, until well combined. Season with salt and pepper. Set aside.
2. For Quinoa Salad, in medium saucepan bring the water, quinoa, and salt to boiling. Reduce heat and simmer, covered, for 10 minutes, until liquid is absorbed. Remove from heat; let stand 10 minutes.
3. Fluff quinoa with a fork. In large bowl toss quinoa with cashews, apricots, cherries, and onion. Add lettuce, then drizzle with ½ cup of the vinaigrette. Season to taste with salt and pepper, then toss again. Pass remaining vinaigrette. Refrigerate remaining vinaigrette up to 5 days in sealed jar. Makes 4 servings.
EACH SERVING *372 cal, 17 g fat, 0 mg chol, 230 mg sodium, 52 g carb, 5 g fiber, 9 g pro.*

HONEY BEAR HISTORY
The squeezable honey bear was created in 1957. Ralph and Luella Gamber, founders of Dutch Gold Honey, were brainstorming packaging ideas with fellow beekeepers when the idea struck. In those early days, the eyes, noses, and sometimes red lips were hand-painted on each bear.

HOW TO USE THE HONEYCOMB
Find honeycomb in two forms. Comb honey is in its original state, honey in the honeycomb. Cut comb honey is liquid honey with chunks of the comb added to the jar—also known as a liquid-cut-comb combination.

The comb is edible, so serve these types as table honey with toast or fruit, or as a sweet addition to cheese plates.

Honey acts as a foil for zingy ingredients like mustard. But don't be fooled into thinking it's all about sweet. Simmer a squeeze of honey with earthy beets and exotic spices, and you'll unleash distinctive, heady notes.

KID FRIENDLY | FAST

Crispy Honey Mustard Pork Chops

Once the chops are dipped in the honey mixture, place them in the fridge a few minutes for the marinade to thicken and adhere to the pork before cooking. Serve the chops with Sweet Beet Chutney.

PREP 15 min. COOK 6 min.
BAKE 8 min. OVEN 450°F

4   pork chops, ½ inch thick (about 1½ lb.)
½   tsp. salt
¼   tsp. freshly ground black pepper
¼   cup honey
¼   cup stone-ground mustard
2   Tbsp. panko (Japanese-style bread crumbs)
2   tsp. chopped fresh marjoram
⅛   tsp. onion powder
¼   cup extra virgin olive oil

1. Preheat oven to 450°F. Trim fat from chops, season with salt and pepper, then set aside. In shallow dish combine honey and mustard. In small bowl combine bread crumbs, 1 tsp. of the marjoram, and the onion powder. Set aside.
2. Dip chops in honey mixture to coat, letting excess drip off. Place on parchment-lined plate. Marinate in refrigerator 5 minutes.
3. Heat 12-inch skillet over medium-high heat. Swirl in olive oil. (If pan isn't large enough to hold 4 chops without crowding, cook in two batches.) Cook chops in hot oil 3 minutes until undersides are crisp and browned. Turn chops; cook 3 minutes. Transfer to oven-safe platter. Sprinkle chops with bread crumb mixture.
4. Bake chops 8 to 9 minutes until crumbs begin to brown. Sprinkle with remaining marjoram. Serve with Sweet Beet Chutney. Makes 4 servings.
EACH SERVING 553 cal, 25 g fat, 64 mg chol, 783 mg sodium, 58 g carb, 4 g fiber, 26 g pro.

Sweet Beet Chutney In a medium saucepan combine 1 lb. peeled and diced beets and ¾ cup water. Bring to boiling, covered. Reduce heat. Boil gently, covered, for 8 minutes. Uncover. Stir in ¼ cup cider vinegar, 3 Tbsp. honey, ½ cup raisins, 1 tsp. ground coriander, ½ tsp. dried mustard, ½ tsp. ground cardamom, and salt to taste. Return to gentle boiling. Cook, uncovered, 20 to 25 minutes, until liquid is syrupy.

CRISPY HONEY
MUSTARD
PORK CHOPS

Honey is the kind of sweet that mates well with all types of heat. Bubble it in a pan until amber brown and it takes on a deep, complex personality—just right for creamy custards.

FLAVOR NOTES

More than 300 varieties of honey are found in the United States; the most common is clover honey. Varietals have flavors that range from herbaceous to floral to earthy, all based on the types of plants from which the bees gathered pollen. Color and flavor in honey are often linked. Typically, dark honey has a strong robust taste; light-color honey is more delicate and sweeter.

KID FRIENDLY

Sticky Honey-Pineapple Custards

The pineapple-infused honey gets thicker as it cooks and reduces. Stir any leftover honey into yogurt or oatmeal, heating it for a few seconds in the microwave to make drizzling easy.

PREP 25 min. BAKE 20 min.
CHILL 1 hr. OVEN 325°F

1¾	cups half-and-half or light cream
5	egg yolks, lightly beaten
¼	cup sugar
1	Tbsp. honey
1	tsp. vanilla
¾	cup honey
4	½-inch slices peeled and cored fresh pineapple rings
	Flaked sea salt (optional)

1. Preheat oven to 325°F. In a small heavy saucepan heat half-and-half over medium-low heat just until bubbly. Remove from heat; set aside.

2. Meanwhile, in a medium bowl combine egg yolks, the sugar, the 1 Tbsp. honey, and vanilla. Beat with wire whisk just until combined. Slowly whisk in the hot half-and-half.

3. Place 4 shallow 8-oz. ramekins or 6- to 10-oz. custard cups in a roasting pan. Pour custard in dishes. Place pan on oven rack. Carefully pour boiling water in pan to halfway up sides of dishes.

4. Bake for 20 to 25 minutes for shallow dishes or 35 to 40 minutes for deep dishes, just until a knife inserted near center comes out clean (centers will jiggle slightly). Carefully remove dishes from water; cool on wire rack. Cover; chill for 1 to 8 hours.

5. Just before serving, in large skillet heat the ¾ cup honey. Arrange pineapple slices in honey in skillet. Bring to gentle boiling over medium-high heat. Boil, uncovered, 15 minutes (honey will bubble) until honey has thickened and begins to darken and pineapple is tender. Place a pineapple ring on each custard. Drizzle with some of the reserved honey. Sprinkle with sea salt if desired. Makes 4 servings.

EACH SERVING *399 cal, 18 g fat, 270 mg chol, 56 mg sodium, 56 g carb, 1 g fiber, 7 g pro.*

STICKY HONEY-
PINEAPPLE
CUSTARDS

LEMON-RASPBERRY
COFFEECAKE

Home Cooking

Throw open the windows and celebrate the end of winter with these luscious, crowd-pleasing recipes that bring fresh-baked goodness to breakfast or brunch.

KID FRIENDLY

Lemon-Raspberry Coffeecake

Cut wedges straight from the pan or transfer the cake to a serving plate for pretty presentation.

PREP **15 min.** BAKE **45 min.**
COOL **10 min.** OVEN **375°F**

1½ cups all-purpose flour
1½ tsp. baking powder
¼ tsp. baking soda
¼ tsp. salt
1¼ cups granulated sugar
½ cup butter, softened
1 egg
1 tsp. vanilla
¾ cup buttermilk
3 oz. cream cheese, softened
1 tsp. finely shredded lemon peel
1 egg
1 cup fresh or frozen raspberries
Powdered sugar (optional)

1. Preheat oven to 375°F. Lightly grease bottom of 9×1½-inch round cake pan. Line bottom of pan with parchment. Grease and lightly flour pan; set aside. For cake, in a medium bowl stir together flour, baking powder, baking soda, and salt; set aside.

2. In medium mixing bowl beat 1 cup of the granulated sugar and the butter with mixer on medium to high until combined. Add 1 egg and the vanilla. Beat on low to medium 1 minute. Alternately add flour mixture and buttermilk to sugar mixture, beating just until combined after each addition; set aside.

3. For cheesecake filling, in small mixing bowl beat cream cheese and remaining ¼ cup granulated sugar on medium to high until combined. Add lemon peel and 1 egg. Beat until combined.

4. Spoon half the cake batter into prepared pan, spreading to edges. Pour cream cheese mixture on cake batter, spreading to edges. Dollop remaining batter on cream cheese layer, carefully spreading to edges of pan.

5. Bake 20 minutes or until puffed. Gently press raspberries into cake. Bake 25 to 30 minutes more or until toothpick inserted near center comes out clean. Cool in pan on wire rack 10 minutes. Loosen edges of cake from pan; remove from pan. Sprinkle with powdered sugar if desired. Makes 10 servings.

EACH SERVING *309 cal, 14 g fat, 72 mg chol, 302 mg sodium, 43 g carb, 1 g fiber, 5 g pro.*

LAYERING THE BATTERS
Keep the cheesecake filling from mixing into the cake layer. Spread half the cake batter into the pan and evenly top with the cheesecake filling. Using two spatulas, dollop remaining cake batter over the filling and carefully smooth top.

The lemony cheesecake center and fresh raspberries make this a springtime-perfect coffeecake. So the raspberries do not sink into the batter, the cake is partially baked, then berries are gently pressed into the top.

These savory cornmeal muffins have scrambled eggs, cheddar cheese, and bacon strips baked right in. To ensure tender muffins, learn to love lumps. Stir the batter together until combined but not completely smooth.

NO-STICK FLAVOR BOOST
Use bacon drippings to grease the muffin cups and add flavor. Dip a pastry brush in the drippings and brush on the bottom and sides of each cup.

KID FRIENDLY

Bacon-and-Egg Muffins

PREP **30 min.** BAKE **15 min.**
COOL **5 min.** OVEN **400°F**

4	slices bacon, cut in thirds
5	eggs
1	cup all-purpose flour
½	cup yellow cornmeal
2	Tbsp. sugar
2½	tsp. baking powder
1	cup milk
¼	cup vegetable oil or butter, melted
½	cup shredded cheddar cheese
	Maple or cane syrup (optional)

1. Preheat oven to 400°F. In large skillet cook bacon just until it begins to crisp. Drain and reserve drippings. Return 2 tsp. drippings to skillet. For scrambled eggs, in small bowl beat 3 of the eggs, 2 Tbsp. water, and a dash each of salt and pepper. Cook eggs in hot skillet over medium heat, without stirring, until eggs begin to set on bottom and around edges. With a spatula, lift and fold for uncooked portion to flow underneath. Cook until set but still moist. Transfer to bowl; set aside.

2. Brush twelve 2½-inch muffin cups with some remaining bacon drippings. In medium bowl stir together flour, cornmeal, sugar, baking powder, and ½ tsp. salt. Combine milk, oil, and remaining 2 eggs in bowl. Stir into flour mixture. Fold in scrambled eggs and cheese. Spoon into muffin cups (cups will be full).

3. Place 1 bacon piece on each muffin. Bake 15 to 17 minutes or until light brown and a toothpick inserted in centers comes out clean. Cool slightly in pan on rack. Run a table knife around edges of muffins to loosen; remove from pans. Serve with syrup if desired. Makes 12 servings.

EACH SERVING *202 cal, 12 g fat, 89 mg chol, 356 mg sodium, 16 g carb, 1 g fiber, 7 g pro.*

BACON-AND-EGG
MUFFINS

**BLUEBERRY CREAM
BISCUITS WITH
BLUEBERRY SAUCE**

The key to melt-in-your-mouth biscuits is a light touch. Don't overwork the dough. Using cream is like having butter and milk combined—you skip a step and the dough is worked very little.

KID FRIENDLY | FAST

Blueberry Cream Biscuits with Blueberry Sauce

This recipe is foolproof—there's no blending in butter, no rolling. Here the biscuits are studded with blueberries for breakfast, but they're just as good for dinner, made without berries and sugar.

PREP 20 min. BAKE 17 min.
OVEN 425°F

2   cups all-purpose flour
2   tsp. baking powder
2   Tbsp. sugar
½   tsp. salt
¼   tsp. grated nutmeg
1   cup blueberries
1½ cups whipping cream
1   recipe Blueberry Sauce

1. Preheat oven to 425°F. In a large bowl stir together flour, baking powder, sugar, salt, and nutmeg to thoroughly mix. Toss blueberries with the flour mixture. Stir cream into the flour mixture just until moistened.
2. Turn dough out onto a floured surface. Gently lift and fold dough four or five times, making a quarter turn between each fold. Place dough on parchment-lined baking sheet. Form dough in a 7- to 8-inch square, approximately 1 inch thick. Using a floured pizza cutter or knife, cut 12 to 16 biscuits, leaving biscuits intact. Bake in upper half of oven for 17 to 20 minutes or until golden brown. Cut or pull apart to serve. Serve with Blueberry Sauce. Makes 12 to 16 biscuits.

Blueberry Sauce In medium saucepan combine 1 cup blueberries, ⅓ cup sugar, and 2 tbsp. water. Bring to a simmer; cook and stir until blueberries pop and sauce has thickened. Remove from heat, then stir in 1 tsp. vanilla and another 1 cup of blueberries. Serve warm or at room temperature.
EACH BISCUIT (WITHOUT SAUCE)
195 cal, 11 g fat, 41 mg chol, 190 mg sodium, 20 g carb, 1 g fiber, 3 g pro.

SCORE AND BAKE
Cut the biscuits with a pizza cutter before baking. Once they come out of the oven, pull the biscuits apart to serve.

The same technique for making fan rolls—layering the dough sideways—is used to create this spin on monkey bread. It makes the loaf more fun to pull apart and eat, and it's quicker than the traditional version that requires shaping dozens of little balls.

CREATING THE LOAF

Making the pull-apart layers is easy. Roll the dough to a rectangle. Top with the melted butter and cinnamon-sugar. Cut in strips and stack. Next, cut the stack in pieces, then stagger them in a loaf pan. Space around the pieces will fill in as the dough rises and bakes.

KID FRIENDLY

Overnight Pull-Apart Cinnamon Loaf

This no-knead dough is made the day before and allowed to slow-rise in the fridge overnight to develop flavor.

PREP 30 min. RISE overnight + 45 min.
BAKE 30 min. COOL 30 min.
OVEN 350°F

¾ cup milk
1 pkg. active dry yeast
¼ cup butter, melted
2 Tbsp. granulated sugar
1 egg, lightly beaten
½ tsp. salt
3 cups all-purpose flour
¼ cup butter, melted
¾ cup granulated sugar
2 tsp. ground cinnamon
1 recipe Quick Glaze
Chopped pistachio nuts (optional)

1. In a small saucepan heat milk just until warm (105°F to 115°F). Pour into a large mixing bowl, then add the yeast. Stir until yeast is dissolved. Let stand 5 minutes or until foamy.

2. With a mixer, beat ¼ cup melted butter, 2 Tbsp. sugar, egg, and salt into the yeast mixture until combined. Add half the flour, then beat on low for 30 seconds, scraping bowl as needed. Increase speed to medium and beat 3 minutes more. Stir in remaining flour. Shape in a ball (dough will not be smooth). Transfer to an oiled bowl. Cover and refrigerate overnight. (Or, to make right away, cover and set aside in a warm place to rise 45 to 60 minutes or until nearly double.)

3. Butter a 9×5×3-inch loaf pan; set aside. Remove dough from refrigerator. On lightly floured surface roll dough to 20×12-inch rectangle (see "Creating the Loaf"). Brush with ¼ cup melted butter and sprinkle with a mixture of ¾ cup sugar and cinnamon. Cut dough rectangle crosswise in five 12×4-inch strips. Stack strips, then cut six 4×2-inch pieces. Loosely stagger pieces in prepared pan, cut sides up.

4. Let rise in a warm place 45 minutes or until nearly double in size. Preheat oven to 350°F. Bake loaf 30 minutes or until golden brown. Cool in pan on wire rack for 10 minutes. Remove from pan and transfer to serving plate. Drizzle with Quick Glaze and sprinkle with nuts if desired. Cool 20 minutes more. Pull apart slices or slice to serve. Makes 12 servings.

Quick Glaze In a small bowl stir together 1 cup powdered sugar, ½ tsp. vanilla, and 1 to 2 Tbsp. milk for drizzling consistency.

EACH SERVING 296 cal, 9 g fat, 37 mg chol, 180 mg sodium, 50 g carb, 1 g fiber, 5 g pro.

OVERNIGHT PULL-APART
CINNAMON LOAF

**LEMON-DILL
SHRIMP AND PASTA**

Everyday Easy

Suppertime Sprint! Win the weeknight race
with this medley of fast, fresh, flavorful dishes.

KID FRIENDLY LOW FAT FAST
Lemon-Dill Shrimp and Pasta

START TO FINISH 25 min.
BUDGET $2.45 per serving

12	oz. frozen peeled and deveined medium shrimp, thawed
1	lemon
8	oz. dried fettuccine
2	Tbsp. olive oil
3	or 4 cloves garlic, thinly sliced
6	cups baby spinach
½	tsp. Italian seasoning, crushed
	Fresh dill sprigs

1. Rinse shrimp; pat dry with paper towels. Finely shred 1 tsp. peel from the lemon; set aside. Juice the lemon over a bowl; set aside juice. Cook pasta according to package directions.
2. Meanwhile, in 12-inch skillet heat olive oil over medium heat. Cook garlic in hot oil for 1 minute. Add shrimp; cook for 3 to 4 minutes, turning frequently until shrimp are opaque. Add spinach and drained pasta; toss just until spinach begins to wilt. Stir in Italian seasoning, lemon peel, and 2 Tbsp. lemon juice. Season to taste with salt and pepper and top with fresh dill. Makes 4 servings.
EACH SERVING *359 cal, 9 g fat, 107 mg chol, 696 mg sodium, 50 g carb, 5 g fiber, 21 g pro.*

GINGERED
CARROT-SWEET POTATO
SOUP

GRILLED HAM AND
PINEAPPLE BURGERS

LOW FAT | **FAST**

Gingered Carrot-Sweet Potato Soup

START TO FINISH 30 min.
BUDGET $1.83 per serving

1   lb. carrots, peeled and thinly sliced
1   large sweet potato, peeled and cut in ½-inch cubes
3   14.5-oz. cans reduced-sodium chicken broth
1   tsp. ground ginger
½   cup sour cream or crème fraîche
2   Tbsp. finely minced green onions or snipped fresh chives
1   19-oz. can no-salt-added cannellini (white kidney) beans, rinsed and drained
    Finely minced green onions or snipped fresh chives (optional)
    Ground ginger (optional)

1. In Dutch oven combine carrots, potato, broth, and ginger. Bring to boiling. Reduce heat. Simmer, covered, 10 to 12 minutes until vegetables are tender.

Meanwhile, in small bowl combine sour cream and green onions; set aside.
2. In blender, puree vegetables with beans, one-fourth at a time, removing cap from blender lid and holding folded kitchen towel over opening. Season with salt and pepper. Top servings with sour cream and green onion mixture. If desired, sprinkle additional green onions and ginger. Makes 4 servings.
EACH SERVING *318 cal, 6 g fat, 12 mg chol, 1,059 mg sodium, 54 g carb, 12 g fiber, 14 g pro.*

KID FRIENDLY | **FAST**

Grilled Ham and Pineapple Burgers

START TO FINISH 30 min.
BUDGET $2.89 per serving

2   cups loosely packed fresh basil leaves
1   lb. ground ham loaf (or ½ lb. each ground ham and ground pork)
4   ½-inch slices fresh pineapple
4   kaiser rolls, split and toasted
¼   cup mayonnaise
2   Tbsp. yellow mustard
1   Tbsp. honey

1. Snip enough basil to equal ⅓ cup. In large bowl combine half the snipped basil and ground ham; shape in four ¾-inch-thick patties.
2. Grill patties on rack of charcoal or gas grill, covered, directly over medium heat for 14 to 18 minutes, turning once, until patties register 160°F with instant-read thermometer. Add pineapple to grill during last 6 minutes of grilling time for patties, turning once. Meanwhile, in bowl combine mayonnaise, mustard, honey, and remaining snipped basil. Spread on cut sides of roll bottoms. Layer patties, remaining basil leaves, pineapple, and roll tops. Makes 4 servings.
EACH SERVING *566 cal, 30 g fat, 78 mg chol, 1,238 mg sodium, 49 g carb, 4 g fiber, 26 g pro.*

CHICKEN, TOMATO, AND CUCUMBER DINNER SALAD

ROAST BEEF QUESADILLAS

Chicken, Tomato, and Cucumber Dinner Salad

START TO FINISH 20 min.
BUDGET $2.57 per serving

5   Tbsp. olive oil
1   to 1¼ lb. chicken breast tenders
     Salt and freshly ground black pepper
¼   cup cider vinegar or white wine vinegar
1   Tbsp. snipped fresh thyme
1   tsp. sugar
1   medium cucumber, cut in thin ribbons
2   tomatoes, sliced
½   cup pitted green olives, halved and/ or sliced
4   oz. feta cheese (optional)

1. In large skillet heat 1 Tbsp. of the olive oil over medium heat. Lightly sprinkle chicken tenders with salt and pepper. Cook chicken in hot oil for 8 to 10 minutes, turning once, until no pink remains.
2. For vinaigrette, in screw-top jar combine remaining oil, vinegar, thyme, sugar, and ¼ tsp. each salt and pepper; shake to combine.
3. On plates arrange chicken, cucumber ribbons, sliced tomatoes, olives, and feta cheese, if desired. Drizzle vinaigrette over salads. Makes 4 servings.
EACH SERVING *336 cal, 3 g fat, 73 mg chol, 569 mg sodium, 7 g carb, 2 g fiber, 25 g pro.*

Roast Beef Quesadillas

START TO FINISH 25 min.
BUDGET $2.67 per serving

1   17-oz. pkg. refrigerated cooked beef roast au jus
¾   cup bottled chunky salsa
1½   cups sliced sweet and hot peppers (2 yellow, 2 jalapeño) (see note, page 69)
4   10-inch flour tortillas
     Nonstick cooking spray
¾   cup shredded cheddar cheese
     Fresh cilantro

1. Preheat broiler. In large skillet combine beef in its juices, salsa, and peppers. Cook, covered, over medium heat for 10 minutes, stirring occasionally to break up beef.
2. For quesadillas, spoon some beef mixture on half of each tortilla. Fold tortillas over meat, then fold in quarters. Place folded tortillas on foil-lined baking sheet. Sprinkle cheese on each quesadilla. Broil 1 to 2 minutes, just until cheese is melted and tortillas begin to crisp. Top with cilantro. Makes 4 servings.
EACH SERVING *428 cal, 18 g fat, 86 mg chol, 983 mg sodium, 34 g carb, 2 g fiber, 34 g pro.*

**LEMON-ROSEMARY
CHEESECAKE**

Cheesecake Lessons

Here's the ultimate make-ahead dessert that suits any occasion.

Lemon-Rosemary Cheesecake

PREP 30 min. BAKE 40 min.
STAND 1 hr. 45 min. CHILL 4 hr.
OVEN 300°F

2   15-oz. cartons ricotta cheese
⅓   cup butter
½   cup sugar
⅓   cup all-purpose flour
1   Tbsp. baking powder
1   tsp. vanilla
3   slightly beaten eggs
1   Tbsp. snipped fresh rosemary
2   tsp. finely shredded lemon peel
¼   cup chopped pistachio nuts

1. Preheat oven to 300°F. Let cheese and butter stand at room temperature for 30 minutes to soften. Grease and lightly flour a 9-inch springform pan.
2. In large mixing bowl beat butter and sugar until light and fluffy. Beat in ricotta, flour, baking powder, and vanilla until combined. Stir in eggs, rosemary, and lemon peel just until combined. Pour into prepared pan.
3. Bake 40 minutes. Turn off oven; let cheesecake remain in oven for 1 hour. Remove; cool cheesecake in pan on wire rack for 15 minutes. Using a small sharp knife, loosen cheesecake from sides of pan; cool for 30 minutes. Remove sides of pan; cool cheesecake completely on rack. Cover and refrigerate at least 4 hours. Top with pistachios. Makes 12 servings.
EACH SERVING *245 cal, 17 g fat, 102 mg chol, 184 mg sodium, 14 g carb, 11 g pro.*

MAKE YOUR FAVORITE CHEESECAKE EVEN BETTER
For traditional cream cheese-based cheesecakes, following these tips will improve your results:

● Soften cream cheese at room temperature before beating. Even quicker—soften cheese for 15 to 30 seconds in the microwave.

● Stir eggs in gently after beating the cheese; overbeaten eggs make the cheesecake rise, then fall, as it bakes.

● Closely watch baking time. The longer cheesecake bakes, the more fine cracks appear across the top.

● Wearing oven mitts, test for doneness by gently shaking cheesecake. The center should be just set. It will look underdone at first but will continue cooking and setting after it's out of the oven. Don't test with a knife or toothpick—that's a sure recipe for cracks.

● To create even, beautiful slices, cut with unflavored, unwaxed dental floss or a sharp knife dipped in warm water.

Fire Up, Party Down

Begin the outdoor cooking season
with an appetizer straight off the grill.

FAST

Grilled Onion Flatbread with Bacon and Arugula

PREP 10 min.   GRILL 8 min.

4   small red onions
1   Tbsp. olive oil
6   oz. cream cheese, softened
¼   cup strong dark ale, such as Chimay (a Belgian beer)
2   tsp. Worcestershire sauce
    Pinch cayenne pepper
2   10-inch packaged soft flatbreads

1½ cups torn arugula
1   cup cherry tomatoes, halved or quartered
6   slices crisp-cooked bacon, crumbled

1. Peel and halve onions. Brush with oil, then sprinkle with salt and freshly ground black pepper.
2. Grill onions on the rack of a covered charcoal or gas grill directly over medium-high heat for 6 to 8 minutes or until charred and slightly softened, turning once halfway through grilling. Cool.
3. In a bowl whisk together cream cheese, ale, Worcestershire sauce, and cayenne pepper until smooth. Chop 2 grilled

onions; stir into cream cheese mixture. Season to taste with salt and pepper. Quarter remaining 2 onions; set aside.
4. Grill flatbreads on rack of a covered grill directly over medium-high heat for 2 to 4 minutes or until crisp, turning once halfway through. Transfer to cutting board. Spread half of cream cheese mixture onto each flatbread. Top with arugula, tomatoes, bacon, and quartered onions. Slice and serve. Makes 8 servings.
EACH SERVING *230 cal, 13 g fat, 32 mg chol, 589 mg sodium, 20 g carb, 1 g fiber, 7 g pro.*

Delicious on a Dollar

This easy, so-pretty lunch or dinner salad features a head of lettuce, fresh veggies, and bacon strips.

Iceberg Wedge Salad with Bacon, Carrots, and Radishes

Our favorite way to prepare bacon is in the oven. It cooks without turning, and the stove top stays clean. Here's how to do it: Preheat oven to 400°F. Place bacon slices side by side on a rack in a shallow, foil-lined baking pan with sides. Bake for 18 to 21 minutes or until crisp-cooked. Drain well on paper towels.

START TO FINISH **15 min.**

- 1 head iceberg lettuce
- 6 slices bacon, crisp-cooked and halved
- 3 carrots, thinly bias-sliced
- 2 green onions, chopped
- 6 radishes, sliced and/or chopped
- ¼ cup olive oil or salad oil such as canola
- ¼ cup red wine vinegar
- 3 cloves garlic, mashed
- ¼ tsp. salt
- ¼ tsp. coarse-ground black pepper

1. Trim stem from lettuce while leaving the core intact. Cut lettuce in quarters, then place the wedges on individual serving plates. Arrange bacon, carrots, green onions, and radishes on and around each wedge.

2. In a screw-top jar combine olive oil, vinegar, garlic, salt, and pepper. Cover tightly and shake until combined. Immediately drizzle over salad. Makes 4 servings.

EACH SERVING (1 WEDGE PLUS 2 TBSP. DRESSING) *232 cal, 19 g fat, 13 mg chol, 473 mg sodium, 10 g carb, 3 g fiber, 6 g pro.*

ICEBERG WEDGE SALAD WITH BACON, CARROTS, AND RADISHES

GNOCCHI, SWEET
CORN, AND ARUGULA
IN CREAM SAUCE

LET'S PARTY Luscious cakes are paired with decorating tricks that turn ordinary ingredients into festive flourishes. And Jamie Purviance adds smoke to your cooking toolbox.

117

120

130

Party Cakes

Cake is about more than just taste—it's also a treat for the eyes. Tender cake layers go two-tone, cut marshmallows become flowers, plain sprinkles take on a wash of color, and basic frosting goes glam with just a twist of the piping bag. With these recipes and techniques, even the simplest cake can become a reason to celebrate.

PINK LEMONADE CAKE

Pink Lemonade Cake

When you cut into this cake, guests will be surprised to see and taste colorful two-tone pink layers bursting with lemonade flavor.

PREP 1 hr. BAKE 35 min. OVEN 350°F

1	cup (2 sticks) butter
4	eggs
3⅓	cups all-purpose flour
1	Tbsp. baking powder
½	tsp. salt
2	cups sugar
	Red food coloring
1⅓	cups milk
¼	cup frozen lemonade concentrate, thawed
1	tsp. pure lemon extract
1	recipe Lemonade Buttercream

1. Allow butter and eggs to stand at room temperature for 30 minutes. Meanwhile, grease two 9×2-inch round pans. Line bottoms with parchment; grease paper. Flour pans, tapping to remove excess; set aside. In medium bowl stir together flour, baking powder, and salt; set aside.

2. Preheat oven to 350°F. In extra-large mixing bowl beat butter with mixer on medium to high for 30 seconds. Gradually add sugar, about ¼ cup at a time, beating on medium until well combined. Scrape sides of bowl; beat 2 minutes more. Add ⅛ tsp. red food coloring; beat to combine. Add eggs one at a time, beating well after each addition.

3. In bowl stir together milk, lemonade concentrate, and extract (mixture will look curdled). Alternately add flour mixture and milk mixture to butter mixture, beating on low after each addition just until combined. Remove half (4 cups) of tinted batter; spread in one pan. In remaining batter in bowl, stir in ¼ tsp. red food coloring. Spread in second pan.

4. Bake about 35 minutes until tops spring back when lightly touched. Meanwhile, prepare Lemonade Buttercream.

5. Cool in pans on wire racks 10 minutes. Remove layers from pans; discard paper. Cool completely on wire racks. Trim off domed tops of layers so cake is flat. Cut each layer horizontally in half to create four layers. Brush crumbs from layers.

6. Place one dark pink layer, cut side down, on a plate. Spread 1 cup frosting just to edges. Top with a light pink layer followed by another dark pink layer, spreading frosting on each just to edges. Stack final light pink layer, cut side down; spread frosting on top and sides as desired. Makes 18 servings.

EACH SERVING 583 cal, 32 g fat, 124 mg chol, 442 mg sodium, 72 g carb, 1 g fiber, 5 g pro.

Lemonade Buttercream

This lemony frosting is based on Karen's go-to Almost-Homemade Vanilla Buttercream recipe on page 110 and makes a generous amount, plenty for between the colorful layers.

START TO FINISH 15 min.

3	cups (6 sticks) unsalted butter, softened
2	16-oz. jars marshmallow creme*
¼	cup frozen lemonade concentrate, thawed
1	cup powdered sugar
2	tsp. pure lemon extract

In very large bowl beat butter with mixer on medium until light and fluffy, about 30 seconds. Add marshmallow creme and lemonade concentrate. Beat until smooth, scraping bowl sides. Add powdered sugar and extract; beat until light and fluffy (if frosting is stiff, soften in microwave for no more than 10 seconds, then beat until smooth). Use to frost Pink Lemonade Cake. Or store, refrigerated, up to 3 days or freeze up to a month. Bring to room temperature before frosting cake. Makes 6 cups.

*If only 13-oz. jars are available in your area, use two jars plus 1½ cups additional marshmallow creme.

CAKE LESSON:
ONE BATTER, FOUR COLORFUL LAYERS

To create four alternating color layers, prepare the batter with ⅛ tsp. of food coloring to make the batter light pink. Pour half the tinted batter (4 cups) into one cake pan. Mix an additional ¼ tsp. food coloring into the remaining batter in the bowl for a darker pink (above top). After the layers have baked and fully cooled, horizontally split each one in half with a long serrated knife, sawing gently back and forth to make two layers from each cake. "To keep my knife level, I use inexpensive balsa wood blocks that are ¾ inch thick," Karen says.

MEET KAREN TACK

We turned to cookbook author and cake decorating innovator Karen Tack to make these cakes look as good as they taste without a lot of fuss. "My coauthor Alan Richardson and I are always on the hunt for new ideas and new goodies to work with," Karen says "Tools, candies, ingredients, and techniques, anything to make it easier to flavor, bake, and decorate, all while creating a wow factor."

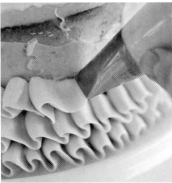

**CAKE LESSON:
FROSTING RUFFLES**

Frost the top of the cake. To create a crumb coat, thinly coat the sides of the cake with frosting, which provides a base for frosting ruffles to adhere. Fit a piping bag with a Wilton #125 or similar petal tip. Begin at the base of the cake with wide end of the tip against the cake. Pipe using a slow, even, back-and-forth sweeping motion to create the ruffles, pausing to turn the cake plate as needed (or use a spinning cake pedestal). Continue piping additional rows to cover the sides of the cake.

KID FRIENDLY

Vanilla Ruffle Cake

To get the hang of making the ruffles, practice on waxed paper, then scoop the frosting back into the pastry bag to pipe onto the cake.

PREP **50 min.**   BAKE **30 min.**   OVEN **375°F**

¾ cup (1½ sticks) butter
3   eggs
2½ cups all-purpose flour
2½ tsp. baking powder
½   tsp. salt
1¾ cups sugar
1½ tsp. vanilla
1¼ cups milk
2   recipes Almost-Homemade Vanilla Buttercream
    Red food coloring

1. Allow butter and eggs to stand at room temperature for 30 minutes. Meanwhile, grease two 8×1½-inch round cake pans. Line bottoms with parchment; grease paper. Flour pans, shaking out excess; set aside. In medium bowl stir together flour, baking powder, and salt; set aside.
2. Preheat oven to 375°F. In large mixing bowl beat butter with mixer on medium to high for 30 seconds. Gradually add sugar, about ¼ cup at a time, beating on medium until well combined. Scrape bowl; beat 2 minutes more. Add eggs one at a time, beating well after each addition. Beat in vanilla. Alternately add flour mixture and milk, beating on low after each addition just until combined. Spread batter in prepared pans.
3. Bake 30 to 35 minutes or until a wooden pick inserted near centers comes out clean. Cool in pans on wire racks for 10 minutes. Remove layers from pans; discard paper. Cool completely on wire racks.
4. Meanwhile, prepare Almost-Homemade Vanilla Buttercream. Tint frosting pale pink (one small drop of red coloring). Place one layer on serving plate. Frost top of layer. Top with second layer. Spread top of cake with frosting, and add a thin crumb coat (see left) to the sides of the cake. To decorate with ruffles, see left, or frost as desired. Makes 18 servings.
EACH SERVING *558 cal, 33 g fat, 116 mg chol, 275 mg sodium, 66 g carb, 0 g fiber, 4 g pro.*

KID FRIENDLY   FAST

Almost-Homemade Vanilla Buttercream

A double batch of this easy silky-smooth frosting is used for the Vanilla Ruffle Cake and Sprinkle-Me-Happy Cake, page 117. For a nice salty-sweet contrast, add ¼ teaspoon of salt.

START TO FINISH **15 min.**

1½ cups (3 sticks) unsalted butter, softened, cut in 1-inch pieces
1   16-oz. jar marshmallow creme*
½   cup powdered sugar
1   tsp. vanilla

In large mixing bowl beat butter with mixer on medium until light and fluffy. Add marshmallow creme and beat until smooth, scraping sides. Add powdered sugar and vanilla; beat until light and fluffy (if too stiff, soften in microwave no more than 10 seconds; beat until smooth). Use to frost cake. Or store, refrigerated, up to 3 days or freeze up to a month. Bring to room temperature before frosting cake. Makes 3 cups.
*If only 13-oz. jars are available in your area, add 3 oz. (¾ cup) additional marshmallow creme.

SALTED VS. UNSALTED BUTTER
"I only purchase unsalted butter, even for buttering bread," Karen says. "I feel that it has a much fresher and cleaner taste, and it enables me to decide how much salt to add to the recipe." For buttercream frostings where the flavor of the butter is really going to come through, use unsalted butter if available.

**VANILLA RUFFLE
CAKE**

**CHERRY FLOWER
POWER CAKE**

Cherry Flower Power Cake

"The Candy Clay flowers can be made a day ahead and stored in an airtight container," Karen says.

PREP 1 hr. 30 min. BAKE 45 min.
OVEN 350°F

¾   cup (1½ sticks) butter
6   egg whites
3   cups all-purpose flour
1½ tsp. baking powder
¾   tsp. salt
½   tsp. baking soda
1¼ cups buttermilk
½   cup juice from maraschino cherries
2¼ cups sugar
1½ tsp. vanilla
¾   tsp. almond extract
1   recipe Cherry Frosting
1   recipe Candy Clay (optional)

1. Allow butter and egg whites to stand at room temperature 30 minutes. Meanwhile, grease 13×9×2-inch baking pan; line bottom with parchment. Grease paper. Flour pan, shaking out excess; set aside. In medium bowl stir together flour, baking powder, salt, and baking soda. In 2-cup glass measuring cup combine buttermilk and cherry juice; set aside.
2. Preheat oven to 350°F. In large mixing bowl beat butter with mixer on medium to high for 30 seconds. Add sugar, vanilla, and almond extract; beat until combined. Add egg whites, a little at a time, beating well after each addition. Alternately add flour mixture and buttermilk mixture, beating on low after each addition until combined.
3. Spoon batter into prepared pan. Bake 45 minutes or until top springs back when lightly touched. Cool in pan on wire rack 10 minutes. Remove from pan; discard paper. Cool completely on wire rack.
4. Meanwhile, prepare Cherry Frosting and Candy Clay (if using). Use a long serrated knife to cut layer in half crosswise, creating two 9×6½-inch layers. Place one half on serving plate. Frost top with about 1 cup of the Cherry Frosting. Stack second half. Thinly frost sides to create a crumb coat. Chill 10 minutes. Spread sides then top of cake with frosting. To decorate with Candy Clay, see right. Makes 24 servings.
EACH SERVING 438 cal, 14 g fat, 37 mg chol, 276 mg sodium, 76 g carb, 0 g fiber, 3 g pro.

Cherry Frosting

Use to frost Cherry Flower Power Cake.
START TO FINISH 15 min.

1   cup (2 sticks) butter, softened
8   cups powdered sugar
6   Tbsp. juice from maraschino cherries
1   tsp. almond extract
    Additional maraschino cherry juice

In very large mixing bowl beat softened butter with mixer on medium until smooth. Gradually beat in 2 cups of the powdered sugar. Slowly beat in cherry juice and almond extract. Gradually beat in remaining powdered sugar. If necessary, beat in additional cherry juice, 1 tsp. at a time, for spreading consistency. Makes 4½ cups frosting.

Candy Clay

Use this delicious, easy-to-shape white chocolate candy clay as you would fondant.
PREP 30 min. STAND 1 hr.

1   12-oz. pkg. white chocolate baking pieces or candy melts
⅓   cup light-color corn syrup
    Food coloring
    Powdered sugar

1. Place white chocolate in a medium microwave-safe bowl. Microwave on 100 percent power (high), stopping to stir every 20 seconds, until melted and smooth, about 1 minute total (do not overheat).
2. Add the corn syrup and stir with a rubber spatula until well-combined. Mixture will look grainy. Cover the clay tightly in plastic wrap and let stand for at least 1 hour to firm up.
3. When ready to use, lightly dust a clean work surface with powdered sugar and knead the clay until smooth. Follow directions for working with the clay in "Cake Lesson," right.

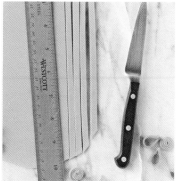

CAKE LESSON:
CANDY CLAY DECORATIONS
For the Candy Clay sheet, tint two-thirds of the clay with food coloring, kneading clay well to blend in color. Roll clay to ⅛-inch thickness. With sharp knife cut an 11×7-inch rectangle. Cut scallop edges along short sides with 1-inch round cutter. Place across frosted cake leaving a 1-inch border of exposed frosting on each end. For the flowers, tint remaining Candy Clay as desired. Roll to ⅛-inch thickness. Cut ¼×1¾-inch strips. Press narrow ends together to make teardrop petals. Press into Candy Clay sheet, using a dot of water to attach. For centers, roll a very thin strip of clay then roll into a coiled disk; attach to petals with a dot of water.

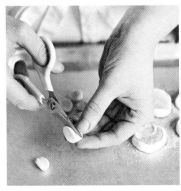

CAKE LESSON: MARSHMALLOW FLOWERS
Prepare tinted sugar (see "Cake Lesson," page 117) or use purchased colored sugar. Cut marshmallows crosswise with scissors. Place on waxed paper and sprinkle or dip cut sides of marshmallows with/in the sugar. Place large dots of melted white chocolate on waxed paper. Arrange five petals on each dot. Chill about 5 minutes until set. Pipe small dot of frosting in each flower center to adhere a sugar pearl. Arrange flowers in a cluster on cake. Use tiny green marshmallows for leaves.

Orange Chiffon Cake with Marshmallow Flowers

Chiffon cakes get their sponge cake-like texture from leavening such as baking powder and stiffly beaten egg whites.
PREP **30 min.** BAKE **25 min.** OVEN **350°F**

2   eggs
2¼ cups all-purpose flour
1½ cups sugar
2   tsp. baking powder
1   tsp. salt
½   cup milk
⅓   cup vegetable oil
½   cup orange juice
1   Tbsp. finely shredded orange or lemon peel
1½ tsp. snipped fresh thyme (optional)
1   recipe Honey Frosting

Flower Decorations
Large and tiny marshmallows
Tinted sugar, see "Cake Lesson," page 117
White baking chocolate, melted
Sugar pearl decorations
Green tiny marshmallows

1. Separate eggs. Allow yolks and whites to stand at room temperature 30 minutes. Meanwhile, grease one 9×1½-inch round cake pan and one 8×1½-inch round cake pan; line bottoms with parchment; grease paper. Flour pans, shaking out excess; set aside.
2. Preheat oven to 350°F. In large mixing bowl stir together flour, 1 cup of the sugar, the baking powder, and salt. Add milk and oil. Beat with mixer on low until combined. Add egg yolks and orange juice; beat 1 minute.
3. Thoroughly wash beaters. In separate large bowl beat egg whites on medium until soft peaks form (tips curl). Gradually add remaining ½ cup sugar; beat until stiff peaks form (tips stand straight).
4. Pour batter in thin stream over beaten egg whites; fold in gently. Fold in orange peel and, if using, thyme. Spoon 3 cups batter into 9-inch pan and 2 cups into 8-inch pan, spreading evenly.

5. Bake 25 to 35 minutes until a toothpick inserted near centers comes out clean. Cool completely on wire racks; remove from pans. Discard paper.
6. Meanwhile, prepare Honey Frosting. Place each layer on wire rack over tray lined with waxed paper. Heat frosting as directed in recipe to soften. Spread softened frosting on each layer to coat. (Microwave frosting 10 seconds at a time if it becomes too firm to spread.) Let layers stand to set.
7. To assemble, on serving plate, stack small layer on large layer. To decorate with Marshmallow Flowers, see "Cake Lessons," left. Makes 16 servings.
EACH SERVING *383 cal, 12 g fat, 41 mg chol, 232 mg sodium, 66 g carb, 1 g fiber, 5 g pro.*

Honey Frosting
PREP **10 min.** STAND **30 min.**

5   oz. mascarpone or cream cheese (⅔ cup)
3   Tbsp. butter
¼   cup honey
½   tsp. vanilla
3   to 3¼ cups powdered sugar

Allow mascarpone cheese and butter to stand at room temperature 30 minutes. In large mixing bowl beat cheese, butter, honey, and vanilla with mixer on medium until light and fluffy. Gradually add 1 cup of the powdered sugar, beating well. Gradually beat in remaining powdered sugar to reach spreading consistency. Place in medium microwave-safe bowl. Microwave on 100 percent power (high) 20 to 30 seconds just to soften (do not melt). Makes 2½ cups.

ORANGE CHIFFON
CAKE WITH
MARSHMALLOW
FLOWERS

SPRINKLE-ME-
HAPPY CAKE

A bagful of colorful sprinkles, plus three rich layers, makes this an outright celebration cake.

KID FRIENDLY

Sprinkle-Me-Happy Cake

Make alternating stripes of color as shown or cover the entire cake with a single color. To catch sprinkles that fall away, place the cake pedestal in a rimmed baking pan or cover the counter with kitchen towels. For even baking, bake only two layers at a time so the oven isn't overcrowded. Plan extra time for baking and cooling the third layer.

PREP 1 hr. 30 min. BAKE 50 min.
OVEN 350°F

4   eggs, lightly beaten
4   cups all-purpose flour
2½   cups sugar
4   tsp. baking powder
1   tsp. salt
¼   tsp. ground cloves
2½   cups mashed ripe bananas (about 5)
1¼   cups vegetable oil
2   tsp. vanilla
2½   cups peeled, shredded uncooked sweet potatoes (about 9 oz.)
1   8-oz. can crushed pineapple (juice pack), drained
2   recipes Almost-Homemade Vanilla Buttercream, page 110

For Decorating

1¾ to 2 cups white jimmies and/or white nonpareils
     Food coloring
1   recipe Candy Clay, page 113
1   Tbsp. light-color corn syrup
     Assorted dragées or small round candies

1. Allow eggs to stand at room temperature 30 minutes. Meanwhile, grease three 8×1½-inch square baking pans; line bottoms with parchment; grease paper. Flour pans, shaking out excess; set aside.
2. Preheat oven to 350°F. In very large bowl stir together the flour, sugar, baking powder, salt, and cloves. Stir in bananas, oil, eggs, and vanilla just until combined. Fold in shredded sweet potatoes and drained pineapple. Evenly divide batter among prepared pans; spread evenly.
3. Refrigerate one layer. Bake two layers on one rack for 50 to 55 minutes, until layers are set in center when gently shaken and tops are golden. Cool layers in pans on wire racks for 10 minutes. Remove layers from pans. Discard paper. Cool completely on wire racks. Bake and cool third layer.
4. Place one layer on serving plate. Frost top with about 1 cup Almost-Homemade Vanilla Buttercream. Add second layer; spread top with 1 cup frosting. Top with final layer. Frost top and sides. (Expect to have more frosting than needed.) To decorate with sprinkles, see right. Makes 32 servings.

EACH SERVING *444 cal, 22 g fat, 57 mg chol, 289 mg sodium, 62 g carb, 1 g fiber, 3 g pro.*

CAKE LESSON:
TINTING SPRINKLES AND SUGAR

"My coauthor, Alan, and I tint our own sprinkles—jimmies, nonpareils, sugars, even coconut," Karen says. "We call it the sugar shake." Line a baking sheet with waxed paper; set it aside. Place sprinkles or sugar in a sealable container, add a drop of gel or liquid food coloring, seal, then shake to evenly coat with color. Use a toothpick to break up any sprinkles that stick together. Spread sprinkles on waxed paper to dry for 15 minutes.

CAKE LESSON:
COLOR STRIPES

Cut 1¼-inch-wide strips of waxed paper. To cover sides in alternating stripes, press waxed paper strips, 1¼ inch apart, against sides of frosted cake. Use spoon to scoop tinted sprinkles. Working from top to bottom, place spoon next to cake and use finger to push sprinkles onto exposed areas of frosting. After each stripe, use a piece of waxed paper to gently press sprinkles into frosting. Chill 10 minutes to firm frosting. Gently peel each strip of waxed paper from cake sides. Using technique above, press white sprinkles into cake. Evenly press stripes of alternating sprinkle colors, reserving some for candy toppers. Combine all remaining sprinkles; evenly press into cake top. For candy toppers, prepare Candy Clay; shape into balls. Coat some of the balls with corn syrup; roll in reserved single-color sprinkles. Arrange on top of cake along with dragées and candies.

Presentation amplifies the fun factor. A stack of mismatched plates, colorful place mats, and tall cake stands enhance any cake and occasion, large or small.

CAKE LESSON: WHITE CHOCOLATE CURLS

Line a 5¾×3×2-inch loaf pan with plastic wrap; set aside. In microwave-safe bowl, heat one 12-oz. pkg. white chocolate candy melts in microwave for 1 minute. Stir. Heat 1 to 2 minutes more, stirring every 30 seconds, until melted; pour in pan. Freeze 15 minutes. To shave curls, let candy stand at room temperature. Line baking sheet with waxed paper. Holding candy with paper towels over waxed paper, use a peeler to shave curls along wide side of candy. If candy becomes soft, refrigerate a few minutes. Chill curls. Using a pick, lift curls; place against cake. Sprinkle with edible glitter.

KID FRIENDLY | FAST

Mini Chocolate Cakes

PREP 1 hr. BAKE 15 min. OVEN 350°F

¾   cup (1½ sticks) butter
3   eggs
1¾ cups all-purpose flour
1   cup unsweetened cocoa powder
1   tsp. baking soda
¾   tsp. baking powder
2   cups sugar
2   tsp. vanilla
1½ cups milk
1   recipe White Chocolate Frosting,

1. Allow butter and eggs to stand 30 minutes. Meanwhile, grease and lightly flour sixteen 3¼-inch (large) muffin cups; set aside. In medium bowl stir together flour, cocoa powder, baking soda, baking powder, and ½ tsp. salt; set aside.
2. Preheat oven to 350°F. In large bowl beat butter with mixer on medium to high 30 seconds. Gradually add sugar, ¼ cup at a time, beating on medium until combined. Scrape bowl; beat 2 minutes more. Add eggs one at a time, beating after each. Beat in vanilla. Alternately add flour mixture and milk; beating on low after each addition just until combined. Beat on medium 20 seconds more. Spoon batter into cups, filling each about two-thirds full. Bake 15 to 18 minutes, until tops spring back when lightly touched. Cool in cups on racks 5 minutes. Remove; cool completely.

3. Meanwhile, prepare White Chocolate Frosting; frost cakes. To decorate, see left. Makes 16 cakes (32 servings).
EACH SERVING *420 cal, 19 g fat, 50 mg chol, 224 mg sodium, 63 g carb, 1 g fiber, 3 g pro.*

KID FRIENDLY | FAST

White Chocolate Frosting

START TO FINISH 15 min.

6   oz. white baking chocolate
½   cup (1 stick) butter, softened
2   tsp. vanilla
6   cups powdered sugar
⅓   cup milk

In saucepan melt white chocolate over low heat, stirring frequently. Set aside; cool. Meanwhile, in large bowl beat butter and vanilla with mixer on medium 30 seconds. Gradually beat in 3 cups powdered sugar. Add milk. Gradually beat in remaining powdered sugar. Beat in melted white chocolate until combined. Beat in 1 to 2 Tbsp. additional milk to make spreading consistency. Use to frost Mini Chocolate Cakes. Makes 3½ cups frosting.

MINI CHOCOLATE
CAKES WITH
WHITE CHOCOLATE
FROSTING

Home Cooking

SMOKING IN A SNAP "Think of smoke as a new flavor for your toolbox," outdoor cooking pro Jamie Purviance says. See how quickly you can add its savory accent to steak, pasta, and cheese using the grill in your backyard. "Lots of people think smoking is just for big, tough cuts of meat," Jamie says. "But just a few minutes of smoke can fill in the bland holes in several kinds of food that lack flavor."

Mesquite Skirt Steak with Corn and Potato Salad

Mesquite is the boldest of the smoking woods. This steak cooks quickly, so the flavor never becomes overpowering.

SMOKE INTENSITY Moderate
PREP 30 min.   COOK 12 to 16 min.

Mesquite Skirt Steak

2   Tbsp. extra virgin olive oil
2   Tbsp. fresh lime juice
2   Tbsp. pure chili powder
2   tsp. ground cumin
1   tsp. minced garlic
1   tsp. kosher salt
1¾ lb. skirt or flank steak, ½ to ¾ inch thick, trimmed of excess surface fat (if too large for your grill, cut into 12-inch sections)

Corn and Red Potato Salad

1   lb. very small red potatoes, scrubbed
2   ears fresh corn, husked
1   ripe Hass avocado, diced
4   medium radishes, thinly sliced
2   scallions (white and light green parts only), thinly sliced
¼   cup finely chopped fresh cilantro leaves
2   Tbsp. fresh lime juice
1   canned chipotle chile pepper in adobo sauce, minced
1   garlic clove, minced
½   cup extra virgin olive oil
     Kosher salt
     Ground black pepper
1   large handful (1 to 1½ cups) mesquite wood chips, soaked in water at least 30 minutes
     Flour tortillas (6 inches) (optional)

1. For Mesquite Skirt Steak, in a small bowl whisk together all ingredients but steak. Spread paste on both sides of steak.

Set aside at room temperature for 15 to 30 minutes before cooking.
2. For Corn and Red Potato Salad, in a medium saucepan cover potatoes with lightly salted water. Bring to boiling over high heat. Reduce heat to medium and cook potatoes until tender when pierced with the tip of a knife, about 20 minutes. Drain, rinse under cold water, and drain again. Cut each potato in half, transfer to a medium bowl, and refrigerate to cool.
3. Preheat gas or charcoal grill for two-zone fire over high heat (450° to 500°F) as directed on page 123.
4. Brush the cooking grate clean. Cook the corn directly over coals or burners, with the lid closed as much as possible, until the kernels are brown in spots all over, 8 to 10 minutes, turning often. Remove from the grill and set aside. When corn is cool enough to handle, cut kernels from cobs. Add to the bowl with the potatoes along with the avocado, radishes, scallions, and cilantro.
5. In a small bowl whisk together lime juice, minced chile pepper, and garlic. Gradually whisk in the oil. Pour over the potato mixture and toss to combine. Season with salt and pepper. Refrigerate while cooking the steaks.
6. Meanwhile drain and add wood chips to charcoal or to gas grill. Cook the steaks over direct high heat (for flank steak use medium) with the lid closed as much as possible until cooked to your desired doneness, 4 to 6 minutes for medium-rare (8 to 10 minutes for flank steak), turning once or twice. Remove from the grill and let rest for 3 to 5 minutes.
7. Cut the steaks across the grain into ½-inch slices. Serve immediately with the salad and, warm tortillas, if desired. Makes 4 servings.
EACH SERVING *503 cal, 34 g fat, 85 mg chol, 667 mg sodium, 24 g carb, 5 g fiber, 30 g pro.*

A GUIDE TO WOOD FLAVORS
Remember that the amount of time food is exposed to smoke is just as important as the type of wood in determining the smoke intensity of the dish.

MILD
Alder: Delicate smoke flavor. Good with fish, including salmon and sturgeon; also chicken, pork.

Apple: Slightly sweet but also dense. Good with beef, poultry, pork—particularly ham.

Cherry: Slightly sweet, fruity. Good with poultry, game birds, pork.

MODERATE
Maple: Nicely smoky, somewhat sweet flavor. Good with poultry, vegetables, ham.

Oak: Assertive but pleasing. Good with beef (particularly brisket), poultry, pork.

Hickory: Pungent, smoky, baconlike flavor. Good with pork, chicken, beef, wild game, cheeses.

Pecan: Rich and more subtle than hickory but similar in taste; burns cool, so ideal for very low-heat smoking. Good with pork, chicken, lamb, fish, cheeses.

STRONG
Mesquite: In a class by itself—a big, bold smoke bordering on bitter. Good with beef and lamb.

"Just a short time on smoke makes a steak much more interesting. But because the smoking time is only a few minutes, you need an assertive wood like mesquite," Jamie says.

"With vegetables, the way you cut them makes all the difference in the smoke flavor," Jamie says. "You want the maximum surface area exposed to the smoke."

Smoked Artichoke Pasta with Lemony Vinaigrette

"I wanted smoke to be the supporting player in this recipe," Jamie says. "That's why only the peppers and artichokes are smoked, and I used oak, a moderate wood, to ensure it stays subtle."

SMOKE INTENSITY Mild
PREP 25 min. COOK 10 to 12 min.

¼ cup fresh lemon juice
¼ cup finely chopped Kalamata olives
1 tsp. finely chopped fresh thyme leaves
⅓ to ½ cup extra virgin olive oil
  Kosher salt
  Ground black pepper
3 medium sweet peppers (red, yellow, and orange), cut into ¼-inch strips
2 14-oz. cans artichoke hearts (not in marinade) or 12 frozen artichoke hearts, thawed, drained, and quartered
¼ cup extra virgin olive oil
2 tsp. minced garlic
1 large handful (1 to 1½ cups) oak or hickory wood chips soaked in water at least 30 minutes
8 oz. dried penne pasta
8 oz. fresh mozzarella cheese, cut into ¼-inch cubes

1. Prepare gas or charcoal grill for two-zone fire over medium heat (350°F to 450°F) as directed, right, and preheat 12-inch grill pan on the cooking grates.
2. In a medium nonreactive serving bowl whisk lemon juice, olives, and thyme. Continue whisking and drizzle the ⅓ to ½ cup oil in a steady stream until dressing is emulsified. Season to taste with salt and pepper. Set aside.
3. In a large bowl toss peppers and artichokes with the ¼ cup olive oil and the garlic.
4. Drain and add wood chips to charcoal or to gas grill; close lid. When the wood begins to smoke, arrange the peppers and artichokes in a single layer on the grill pan. Cook over direct medium heat, with the lid closed as much as possible, until slightly charred and softened, 10 to 12 minutes, turning occasionally. Wearing insulated barbecue mitts, remove the pan from the grill and set it on a heatproof surface. Transfer the vegetables to the serving bowl with the dressing.
5. Cook pasta in a large pot of boiling, salted water according to package directions. Drain pasta and add to serving bowl. Add cheese; toss to combine. Serve warm or at room temperature. Makes 6 to 8 servings.

EACH SERVING *351 cal, 20 g fat, 27 mg chol, 474 mg sodium, 30 g carb, 4 g fiber, 15 g pro.*

TWO-ZONE FIRE

It's a good time to give smoking a try because the wood chips you need are widely available in home centers, barbecue shops, and hardware stores. And Jamie has created a foolproof technique for getting great results. It starts with what he calls a "two-zone" fire.

FOR CHARCOAL

Arrange coals on one side of the charcoal grate and leave the other side empty to create two heat zones. The empty side is for cooking foods that require indirect heat; you can also move food there when you get flare-ups. To smoke, once coals are lit, scatter soaked and well-drained wood chips evenly over the charcoal. Wait for smoke to appear before you begin cooking.

FOR GAS

Gas grills are a little different because they require preheating to generate smoke, and wood chips need to be contained. You can either purchase a metal smoker box or make your own by placing wood chips in a small foil pan. Cover the top with aluminum foil, then poke holes in the foil to let smoke out. Before you light the grill, remove cooking grates and place the aluminum pan directly on bars, preferably in a back corner. Replace cooking grates, light grill with all the burners on high, and close the lid. If you are using a box, place it on top of the grate, directly over a lit burner. When smoke appears, turn one burner completely off, adjust remainder as directed in the recipe, and begin cooking.

JAMIE'S FIVE RULES FOR SMOKING SUCCESS

START RAW.

Many of the flavor compounds in smoke are fat- and water-soluble, which means that what you are cooking will absorb smoky flavors best when it is raw. As the surface cooks and dries out, the smoke will not penetrate as well.

DON'T OVERDO IT.

The biggest mistake rookies make is adding too much wood to the point the food tastes bitter. The first time you make a recipe, try one or two handfuls of chips. You can always go up next time.

WHITE SMOKE IS GOOD; BLACK SMOKE IS BAD.

Clean streams of whitish smoke can layer your food with the intoxicating scents of smoldering wood. But if your fire lacks enough ventilation (or your food is directly over the fire and its juices are burning), a blackish smoke will result that can taint your food.

DON'T PEEK.

Every time you open a grill, you lose heat and smoke—two of the most important elements for making a great meal. Open the lid only when you really need to tend to the fire.

KEEP THE AIR MOVING.

Open the vents on your charcoal grill and position coals on the side opposite the lid vent. The open vents will draw smoke from the charcoal and wood below so that it swirls over your food and out the top properly, giving you the cleanest smoke.

KID FRIENDLY

Chile con Queso

Jamie makes this on a water smoker, but we've adapted it to a backyard grill.

SMOKE INTENSITY Strong
PREP 15 min. **COOK** 30 min. to 1 hour

- 12 oz. Monterey Jack cheese
- 12 oz. mild cheddar cheese (do not use sharp)
- 4 large handfuls (4 cups) mesquite wood chips, soaked in water at least 30 minutes
- 1 medium yellow onion, chopped
- 1 medium jalapeño chile pepper, seeded and finely chopped (see note, page 69)
- 1 large garlic clove, finely chopped
- 1 Tbsp. extra virgin olive oil
- 3 plum tomatoes, seeded and diced
- 2 tsp. dried Mexican oregano* or oregano
- 1 Tbsp. finely chopped fresh cilantro leaves
- 1 12 oz. bag tortilla chips

1. Prepare gas or charcoal grill for two-zone fire over low heat (175°F) as directed on page 123. For charcoal, use 15 briquettes, adding more briquettes if temperature falls below 175°F.

2. In a 10- to 12-inch cast-iron skillet place the blocks of cheese about 2 inches apart.
3. Drain and add wood chunks to grill. When smoke appears, place the skillet on grill away from coals or over unlit burner, cover, and cook just until cheeses melt and run together, 30 to 60 minutes. Check occasionally and rotate pan as needed to melt both sides evenly. Do not overcook or cheese will separate.
4. Meanwhile, for salsa, in a medium skillet over medium heat cook onion, jalapeño, and garlic in hot oil until onion softens, 3 minutes, stirring occasionally. Add tomatoes and oregano; cook until tomatoes give off juices, about 5 minutes, stirring occasionally. Season with kosher salt.
5. Spoon salsa over the melted cheese in the skillet and sprinkle with the cilantro. Serve warm with tortilla chips. Makes 8 to 10 servings.
*Mexican oregano is stronger than regular oregano; find it in supermarkets or at penzeys.com.

EACH SERVING 226 cal, 15 g fat, 33 mg chol, 294 mg sodium, 13 g carb, 1 g fiber, 10 g pro.

These recipes and tips were adapted from Jamie Purviance's latest book, *Weber's Smoke* (Oxmoor House, $22).

"The key to smoking cheese," Jamie says, "is getting the smoke on right at the start. Wait to add your food until the smoke is pouring out of the grill."

Everyday Easy

Spring Time-Savers! Serve your family deliciously healthful weeknight meals even when crunched for time.

FAST

Pan-Seared Pork and Fried Green Tomato Salad

START TO FINISH 30 min.
BUDGET $3.16 per serving

1   lb. pork tenderloin
½   cup cornmeal
1   egg, well beaten
2   small green tomatoes, sliced ½ inch thick
2   Tbsp. olive oil

1   cup watercress
2   oz. crumbled blue cheese
⅓   cup bottled sweet-and-sour sauce

1. Slice tenderloin crosswise in 12 slices. Slightly flatten with palm of hand. Sprinkle with salt and pepper. In shallow dish combine cornmeal, ½ tsp. salt, and ½ tsp. pepper. Place egg in second shallow dish. Dip tomato slices in egg, then coat in cornmeal mixture; set aside.
2. In 12-inch skillet heat 1 Tbsp. oil over medium-high heat. Cook pork for 3 minutes each side until golden brown on outside and slightly pink inside. Transfer to platter; cover to keep warm. Add 1 Tbsp. oil to skillet. Cook tomato slices for 2 to 3 minutes each side until golden, adding oil if necessary. Serve pork and tomatoes with watercress and blue cheese. Drizzle sweet-and-sour sauce. Makes 4 servings.

EACH SERVING *354 cal, 16 g fat, 113 mg chol, 918 mg sodium, 22 g carb, 2 g fiber, 29 g pro.*

PANCETTA-WRAPPED CHICKEN WITH GLAZED DATE SAUCE

DOUBLE-PLAY SALMON BURGERS

FAST

Pancetta-Wrapped Chicken with Glazed Date Sauce

START TO FINISH 30 min.
BUDGET $2.72 per serving

2   8-oz. chicken breast halves
½   5.2-oz. pkg. semisoft cheese with garlic and fines herbes
4   thin slices pancetta or prosciutto (about 1 oz.)
1   Tbsp. olive oil
½   cup pitted whole dates, chopped
½   cup balsamic vinegar
⅓   cup water

1. Cut chicken in half horizontally. Top each with one-fourth of the cheese. Wrap pancetta around cheese; tuck ends under chicken. In large skillet heat oil over medium-high heat. Cook chicken, cheese sdse up first, over medium heat for 4 to 5 minutes. Turn; cook 4 to 5 minutes until golden brown and no pink remains in chicken. Transfer to platter; cover to keep warm.

2. Remove skillet from heat. Add dates, vinegar, and the water to skillet. Return to heat. Cook, uncovered, 5 to 7 minutes until sauce is thickened and dates are soft, stirring to scrape up browned bits. Spoon over chicken. Sprinkle with salt and pepper. Makes 4 servings.

EACH SERVING *343 cal, 16 g fat, 76 mg chol, 282 mg sodium, 22 g carb, 2 g fiber, 27 g pro.*

KID FRIENDLY   FAST

Double-Play Salmon Burgers

START TO FINISH 30 min.
BUDGET $3.65 per serving

5   ciabatta buns
12   oz. skinless, boneless salmon fillets
3   green onions
1   egg
1   tsp. seafood seasoning
3   oz. smoked salmon, hot style (skinned and boned) or lox
1   Tbsp. olive oil
⅓   cup mayonnaise
     Cucumber, green onions, and lemon

1. In food processor, process 1 bun to coarse crumbs. Transfer crumbs to large bowl. Coarsely chop salmon fillets and green onions, then pulse to coarsely grind in processor. Add egg, ½ tsp. seafood seasoning, and two-thirds of the smoked salmon. Pulse to combine. Transfer to bowl with crumbs. Mix, then shape in four 3½-inch-diameter patties.

2. In 12-inch nonstick skillet heat oil over medium heat. Cook patties 5 to 6 minutes per side, just until golden and cooked through. Meanwhile, toast buns and finely chop remaining smoked salmon. For sauce, combine chopped salmon, mayo, and remaining seasoning. Spoon some sauce on bun bottoms. Top with patty, then slices of cucumber and onions. Serve with sauce and lemon wedges. Makes 4 servings.

EACH SERVING *659 cal, 33 g fat, 110 mg chol, 882 mg sodium, 59 g carb, 2 g fiber, 34 g pro.*

FIVE-SPICE BEEF
KABOBS

GNOCCHI, SWEET CORN, AND ARUGULA IN CREAM SAUCE

KID FRIENDLY | LOW FAT | FAST
Five-Spice Beef Kabobs
START TO FINISH 20 min.
BUDGET $2.43 per serving

1   lb. beef flank steak or boneless beef sirloin
2   Tbsp. reduced-sodium soy sauce
1   to 1½ tsp. Chinese five-spice powder
1   6-oz. carton plain Greek yogurt
1   Tbsp. snipped fresh mint leaves
2   small limes
     Fresh mint leaves

1. Thinly slice beef across grain. If necessary, flatten slices with palm of hand or meat mallet to ¼-inch thickness. In medium bowl combine beef, soy sauce, and five-spice powder; toss to coat beef. Thread beef on skewers (soak wooden skewers in water for 30 minutes before threading).
2. Grill kabobs on rack of covered charcoal or gas grill, directly over medium heat, for 4 to 6 minutes or to desired doneness, turning once. Meanwhile, in small bowl combine yogurt and snipped mint. From 1 lime, finely shred 1 tsp peel. Juice the lime. Stir peel and 1 Tbsp. juice into yogurt. Cut remaining lime in wedges if desired. Serve kabobs with yogurt sauce, mint, and lime. Makes 4 servings.
EACH SERVING *213 cal, 8 g fat, 74 mg chol, 366 mg sodium, 5 g carb, 1 g fiber, 29 g pro.*

Carrot Salad Shred ribbons of carrot using a peeler. Toss the ribbons with a squeeze of lime juice; sprinkle with five-spice powder or other seasoning.

FAST
Gnocchi, Sweet Corn, and Arugula in Cream Sauce
START TO FINISH 20 min.
BUDGET $2.24 per serving

12   oz. frozen or shelf-stable potato gnocchi
2   small ears fresh sweet corn or 2 cups frozen whole kernel corn
1   cup half-and-half
1   3-oz. pkg. cream cheese, cut up
½   tsp. each salt, garlic powder, and dried basil or oregano
¼   tsp. freshly ground black pepper
3   cups torn fresh arugula
     Crushed red pepper (optional)

1. In Dutch oven cook gnocchi according to package directions, adding corn the last 5 minutes of cooking time. Use tongs to transfer ears of corn (if using) to cutting board. Drain gnocchi and corn kernels (if using), reserving ½ cup pasta water. Do not rinse.
2. Meanwhile, for cream sauce, in medium saucepan combine half-and-half, cream cheese, salt, garlic powder, dried herb, and pepper. Cook over medium heat for 10 minutes, stirring frequently. Stir in reserved pasta water. Return cooked pasta to Dutch oven. Cut corn from cob and add to pasta. Pour cream sauce over pasta. Stir in arugula. Serve in bowls. Sprinkle with additional salt, pepper, and dried herb, and, if desired, crushed red pepper. Makes 4 servings.
EACH SERVING *328 cal, 13 g fat, 40 mg chol, 908 mg sodium, 46 g carb, 1 g fiber, 8 g pro.*

Delicious on a Dollar

Party meatballs bring spicy, garlicky goodness to your next get-together.

KID FRIENDLY

Spicy Apple-Glazed Meatballs

PREP 20 min. STAND 10 min.
COOK 12 min.

Spicy Meatballs

1	egg
¼	cup milk
2	slices white or whole wheat bread, torn
1	lb. 85-percent-lean ground beef
4	cloves garlic, minced
½	tsp. freshly ground black pepper
¼	tsp. salt
¼	tsp. cayenne pepper
1	Tbsp. vegetable oil

Apple Glaze

1	cup apple juice
¼	cup reduced-sodium soy sauce
3	Tbsp. packed brown sugar
1½	tsp. cornstarch
1	tsp. ground ginger
¼	tsp. cayenne pepper
6	green onions, sliced

1. For Spicy Meatballs, in large bowl whisk together egg and milk. Add bread. Let stand 10 minutes, just until bread is softened. Add ground beef, garlic, black pepper, salt, and cayenne pepper; mix thoroughly with hands or wooden spoon. Shape beef mixture into about forty-eight 1-inch balls.

2. In 12-inch skillet heat oil over medium heat. Cook meatballs, half at a time, turning occasionally, until brown and crusty on the outside and no longer pink inside, about 6 minutes per batch. Transfer meatballs to covered dish to keep warm. Drain fat from skillet; wipe out skillet.

3. For Apple Glaze, in bowl combine juice, soy sauce, brown sugar, cornstarch, ginger, and cayenne. In the same skillet over medium heat cook and stir sauce until thickened and bubbly (should be at a full boil). Cook and stir 2 minutes more. Return meatballs to skillet to glaze and heat through. Transfer to serving dish. Top with green onions. Makes 12 (4-meatball) appetizer servings.

EACH SERVING *143 cal, 8 g fat, 42 mg chol, 297 mg sodium, 10 g carb, 0 g fiber, 9 g pro.*

SPICY APPLE-GLAZED MEATBALLS

STUFFED
POBLANO CHILES
WITH SAUSAGE
AND CORN

SUMMER MADE SIMPLE Chef Domenica Catelli keeps things simple so she and her guests can enjoy one another as much as the food. And five celebrity chefs share dinner ideas—grilling-style.

142

151

152

Time for Dinner

For chef and cookbook author Domenica Catelli there's a rule of thumb for entertaining, and it goes like this: The simpler the menu, the more time for the meal.

These delicious recipes reflect how Sonoma Valley chef and cookbook author Domenica Catelli eats and entertains—simply enough that guests can jump in and lend a hand. "Gone are the days of one person doing it all," Domenica says. "Part of the joy is involving others. And we're drinking wine, talking, and laughing while we work."

Having a few store-bought ingredients on hand gives even inexperienced cooks something to do. "One of my favorite appetizers involves basically no prep— fresh mozzarella, a pile of fresh arugula, grilled bread, and prosciutto," Domenica says. She simply gets out a serving platter and asks someone to pile on the ingredients.

By relying on ready-to-use items, Domenica can keep entertaining simple. To set the scene, she takes inspiration from local spots such as design retailer Saint Dizier Home (saintdhome.com)and Hotel Healdsburg (hotelhealdsburg.com). "I keep pillows on hand to add to dining chairs when entertaining. It's something I picked up from the laid-back, comfy style of Hotel Healdsburg," she says. "I love the easy way they make guests feel welcome."

Once the food is prepped and the scene is set, it's time for the heart of the evening to begin. "To me, sitting around the table, eating with people you love is one of life's greatest pleasures," Domenica says. "In our busy lives, we have to work to make time for occasions that once were traditions. And it's worth the effort."

For more information on Catelli's restaurant, go to mycatellis.com.

Fresh local blackberries flavor Domenica's signature cocktail, an icy blend of vodka, mint, and elderflower liqueur.

LOW FAT | FAST

Mom-A-Licious Summer-Tini

Inspiration for this drink came from Spoonbar in the h2 hotel in Healdsburg, California, where cocktails are created from fresh local fruits and herbs. The drink's name comes from Domenica's blog, Be Mom-A-Licious.

START TO FINISH **5 min.**

6   fresh ripe blackberries, plus more for garnish

3   mint or basil leaves
3   oz. vodka (6 Tbsp.)
1   oz. elderflower liqueur, such as St. Germain (2 Tbsp.)

In a martini shaker muddle berries and mint, slightly mashing berries. Add vodka, liqueur, and ice to shaker. Shake vigorously for approximately 30 seconds. Strain into a chilled martini glass. Garnish with blackberries. Makes 1 cocktail.

EACH SERVING *330 cal, 0 g fat, 0 mg chol, 4 mg sodium, 20 g carb, 4 g fiber, 0 g pro.*

PESTO-RUBBED
PORK ROAST WITH
GRILLED FRUIT

Pesto-Rubbed Pork Roast with Grilled Fruit

For contrasts in color, texture, and taste, slices of slow-roasted grilled pork are served with grilled fresh stone fruits.
PREP 20 min. STAND 15 min.
GRILL 1 hr.

3 to 4 lb. boneless pork top loin roast (single loin)
1 recipe Mixed Herb Pesto or purchased pesto
4 to 5 apricots, plums, and/or peaches, halved and pitted
3 Tbsp. balsamic vinegar

1. Coat pork with ¼ cup pesto. Let stand for 15 minutes.
2. For charcoal grill, arrange medium-hot coals around a drip pan. Test for medium heat above pan. Place pork, fat side up, on grill rack over pan. Cover grill. Grill for 1 to 1½ hours, until instant-read thermometer registers 145°F. (For gas grill, preheat grill. Reduce heat to medium. Adjust for indirect cooking. Place pork on grill rack over unheated burner. Grill as directed.)
3. Meanwhile, in large bowl toss halved and pitted fruit with balsamic vinegar. Sprinkle with salt and pepper. Let stand 30 minutes, turning to coat occasionally. Grill over direct heat 5 to 7 minutes, until tender, turning once.
4. Remove pork from grill. Cover and let stand for 3 minutes. Slice pork. Serve with grilled fruit. Pass remaining Mixed Herb Pesto. Makes 8 servings.
EACH SERVING *336 cal, 17 g fat, 108 mg chol, 204 mg sodium, 5 g carb, 1 g fiber, 37 g pro.*

GRILLED FRUIT

Cooking fruit on a grill caramelizes the natural sugars while the fruit softens and becomes even juicier. Smoky grill marks make the chunks or halves of fruit savory companions to serve alongside grilled meat. For grilling, select apricots, plums, or peaches that are firm (rather than overripe) so they'll keep their shape and not fall apart while cooking.

Mixed Herb Pesto

Domenica makes this recipe according to what's fresh from the garden and what's at local farmer's markets.
START TO FINISH 15 min.

½ cup pine nuts, toasted
9 large cloves garlic
4½ cups fresh flat-leaf parsley
3 cups mixed fresh herbs (mint, basil, dill, oregano, and/or thyme)
¾ cup freshly grated Parmesan cheese
1½ tsp. salt
1½ cups extra virgin olive oil

In processor combine pine nuts, garlic, parsley, herbs, cheese, and salt. Pulse a few times to chop and combine. With processor running, slowly pour oil through opening. Process until well blended. Spoon pesto into airtight container. Refrigerate up to 1 week or freeze up to 6 months. Makes 2½ cups.

Domenica Catelli believes in making time for dinner. "It's not just about putting food on the table," she says. "It's about enjoying the preparation as much as you do the meal itself."

Catelli's Mini Summer Meatballs

Ricotta makes these meatballs tender and flavorful. Wrap and freeze extra meatballs up to a month.

PREP 25 min. COOK 20 min.
BAKE 10 min. OVEN 450°F

1   egg, slightly beaten (1 cup)
1   lb. ground beef
1   lb. bulk Italian sausage
1½   cups ricotta cheese (12 oz.)
1   cup panko (Japanese-style bread crumbs)
½   cup finely chopped onion
½   cup grated Parmesan cheese
¼   cup fresh minced garlic
2   Tbsp. chopped fresh thyme
1   Tbsp. chopped fresh parsley
1½   tsp. kosher salt
2   to 4 cups Domenica's Simple Tomato-Garlic Sauce (right) or jarred sauce, heated
     Additional chopped parsley (¼ cup) and grated Parmesan cheese (2 Tbsp.)

1. Preheat oven to 450°F. In large bowl combine egg, beef, sausage, ricotta cheese, panko, onion, ½ cup Parmesan, garlic, thyme, 1 Tbsp. parsley, and salt with hands. Form into forty 1½-inch meatballs.
2. Heat a very large cast-iron skillet with olive oil. Half at a time, brown meatballs in hot skillet about 10 minutes per batch. Return all meatballs to skillet. Bake 10 minutes, until done (160°F).

3. Spoon sauce into two small cast-iron skillets or serving dishes (can reheat skillets on grill set to medium heat). Place baked meatballs in sauce, turning to coat. Sprinkle chopped parsley and Parmesan. Serve meatballs with bamboo skewers. Makes 20 servings (2 meatballs + ½ Tbsp. sauce).

EACH SERVING *217 cal, 16 g fat, 53 mg chol, 468 mg sodium, 6 g carb, 1 g fiber, 11 g pro.*

Domenica's Simple Tomato-Garlic Sauce

Serve this sauce—made quickly from ingredients in the pantry—with Catelli's Mini Summer Meatballs, over pasta, or in any recipe that calls for tomato sauce. It's so easy and delicious, it's sure to become a favorite.

START TO FINISH 25 min.

4   to 5 garlic cloves, chopped
½   tsp. dried crushed red pepper
2   Tbsp. extra virgin olive oil
1   28-oz. can crushed tomatoes
½   tsp. salt

In a large saucepan cook garlic and crushed pepper in hot oil over medium heat for 1 minute. (Do not let garlic brown, which causes bitterness.) Stir in tomatoes and salt. Bring sauce to boiling. Reduce heat to low. Simmer, uncovered, for 15 minutes, stirring occasionally. Makes 3 cups.

CATELLI'S MINI
SUMMER
MEATBALLS

Simple Summer Spaghetti

This recipe can evolve as summer progresses. Grill available garden-fresh or farmer's market veggies.
PREP 20 min. COOK 20 min.

- 12 oz. packaged dry spaghetti or spaghettini
- ¼ cup extra virgin olive oil
- 5 cloves garlic, coarsely chopped
  Pinch crushed red pepper, or more to taste
- 2 cups cut-up grilled zucchini and/or summer squash
- 2 cups red and/or yellow cherry tomatoes, quartered
- ¼ cup fresh basil leaves, torn
- ¼ to ½ cup grated Parmesan cheese
- 2 Tbsp. chopped fresh basil or Italian parsley

1. Bring large pot of salted water to boiling. Stir in spaghetti. Cook 9 to 10 minutes, just until tender. Strain pasta, reserving 1 cup cooking liquid.
2. Meanwhile, in extra-large skillet combine olive oil, garlic, and crushed red pepper. Cook over medium heat about 3 minutes, until garlic begins to soften. Do not let garlic brown. Stir in zucchini, tomatoes, and torn basil. Season with salt and pepper.
3. Reduce heat to low; stir pasta liquid and spaghetti into vegetables in skillet. (If skillet is too small, mix all ingredients in large pot.) Heat thoroughly. Sprinkle with Parmesan. Transfer to large serving bowl. Sprinkle with chopped fresh basil. Makes 4 to 8 servings.
EACH SERVING *511 cal, 18 g fat, 9 mg chol, 459 mg sodium, 71 g carb, 5 g fiber, 17 g pro.*

HOMEMADE CROUTONS

You can use purchased croutons in the Lemony Kale Salad with Tomatoes, but homemade are easy, quick, and fresh. Remove crust from a chunk of ciabatta or baguette. Tear the bread in enough pieces to equal about a cup. Transfer to a large bowl. Combine 2 Tbsp. olive oil or melted butter with a small clove of minced garlic. Drizzle over bread and toss to coat. Spread on a baking sheet, sprinkle with salt, then bake at 350°F for 9 to 11 minutes, tossing once halfway through baking time.

> "If you want to enjoy entertaining," Domenica says, "do not rush to do anything. Slow down, relax, take time to enjoy the process, and watch things evolve."

Lemony Kale Salad with Tomatoes

Domenica loves the combo of hearty kale plus light and bright lemon. Other greens, such as romaine, Bibb, or arugula, can be added, or they can replace the kale.
START TO FINISH 25 min.

- 2 bunches dinosaur kale
- 3 cups red and/or yellow cherry tomatoes, halved
- 1 cup Homemade Croutons, left
- ½ cup chopped walnuts
- ⅓ cup grated Parmesan cheese
- 3 to 4 lemons
- ½ cup extra virgin olive oil
  Salt and pepper, to taste
- ½ cup shaved Parmesan

1. Rinse and dry kale. Trim and discard tough stems. Stack leaves, then cut ¼-inch strips across the leaves.
2. In an extra-large salad bowl combine kale, tomatoes, croutons, nuts, and the ⅓ cup grated Parmesan cheese. Juice lemons over salad ingredients. Drizzle olive oil, sprinkle salt and pepper, then toss. To serve, sprinkle salad with shaved Parmesan. Makes 8 servings.
EACH SERVING *297 cal, 23 g fat, 7 mg chol, 326 mg sodium, 19 g carb, 4 g fiber, 9 g pro.*

"I've never had a big sweet tooth," Domenica says. "But I can't resist summer fruit. Pairing fruit with herbs is one of my favorite ways to enjoy dessert."

KID FRIENDLY

Rosemary-Strawberry Shortcake Pizza

This easy-to-make shortcake is enough to serve a crowd. Hope for some leftovers to nibble over coffee the next morning. Make it an outdoor favorite by pulling it together on the grill.

PREP **30 min.** BAKE **22 min.**
OVEN **400°F**

1	quart strawberries, rinsed, then halved or quartered (4 cups)
¼	cup honey or agave nectar
3	cups all-purpose flour
¼	cup granulated sugar
2	Tbsp. chopped fresh rosemary or thyme (optional)
4½	tsp. baking powder
¾	tsp. salt
½	cup cold unsalted butter, cut in small pieces
1¾	cups whipping cream
1	egg white, lightly beaten
2	Tbsp. sugar
	Sweetened whipped cream

1. Preheat oven to 400°F. In a large bowl combine strawberries and honey. Let stand, stirring occasionally, while preparing shortcake.

2. For shortcake, in a food processor combine flour, ¼ cup sugar, rosemary, baking powder, and salt; pulse to mix. (Or whisk together in large bowl.) Add butter to flour mixture; pulse several times. (Or cut in butter with pastry blender or two knives.) While pulsing, add cream, pulsing until dough begins to come together. (Or make a well in center of flour mixture. Pour cream into well. Mix with fork just until dough is evenly moistened.)

3. Turn out dough on lightly floured surface. Knead quickly. Roll dough to 9×13-inch rectangle (½-inch thickness). Transfer dough to large parchment-lined baking sheet. With sharp knife, score dough (cutting not quite through) in 1½-inch squares. Brush dough with egg white; sprinkle with 2 Tbsp. sugar. Bake 22 to 26 minutes, until golden brown.

4. Transfer shortcake and parchment to wooden board or platter. Spoon strawberries on shortcake. Drizzle with juices. Serve in tumblers or bowls with whipped cream. Makes 15 (2-square) servings, plus leftovers.

Grill Option On charcoal grill large enough to accommodate large skillet placed in center of grill rack, arrange medium-hot coals around perimeter of grill (for indirect cooking). Prepare shortcake as directed. After kneading, pat dough into generously buttered 12-inch cast-iron skillet. Test for medium heat above center of grill. Place skillet in center of grill (not over coals). Cover and grill 25 to 30 minutes, until set in center. Remove from grill; let stand 10 minutes. Cut in wedges. Serve with strawberries and whipped cream.

EACH SERVING *348 cal, 23 g fat, 77 mg chol, 285 mg sodium, 33 g carb, 1 g fiber, 4 g pro.*

ROSEMARY-
STRAWBERRY
SHORTCAKE PIZZA

SERRANO "The smaller the pepper, the hotter the burn," Robert says. These skinny 2- to 4-inch peppers have a sudden, intense bite and add welcome heat to salsa, sauces, and guacamole.

POBLANO/PASILLA Known by two names, depending on where you find them, medium-hot poblanos have a rich, sweet flavor. They are especially delicious stuffed.

Home Cooking

CHILE PEPPERS Produce expert Robert Schueller used to shun the potent pods. Now he can't get enough. Here he shares delicious ways to serve them—fresh, roasted, peeled, and pickled.

ANAHEIM Often served stuffed in dishes such as chiles rellenos, mildly spicy Anaheims are also good in stews. Raw, their flavor is peppery and green; cooked, they become mellow.

JALAPEÑO These medium-hot peppers are popular across America for good reason. In addition to heat, they add a distinctive green sweet-pepper flavor to any dish.

FRESH UNCOOKED Chiles give a dish crunchy texture. "When buying fresh chiles," Robert says, "here's how to choose between hotter or milder: Small cracks or light brown veins at the base of the chile or near the top mean the pepper is mature, and it's going to be hotter."

LOW FAT | FAST

Chilled Raspberry-Chile Soup

"Serve this blender soup as either a lively appetizer or a memorable dessert," Robert says.

PREP 15 min.   CHILL 1 hr.

4   cups fresh raspberries
4   ripe bananas, peeled and cut up
1   cup fresh orange juice
1   6-oz. carton plain low-fat yogurt
2   Tbsp. agave syrup or corn syrup
2   fresh jalapeño peppers, minced (see note, page 69)
    Whole or sliced fresh raspberries (optional)
    Sliced fresh jalapeño or serrano peppers (see note, page 69) (optional)

In a blender combine the 4 cups raspberries, bananas, orange juice, yogurt, and syrup. Cover and blend until smooth. Stir in minced jalapeño peppers, then refrigerate at least 1 hour. Serve the soup in small bowls. Garnish with raspberries and sliced chiles, if desired. Makes 6 servings.

EACH SERVING *170 cal, 1 g fat, 2 mg chol, 22 mg sodium, 40 g carb, 8 g fiber, 4 g pro.*

SEEDING PEPPERS
Use a spoon with a narrow tip to easily remove seeds and ribs from chiles. A knife also works well for tough flesh.

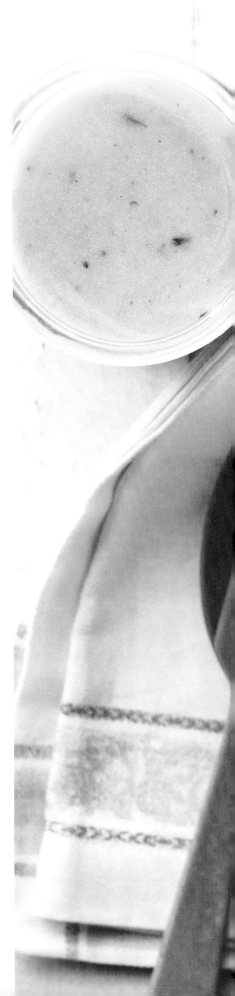

ROASTED "High heat gives toasty flavor to chiles. But stop roasting when skins begin to wrinkle and color. The skins should just be brown."

Potato Salad with Caramelized Onions and Roasted Chile Vinaigrette

PREP 30 min.   ROAST 45 min.
OVEN 425°F

Potato Salad

3 lb. Dutch yellow potatoes, halved
3 Tbsp. extra virgin olive oil
   Kosher salt and freshly ground pepper
1 large sweet onion, thinly sliced
2 Tbsp. olive oil
1 Tbsp. butter

Roasted Chile Vinaigrette

½ cup seasoned rice vinegar
2 Tbsp. granulated sugar
1½ lb. fresh Anaheim chiles, roasted (see directions, right) and coarsely chopped, divided (see note, page 69)
1 clove garlic, peeled
⅓ cup canola oil
   Kosher salt and freshly ground pepper, to taste
   Fresh cilantro

1. For potato salad, preheat oven to 425°F. In a shallow roasting pan toss together potatoes, the 3 Tbsp. olive oil, salt, and pepper. Roast potatoes, uncovered, for 25 to 30 minutes, until the potatoes can easily be pierced with a fork. Remove from oven to cool.
2. Meanwhile, in a large skillet cook and stir onion in the 2 Tbsp. olive oil and butter over medium heat about 15 minutes, until softened and caramel color.

3. For vinaigrette, in a blender combine vinegar, sugar, about ½ cup of the roasted chiles, and the garlic. Cover and blend until well combined. With blender running, slowly add canola oil in a steady stream until vinaigrette is thickened. Season to taste with salt and pepper.
4. In a large bowl gently toss roasted potatoes, caramelized onion, and remaining chiles. Add 1 cup of the Roasted Chile Vinaigrette, then toss to coat. Sprinkle with cilantro. Pass remaining vinaigrette. Makes 10 to 12 (⅔-cup) servings.
EACH SERVING *284 cal, 15 g fat, 3 mg chol, 202 mg sodium, 35 g carb, 5 g fiber, 4 g pro.*

ROASTING CHILES
To roast Anaheims, arrange them on a baking sheet, leaving room between chiles. Roast in a 425°F oven about 20 minutes or until skins are browned. No need to brush with oil.

PEELED "Think of it as giving chiles a makeover. After steaming, they will deflate, shrivel, and look rather sad, but the skin will easily lift off, revealing silky flesh underneath."

LOW FAT

Stuffed Poblano Chiles with Sausage and Corn

When chiles such as poblanos are to be used whole, the skin can be tough, so they're best peeled.

PREP 45 min. COOK 20 min.
STAND 20 min. BAKE 10 min.
OVEN 350°F

1½ cups water
½ cup farro, rinsed
1 dried chipotle pepper
¼ tsp. cayenne pepper
8 oz. sweet or hot Italian sausage (remove casings, if present)
½ cup finely chopped sweet onion
½ cup sliced celery
⅓ cup finely chopped green sweet pepper
1 fresh serrano pepper, sliced (see note, page 69)
2 cloves garlic, minced
¼ cup bottled diced pimiento or roasted red sweet pepper
¾ cup steamed red kidney beans, or canned red kidney beans, rinsed and drained
1 tsp. dried oregano, crushed
1 tsp. chili powder
⅛ tsp. cayenne pepper
1 cup fresh corn cut from the cob
Sea salt
8 fresh poblano/pasilla peppers, roasted, seeded, and peeled (see "Peeling Peppers," right) (see note, page 69)
Salsa (optional)

1. For stuffing, in a small saucepan combine the water, farro, chipotle, and cayenne pepper. Bring to boiling. Reduce heat and simmer, covered, 20 minutes or until farro is tender; drain. If desired, remove stem and seeds from chipotle; chop and stir into farro.
2. Preheat oven to 350°F. Meanwhile, in a 12-inch skillet cook sausage 5 minutes. Add onion, celery, sweet pepper, serrano pepper, and garlic. Cook 5 minutes, until vegetables are tender and sausage is no longer pink. Stir in pimiento, beans, oregano, chili powder, cayenne pepper, farro, and corn. Heat through. Season to taste with salt.
3. Fill roasted peppers with farro-sausage mixture. Transfer to a shallow baking pan and roast stuffed peppers 10 to 15 minutes, until heated through. Top with salsa if desired. Makes 8 servings.
EACH SERVING *181 cal, 3 g fat, 9 mg chol, 325 mg sodium, 28 g carb, 4 g fiber, 11 g pro.*

PEELING PEPPERS
For easiest peeling, broil peppers, cut sides down, on a foil-lined baking sheet, 4 to 5 inches from heat, for 8 to 10 minutes until blackened and blistered. Seal in bowl or bag to steam; when still slightly warm, lift off skin, using a knife tip to loosen stubborn sections.

PICKLED "This is one of my favorite techniques because in just an hour, vinegar works its magic on the peppers, giving them a more tender texture and a softer edge to their heat."

LOW FAT

Black-Eyed Pea Relish

A single fiery serrano is all this dish needs for heat; serve it either with bruschetta as an appetizer or as an alternative to traditional baked beans at a cookout.

PREP 15 min. CHILL 1 hr.

¼ small red onion, diced (about ¼ cup)
1   yellow sweet pepper, diced
½   red sweet pepper, diced
½   green sweet pepper, diced
1   fresh serrano chile, thinly sliced
    (see note, page 69)
1   clove peeled garlic, minced
2   Roma tomatoes, diced
1   11-oz. pkg. steamed ready-to-eat
    black-eyed peas, rinsed and drained;
    or one 15-oz. can black-eyed peas,
    rinsed and drained
¼   cup seasoned rice vinegar
    Sea salt and freshly ground pepper
1   Roma tomato, sliced (optional)

In a large bowl gently combine red onion, sweet peppers, chile, garlic, diced tomatoes, black-eyed peas, and vinegar. Season to taste with salt and pepper. Top with tomato slices, if desired. Refrigerate 1 hour for flavors to blend and for chiles to pickle. Makes 6 servings.

EACH SERVING 50 cal, 0 g fat, 0 mg chol, 72 mg sodium, 9 g carb, 2 g fiber, 3 g pro.

QUICK PICKLING
Submerge chiles in a vinegar bath for 30 minutes to soften texture and mellow flavor. Robert prefers seasoned rice vinegar in this recipe because it has just the right amount of sweetness.

Delicious on a Dollar

These two-bite appetizers have a crisp Parmesan crust and a savory custard filling.

Mini Party Quiches

PREP 30 min. BAKE 28 min.
OVEN 425°F/350°F

	Nonstick cooking spray
2	cups all-purpose flour
2	Tbsp. grated Parmesan cheese
½	tsp. salt
⅓	cup olive oil or vegetable oil (such as canola)
5	to 7 Tbsp. ice-cold water
1	egg
⅓	cup milk
	Dash ground black pepper
⅓	cup finely shredded Monterey Jack or Gruyère cheese
1	Tbsp. chopped green onion
5	to 6 pear or cherry tomatoes, thinly sliced, and/or 24 small herb leaves
	Fresh thyme leaves (optional)

1. Preheat oven to 425°F. Coat twenty-four 1¾-inch muffin cups with cooking spray; set aside. For pastry, in a large bowl stir together flour, Parmesan cheese, and salt. Add oil all at once. Mix until crumbly. Add 2 Tbsp. of the ice-cold water; stir to combine. Add enough remaining water, 1 Tbsp. at a time, until flour is moistened. Gather in a ball, then knead gently just until pastry holds together.

2. Divide pastry in 24 portions. Press each portion in a muffin cup. Do not prick. Bake for 8 to 10 minutes or just until pastry begins to brown. Remove from oven; set aside. Reduce oven to 350°F.

3. For quiche filling, in a small bowl whisk together egg, milk, and pepper. Stir in cheese and onion. Fill each pastry cup with about 1 tsp. filling. Top each quiche with a tomato slice or, if desired, herb leaves.

4. Bake quiches for 20 minutes or until filling is puffed and set. Cool in muffin cups on a wire rack for 5 minutes. Remove from cups; serve warm. Makes 12 (2-quiche) servings.

EACH SERVING 156 cal, 8 g fat, 20 mg chol, 141 mg sodium, 17 g carb, 1 g fiber, 4 g pro.

Mini Party Quiches

Hot off the Grill

Take it from five celebrity chefs: Any meal tastes better when it's cooked over fire.

**HEARTY BOYS'
GREEK LAMB AND
FETA BURGERS**

FAST

Hearty Boys' Greek Lamb and Feta Burgers

PREP 15 min.   GRILL 12 min.

1½ lb. ground lamb
2   Tbsp. minced fresh shallot
3   tsp. dried oregano, crushed
1¼ tsp. ground cinnamon
½   tsp. salt
¾   tsp. ground black pepper

2   Tbsp. water
4   crusty buns, split
4   to 8 oz. feta cheese, crumbled
¼   cup sour cream
     Sliced tomatoes (optional)

1. In large bowl combine lamb, minced shallot, 2 tsp. of the oregano, the cinnamon, salt, pepper, and the water. Form in four ¾-inch-thick patties.
2. Grill patties, covered, directly over hot coals for 4 to 5 minutes per side, until

done (instant-read thermometer reads 160°F), turning once halfway through grilling time. Toast buns, cut sides down, the last 1 to 2 minutes of grilling time.
3. Meanwhile, for sauce, combine feta, sour cream, and remaining oregano. Serve grilled patties on toasted buns with sauce and sliced tomatoes if desired. Makes 4 burgers.
EACH BURGER *708 cal, 51 g fat, 156 g chol, 1, 018 mg sodium, 41 g carb, 3 g fiber, 39 g pro.*

STEPHANIE IZARD'S JUNIPER-GRILLED FISH STUFFED WITH FENNEL AND ONION

GALE GAND'S GRILLED ASPARAGUS WITH FRIED EGGS AND PARMESAN

LOW FAT

Stephanie Izard's Juniper-Grilled Fish Stuffed with Fennel and Onion

PREP 15 min. COOK 9 min.
GRILL 14 min.

1 medium fennel bulb, cut in bite-size strips
1 red onion
3 cloves garlic, minced
1 tsp. juniper berries* (spice or gourmet section)
1 Tbsp. extra virgin olive oil
2 Tbsp. quality gin
1 whole black sea bass or red snapper (about 2 lb.), head and tail intact (ask fish counter to remove bones and backbone to make pocket)

1. For stuffing, in large skillet cook fennel, onion, garlic, and juniper berries slowly in hot oil over medium heat for 7 to 8 minutes or until fennel is tender. Season with salt and pepper. Carefully add gin (mixture may flare up briefly); cook about 2 minutes, allowing liquid to absorb into vegetables. Remove from heat. Cool slightly.
2. Heat grill to medium-high. Score the skin of the fish. Season inside with salt and pepper, then stuff. Season outside with salt and pepper. Transfer fish to well-oiled rack. Grill 7 to 8 minutes each side, checking inside for doneness. Cut into portions to serve. Makes 4 servings.
*Note: Use only berries labeled as food-safe.

EACH SERVING *316 cal, 10 g fat, 92 mg chol, 331 mg sodium, 7 g carb, 21 g fiber, 43 g pro.*

FAST

Gale Gand's Grilled Asparagus with Fried Eggs and Parmesan

PREP 20 min. GRILL 5 min.

2 1-lb. bunches asparagus spears
1 Tbsp. extra virgin olive oil
1 clove garlic, minced
   Salt and ground black pepper
2 tsp. butter
8 eggs
   Coarsely grated Parmesan cheese

1. Snap off and discard woody bases from asparagus spears. In large bowl toss asparagus with olive oil, minced garlic, salt, and pepper. Massage oil onto asparagus to evenly coat.
2. Grill asparagus, covered, directly over medium-hot coals for 5 minutes, turning once.
3. Meanwhile, heat a 12-inch skillet over medium heat. Add butter and wait until it foams. Add eggs to hot butter; sprinkle with salt and pepper. Reduce heat to low. Cook eggs 3 to 4 minutes, until whites are completely set and yolks begin to thicken. Divide asparagus among four plates. Place 2 eggs on each mound of asparagus. Sprinkle with Parmesan cheese. Makes 4 servings.

EACH SERVING *226 cal, 16 g fat, 381 mg chol, 381 mg sodium, 4 g carb, 1 g fiber, 16 g pro.*

GUY FIERI'S
GRILLED CHICKEN
TORTAS WITH
CHIPOTLE CREMA

Guy Fieri's Grilled Chicken Tortas with Chipotle Crema

PREP 35 min. GRILL 5 min.

- 2 oz. achiote paste (ground annatto seed)
- 2 cloves garlic, minced
- 2 Tbsp. plus 1 tsp. lime juice
- 1 Tbsp. paprika
- 1 tsp. ground cumin
- 4 boneless, skinless chicken breast halves (2½ lb.)
- 1 recipe Chipotle Crema
- 4 ciabatta rolls (4- to 5-inch diameter), split
- 2 Roma tomatoes, cut in ¼-inch slices
- ¼ cup thinly sliced sweet onion
- 1½ cups finely shredded iceberg lettuce
- 1 ripe avocado, pitted, peeled, and sliced
- ¼ cup crumbled Cotija cheese or queso fresco

1. Break up achiote. Combine with garlic, 1 Tbsp. of the lime juice, paprika, cumin, pinch cayenne pepper, and kosher salt. Thinly slice chicken horizontally. Mix with garlic-lime juice mixture to coat. Cover and refrigerate 30 minutes. Prepare Chipotle Crema.
2. Heat grill to high. Using tongs, wipe grill with oil-blotted paper towel. Grill chicken 3 to 4 minutes per side until well marked. Transfer to plate. Drizzle remaining lime juice on chicken. Drizzle cut sides of buns with olive oil. Grill 1 minute. Turn; grill 30 seconds. Slather buns with Crema. On bottom buns layer chicken, tomatoes, onion, lettuce, avocado, cheese, and buns top. Makes 4 sandwiches.
Chipotle Crema In a bowl mix ¼ cup sour cream, 1 Tbsp. sauce from a container of chipotles in adobo sauce, 1 tsp. lime juice, and ½ tsp. honey. Season with kosher salt; set aside.
EACH SERVING *600 cal, 25 g fat, 81 mg chol, 1,049 mg sodium, 58 g carb, 5 g fiber, 36 g pro.*

ADAM PERRY LANG'S BUTTER-BASTED STRIP STEAK

KID FRIENDLY
Adam Perry Lang's Butter-Basted Strip Steak

PREP 10 min. STAND 1 hr. 10 min. GRILL 12 min.

- 4 8- to 10-oz. boneless strip steaks, 1¼ inches thick
- ½ cup unsalted butter
- 5 cloves garlic, peeled and crushed
- 1 Tbsp. garlic salt
- 1½ tsp. freshly ground black pepper
- ½ tsp. cayenne pepper
- 1 bunch rosemary

1. Let steaks stand at room temperature 1 hour. For butter baste, in a small saucepan simmer butter and garlic over medium heat 2 to 4 minutes. Let stand 1 hour. Remove 2 Tbsp. of butter-garlic mixture, set aside.
2. Combine garlic salt and peppers; use to season both sides of steaks. Moisten hands with water; work seasoning into meat. Let stand 5 minutes. For basting brush, tie rosemary to wooden spoon handle. Brush some of the butter baste on steaks. Grill steaks directly over hot coals 8 minutes. Turn steaks; baste every 2 minutes. Stand steaks on edge, fat edges down, leaning against one another. Grill 1 minute. Turn. Grill until steaks reach internal temperature of 145°F. Transfer to cutting board. With fresh basting brush, baste steaks with reserved butter. Let stand 5 minutes. Makes 4 servings.
EACH SERVING *756 cal, 57 g fat, 57 mg chol, 973 mg sodium, 3 g carb, 0 g fiber, 60 g pro.*

**BOILED-IN-THE-HUSK
CORN ON THE COB**

SUMMER FUN Gather friends together with reinvented summer classics—burgers, dogs, and shakes. Whether you like your corn on the cob or off, July is when it's at its scrumptious best.

159

165

177

Start the Fireworks

Summer means party season, so begin it with a bang. This mixed-berry tart practically screams Fourth of July.

KID FRIENDLY

Berry Patchwork Tart

On a crust of packaged crescent dough, spread a creamy mascarpone filling, then top with blueberries, strawberries, raspberries, and blackberries lightly glazed with a quick homemade syrup.

PREP **20 min.** BAKE **12 min.**
CHILL **2 hr.** OVEN **375°F**

	Nonstick cooking spray
1	8-ounce refrigerated crescent dough
½	cup honey
⅓	cup water
¼	cup loosely packed mint or basil leaves
⅔	cup mascarpone or cream cheese, softened
2	tablespoons honey
¾	cup whipping cream
6	cups berries (red and/or golden raspberries, blueberries, blackberries, and halved or sliced small strawberries), not mixed together

1. Preheat oven to 375°F. Line a 13×9×2-inch baking pan with heavy foil, extending foil beyond pan edges. Lightly coat foil with nonstick cooking spray. Press dough evenly into bottom of pan. Bake for 12 to 15 minutes, until golden. Cool on a wire rack.

2. Meanwhile, for syrup, in a small saucepan combine the ½ cup honey, the water, and mint or basil. Bring to boiling. Simmer, uncovered, for 5 minutes. Remove from heat; let stand to cool. Strain syrup, discarding herbs. Set aside.

3. For cheese layer, in a medium bowl stir together mascarpone and 2 Tbsp. honey. (If using cream cheese, beat until smooth, then beat in honey.) In a chilled mixing bowl beat whipping cream to soft peaks; gradually stir into cheese. Spread cheese layer on crust. Use a knife tip to mark two lengthwise lines and three crosswise lines to form 12 squares.

4. In separate bowls toss berries with about 1 Tbsp. syrup for each cup of berries. Spoon about ½ cup berries in each square. Cover and refrigerate at least 2 hours. Drizzle with remaining syrup if desired.

5. Lifting foil edges, transfer tart from pan to serving platter. Serve immediately or chill up to 4 hours. Tart is best when served the same day it is prepared. Makes 12 servings.

EACH SERVING *253 cal., 14 g fat, 37 mg chol, 164 mg sodium, 31 g carb, 4 g fiber, 5 g pro.*

The New All-Americans

Summer gatherings just got a whole lot more fun with these deliciously clever spins on three ever-popular eats—burgers, dogs, and shakes.

CHORIZO-CHILE BURGERS

PEPPERCORN-BLUE CHEESE BURGERS WITH TANGY CHERRY COMPOTE

CLASSIC CHEESEBURGERS WITH GRILLED ROMAINE AND ONIONS

Classic Cheeseburgers with Grilled Romaine and Onions

For purists, grinding the meat by hand is a must. Give it a try at home using your food processor.
PREP 30 min. GRILL 12 min.

1 large red onion, sliced ½ inch thick
2 Tbsp. extra virgin olive oil
 Kosher or sea salt and freshly ground black pepper
1 recipe Home-Ground Beef or 1¼ lb. ground meat of choice
6 oz. sharp cheddar cheese, thinly sliced
6 hamburger buns, split
½ small heart romaine lettuce
¼ cup mayonnaise

1. In a large skillet over medium-low heat, cook onion in 1 Tbsp. hot olive oil, keeping slices intact. Lightly season with salt and pepper. Cook slowly for 5 minutes, occasionally pressing with spatula to cook evenly. Turn onions carefully, keeping slices intact; cook 5 minutes more, until softened and light brown. (Or brush slices with oil; grill with burgers 5 minutes each side, until browned.)
2. Build charcoal fire or preheat gas grill for direct cooking. Form ground meat in six ¾-inch-thick patties. Slightly indent center of each patty. Season patties with salt. Cook patties on covered grill rack over medium heat for 12 to 14 minutes, until done (160°F), turning once. Top with cheese the last 1 minute of cooking time.
3. Meanwhile, lightly toast buns on grill. Brush romaine heart with remaining 1 Tbsp. oil. Grill 3 minutes, until browned, turning once. Remove from grill; separate into leaves. Spread buns with mayonnaise. Layer patties, onion, and romaine. Makes 6 burgers.
Home-Ground Beef Cut 1¼ lb. boneless chuck roast (or other meat) in large cubes, place on a tray, and freeze about 20 minutes. Half at a time, place cubes in food processor; sprinkle with pepper. Pulse until coarsely ground. (If using meat grinder, process through large die. Mix pepper into ground meat, then grind a second time.)
EACH BURGER *506 cal, 32 g fat, 93 mg chol, 724 mg sodium, 26 g carb, 2 g fiber, 28 g pro.*

Chorizo-Chile Burgers

Mexican chorizo is super spicy. It's also fresh, which means it must be cooked.
PREP 30 min. STAND 30 min.
GRILL 10 min.

1 recipe Poblano-Avocado Spread or purchased avocado spread
1 medium red onion, thinly sliced
 Juice of 1 lime (2 Tbsp.)
1 Tbsp. white vinegar
½ tsp. ground cumin
 Kosher or sea salt and freshly ground black pepper, to taste
6 oz. uncooked chorizo sausage
1¼ lb. ground beef chuck
6 hamburger buns

1. Prepare Poblano-Avocado Spread. Cover and refrigerate. For pickled onions, in medium saucepan of boiling water, heat onion slices 30 seconds. Transfer to bowl of ice water to cool. Drain. In second bowl combine cooled onions, lime juice, vinegar, cumin, salt, and pepper. Toss to coat. Let stand 30 minutes.
2. In large skillet over medium-high heat, cook chorizo about 5 minutes, until slightly browned and becoming crisp, breaking up meat with a spatula. Remove from heat. Spread on plate lined with paper towels to cool.
3. Build charcoal fire or preheat gas grill for direct cooking. In bowl combine cooled chorizo with ground beef. Form into six ¾-inch-thick patties. Indent center of each patty. Grill over medium heat, covered, for 10 to 12 minutes, until done (160°F), turning once midway through grilling time. Spread Poblano-Avocado Spread on buns. Layer patties and pickled onions on buns. Makes 6 burgers.
Poblano-Avocado Spread Char 1 fresh poblano pepper by holding with tongs over gas flame, placing on broiler rack, or baking on foil-lined baking sheet at 425°F 20 to 25 minutes (until skin is blistered and brown). Wrap pepper in foil. Let stand 20 to 30 minutes, until cool enough to handle. Slip off blackened skin, twist off stem, and scoop out seeds; discard skin, stem, and seeds. Coarsely chop, then transfer to small bowl. Halve, pit, and peel 1 avocado. Mash half the avocado; add to chopped pepper. Slice remaining avocado half and stir into poblano-avocado in bowl. Stir in 2 Tbsp. lime juice, 1 Tbsp. chopped cilantro, 1 tsp. mayonnaise, and kosher salt to taste.
EACH BURGER *514 cal, 31 g fat, 9 mg chol, 759 mg sodium, 28 g carb, 3 g fiber, 30 g pro.*

Peppercorn-Blue Cheese Burgers with Tangy Cherry Compote

This burger pairs sweet and tart cherries with peppery beef and creamy blue cheese.
PREP 30 min. COOK 20 min.
GRILL 10 min.

1¼ lb. ground beef chuck
½ tsp. kosher salt
2 Tbsp. coarsely cracked black peppercorns
6 oz. blue cheese, such as Gorgonzola dolce
1 recipe Tangy Cherry Compote or purchased compote of choice
6 hamburger buns, lightly toasted

1. In medium bowl season beef with salt. Form beef in six ¾-inch thick patties. Spread cracked peppercorns on plate; press one side of each patty into pepper. Indent center of each patty.
2. Grill patties on rack of covered charcoal or gas grill 10 to 12 minutes, directly over medium heat until done (160°F), turning once midway through. Spread patties with blue cheese; let stand 5 minutes to melt cheese. Serve patties, topped with Tangy Cherry Compote, on buns. Pass remaining compote. Makes 6 burgers.
Tangy Cherry Compote In medium saucepan combine 1 lb. (3 cups) pitted fresh or frozen tart cherries (thawed and drained), ⅓ cup sugar, ¼ cup dried cherries, 2 Tbsp. red wine vinegar, and 1 tsp. snipped fresh rosemary. Bring to boiling over medium-high heat, stirring frequently. Reduce heat. Boil gently, uncovered, 20 minutes until thickened. Makes 1¼ cups.
EACH BURGER *523 cal, 24 g fat, 85 mg chol, 841 mg sodium, 49 g carb, 3 g fiber, 29 g pro.*

Mushroom-Topped Burgers with Slow-Roasted Tomato Ketchup

This special burger deserves extraordinarily flavorful ketchup.

PREP 35 min. BAKE 10 min.
GRILL 10 min. OVEN 400°F

1 recipe Slow-Roasted Tomato Ketchup, or purchased ketchup of choice
6 oz. aged Gouda cheese, coarsely shredded (1 cup)
6 oz. oyster mushrooms, coarsely sliced
1 tsp. snipped fresh thyme
¼ tsp. kosher or sea salt
1 Tbsp. extra virgin olive oil
1¼ lb. ground beef chuck (80 percent lean)
3 cloves garlic, minced
Kosher salt and freshly ground black pepper
6 large leaves butterhead Boston lettuce
6 hamburger buns, split and toasted

1. Prepare Slow-Roasted Tomato Ketchup; set aside.
2. For cheese crisps, heat oven to 400°F. Line a large baking sheet with parchment. Space eight 2-Tbsp. mounds of cheese at least 3 inches apart. Bake 10 minutes, until bubbly and lightly browned. Cool on baking sheet.
3. Meanwhile, in large skillet over medium-high heat cook mushrooms, thyme, and salt in hot oil for 5 minutes, until mushrooms are tender.
4. Build charcoal fire or preheat gas grill for direct cooking. In large bowl gently mix ground chuck with garlic, salt, and pepper; form in six ¾-inch patties. Indent each patty. Grill patties over medium heat, covered, for 10 to 12 minutes, until done (160°F), turning once midway through grilling time. Layer lettuce, cheese crisps, patties, ketchup, and mushrooms on buns. Makes 6 burgers.
Slow-Roasted Tomato Ketchup Preheat oven to 275°F. On baking sheet lined with parchment paper place 1 medium onion cut in large chunks and 1 lb. (6 or 7) halved and seeded Roma tomatoes, cut sides up. Sprinkle tomatoes with 2 Tbsp. brown sugar and ¼ tsp. kosher or sea salt. Drizzle tomatoes and onion with 1 Tbsp. extra virgin olive oil. Roast, uncovered, 2 hours, until onions are browned and tomatoes are softened yet moist. In blender or food processor, blend or process tomatoes and onions until smooth. Transfer to small bowl. Stir in 1 Tbsp. hoisin sauce. Let stand until ready to use. Cover and refrigerate remaining ketchup up to 1 week. Makes ¾ cup.
EACH BURGER *556 cal, 33 g fat, 99 mg chol, 729 mg sodium, 35 g carb, 3 g fiber, 30 g pro.*

FAST
Spicy Kimchi Burgers

Korean kimchi, a spicy fermented cabbage dish, goes beautifully with beef.
PREP 20 min. GRILL 10 min.

1 recipe Sesame-Scallion Mayonnaise, or mayonnaise of choice
1 cup shredded red cabbage
1 cup bottled spicy kimchi, chopped
1¼ lbs. ground beef chuck
1 Tbsp. fish sauce
6 hamburger buns

1. Prepare Sesame-Scallion Mayonnaise. In medium bowl toss red cabbage with kimchi and 1 Tbsp. of the Sesame-Scallion Mayonnaise; set aside.
2. In large bowl gently mix beef and fish sauce; form in six ¾-inch-thick patties. Indent each patty. For charcoal or gas grill, cook patties on rack of covered grill directly over medium heat for 10 to 12 minutes, or until done (160°F), turning once midway through grilling. For each burger, spread 1 Tbsp. Sesame-Scallion Mayonnaise on bun. Layer patty and some kimchi mixture. Makes 6 burgers.
Sesame-Scallion Mayonnaise In small bowl whisk 1 pasteurized egg yolk, 1 Tbsp. Dijon mustard, l Tbsp. white vinegar, and 1 Tbsp. chili sauce until combined. In a thin steady stream slowly whisk in ⅓ cup sesame oil and ⅓ cup peanut oil (mayonnaise will thicken). Stir in 2 green onions and 1 tsp. sesame seeds. Refrigerate, covered, up to 3 days; stir before using. Makes 1 scant cup.
EACH BURGER *426 cal, 26 g fat, 77 mg chol, 719 mg sodium, 24 g carb, 2 g fiber, 23 g pro.*

Double Cheeseburgers with Basil, Bacon, and Egg

This oh-so-indulgent butter burger is worth the splurge.
PREP 30 min. GRILL 12 min.

1 recipe Bacon Aïoli or garlic-and-bacon-flavor mayonnaise
1½ lb. ground beef chuck (80 percent lean)
¼ cup finely snipped fresh flat-leaf Italian parsley
2 Tbsp. unsalted butter, melted, then cooled to room temperature
4 oz. mozzarella or smoked mozzarella cheese, coarsely shredded
1 Tbsp. extra virgin olive oil (optional)
4 eggs (optional)
4 hamburger buns
Fresh basil leaves

1. Prepare Bacon Aïoli; set aside.
2. Build charcoal fire or preheat gas grill for direct cooking. In a large bowl gently mix ground beef, parsley, butter, ½ tsp. salt, and ¼ tsp. pepper; form into 8 thin patties. Equally divide cheese in 4. Place cheese between 2 thin patties; press and pinch edges to seal.
3. For fried eggs, in large skillet heat oil over medium heat. When oil shimmers, crack each egg into small bowl; tip egg into skillet. Sprinkle with salt and pepper. Cook, covered, to desired doneness.
4. Grill patties over medium heat (about 400°F), covered, for 12 to 14 minutes, turning once midway through grilling. Spread each bun with 2 Tbsp. Bacon Aïoli; layer a patty and egg. Top with basil. Makes 4 burgers.
Bacon Aïoli Preheat oven to 350°F. Place 16 unpeeled cloves of garlic on a sheet of aluminum foil. Drizzle with 1 Tbsp. olive oil, then bring up foil edges, roll, and seal to form a packet. Bake about 20 minutes, until garlic is very soft. Meanwhile, heat large skillet over medium-high heat. Cook 8 slices thick-sliced bacon, chopped, for 7 to 8 minutes, until crisp, stirring occasionally. Drain bacon on paper towels. When garlic is cool enough to handle, squeeze cloves from skins into small bowl. Mash with fork. Stir in bacon and 1 cup of mayonnaise. Makes 1¼ cups.
EACH BURGER *(with 2 tbsp. aïoli) 893 cal, 68 g fat, 169 mg chol, 1,080 mg sodium, 25 g carb, 1 g fiber, 44 g pro.*

From fast food to fine dining, the basic burger has become a canvas for flavor.

SPICY KIMCHI BURGERS

MUSHROOM-TOPPED BURGERS WITH SLOW-ROASTED TOMATO KETCHUP

DOUBLE CHEESEBURGERS WITH BASIL, BACON, AND EGG

CLASSIC DOGS WITH TANGY-SWEET RELISH

FARMSTAND SLAW DOGS

PICKLED PEACH AND BACON DOGS WITH ARUGULA MAYO

The humble hot dog has long been a starting point for building flavor—think classic toppings like crunchy slaw or sweet relish.

Classic Dogs with Tangy-Sweet Relish

Make a quick relish by combining two types of pickles.
PREP 40 min.　BROIL 4 min.　OVEN 500°F

- 8 hot dogs of choice*
- ½ cup coarsely chopped bread and butter pickles
- ¼ cup coarsely chopped dill pickles
- 8 hot dog buns
- ¼ cup finely chopped red onion
- ½ English cucumber cut in wedges
  Mustard

1. Preheat broiler. Place hot dogs on baking sheet lined with foil. Broil 4 to 5 minutes, turning often, until heated through. Meanwhile, in small bowl stir together pickles. Serve hot dogs in buns with pickles, onion, cucumber, and mustard. Makes 8 servings.

EACH SERVING *350 cal, 18 g fat, 25 mg chol, 1,115 mg sodium, 33 g carb, 3 g fiber, 13 g pro.*

* We like classic all-beef dogs in these recipes, but you can substitute your favorite type. From basic to gourmet, you can now find hot dogs in a wide variety such as turkey, pork, and meatless.

Farmstand Slaw Dogs

Anything goes for this slaw. Substitute whatever vegetables are popping up at farmer's markets or in the garden, and serve some of the slaw on the side.
PREP 20 min.　COOK 5 min.　GRILL 6 min.

- 4 oz. fresh green beans, trimmed
- 3 ears corn, husks and silks removed
- 5 small radishes, sliced
- 1 medium carrot, shaved in ribbons with vegetable peeler
- 1 small green sweet pepper, cut in narrow strips
- ¼ cup canola or olive oil
- 1 lemon, juiced (3 Tbsp.)
- 1 Tbsp. sugar
- 1 tsp. snipped fresh tarragon
- 1 tsp. Dijon-style mustard
- 8 hot dogs of choice*
- 8 hot dog buns, split and lightly toasted

1. In a large saucepan cook beans and corn, covered, in lightly salted boiling water for 5 minutes. Drain and rinse with cold water. Cut corn from cobs. For slaw, in large bowl combine beans, corn, radishes, carrot, and sweet pepper. For dressing, in screw-top jar combine oil, lemon juice, sugar, tarragon, mustard, and ⅛ tsp. each salt and pepper. Cover and shake. Drizzle dressing on vegetables; toss to combine. Set aside to marinate while grilling hot dogs (or refrigerate up to 6 hours).
2. Preheat grill to medium. Grill hot dogs, covered, 6 minutes, turning until grill marks form. Serve in buns, topped with slaw. Makes 8 servings.

EACH SERVING *368 cal, 21 g fat, 25 mg chol, 746 mg sodium, 34 g carb, 2 g fiber, 11 g pro.*

Pickled Peach and Bacon Dogs with Arugula Mayo

Bacon on a hot dog? Oh, yeah. Sweet-tart pickled peaches balance the rich meaty flavor—and mayo pulls it all together.
PREP 30 min.　GRILL 5 min.

- ½ cup rice vinegar
- 1 Tbsp. honey
- 1 tsp. fennel seeds, crushed
- ½ tsp. salt
- 2 peaches, halved, pitted, and thinly sliced
- ½ cup arugula, finely chopped
- ½ cup basil leaves, finely chopped
- ¾ cup mayonnaise
- 8 hot dogs of choice*
- 8 hot dog buns
- 8 slices bacon, crisp-cooked
  Arugula leaves (optional)

1. For pickled peaches, in small bowl whisk together vinegar, honey, fennel seeds, and salt. Place peaches in large resealable plastic bag set in shallow dish; pour marinade over peaches. Seal bag; rotate to coat. Let sit at least 20 minutes.
2. Meanwhile, preheat grill to medium. For Arugula Mayo, in small bowl combine chopped arugula and basil and the mayonnaise; set aside.
3. Grill hot dogs on rack of covered charcoal or gas grill, directly over medium heat, 5 to 7 minutes, turning occasionally. On each bun, spread 1 Tbsp. Arugula Mayo. Layer bacon and hot dog. With slotted spoon, scoop some peaches on dogs. Top with arugula if desired. Serve with remaining peaches. Cover and refrigerate Arugula Mayo up to 3 days. Refrigerate peaches up to 1 day. Makes 8 servings.

EACH SERVING *573 cal, 34 g fat, 48 mg chol, 1,177 mg sodium, 50 g carb, 2 g fiber, 18 g pro.*

Go along with summer's carefree, playful air—throw a mix-and-match party, encouraging guests to swap different dogs and toppings any which way. There are no rules when it comes to creating something totally tasty.

KID FRIENDLY | FAST
Lime Beer-Braised Salsa Dogs

Homemade salsa gives these dogs a vibrant boost of flavor and spice.
PREP 20 min. COOK 7 min.

1   pint red and yellow grape, pear, or cherry tomatoes, halved or chopped
½   cup sliced green onions (4)
½   cup coarsely chopped cilantro
1   jalapeño pepper, stemmed, halved lengthwise, and seeded if desired (see note, page 69)
     Salt and ground black pepper
2   limes
1   12-oz. can or bottle beer
8   hot dogs of choice*
8   hot dog buns, split and toasted
½   cup crumbled queso blanco or shredded Monterey Jack cheese (2 oz.)

1. For salsa, in medium bowl combine tomatoes, onions, cilantro, and half the jalapeño, thinly sliced. Season with salt and pepper; set aside.
2. For lime-beer cooking liquid, cut 1 lime in half; juice both halves, retaining halves. In large skillet combine beer, remaining jalapeño, lime juice, and lime halves. Bring to simmering. Add hot dogs; return to simmering. Cook, uncovered, for 7 minutes. Remove hot dogs. Discard cooking liquid and solids.
3. Cut remaining lime in wedges. Serve hot dogs in buns with queso blanco and salsa. Serve with lime wedges. Makes 8 servings.
EACH SERVING *314 cal, 16 g fat, 30 mg chol, 810 mg sodium, 28 g carb, 1 g fiber, 11 g pro.*

KID FRIENDLY
Barbecue Potato Chip Crunch Dogs

Homemade sauce from pantry items gives this dog zing. Bottled barbecue sauce is a quick substitute. Top with chips right before serving so they stay crisp.
PREP 15 min. COOK 25 min.

1   cup ketchup
½   cup cider vinegar
1   Tbsp. honey
1   Tbsp. Worcestershire sauce
1   tsp. chili powder
½   tsp. garlic powder
8   hot dogs of choice*
2   cups finely shredded napa or white cabbage
8   hot dog buns
     Barbecue-flavor potato chips

1. For sauce, in medium saucepan combine ketchup, vinegar, honey, Worcestershire sauce, chili powder, and garlic powder. Bring to boiling. Reduce heat; simmer, uncovered, 20 minutes, stirring often.
2. Add hot dogs to sauce. Simmer, uncovered, 5 to 10 minutes, until plump and heated through. (If desired, thin remaining sauce with water for dipping.) Sprinkle cabbage in each bun. Top with hot dog and chips. Serve immediately. Makes 8 servings.
EACH SERVING *329 cal, 17 g fat, 25 mg chol, 930 mg sodium, 34 g carb, 1 g fiber, 10 g pro.*

KID FRIENDLY | FAST
Mac and Cheese Dogs

These two classic tastes are better eaten together. In a hurry? Heat frozen or leftover mac and cheese.
PREP 15 min. BAKE 10 min.
OVEN 400°F

2   cups dried elbow macaroni
2   Tbsp. butter
2   Tbsp. all-purpose flour
2   cups milk
6   oz. cheddar cheese, shredded (1½ cups)
6   oz. American cheese, shredded (1½ cups)
8   hot dogs of choice*
8   hot dog buns
½   cup toasted bread crumbs
     Chili powder (optional)

1. Preheat oven to 400°F. Cook pasta according to package directions; set aside. In medium saucepan melt butter over medium heat. Stir in flour; cook 1 minute. Stir in milk all at once. Cook and stir until slightly thickened and bubbly. Stir in cheeses until melted. Stir in pasta. Remove from heat. Cool slightly.
2. Line a 13×9×2-inch baking pan with foil. Place hot dogs in buns on pan. Top each hot dog with about ⅓ cup macaroni and cheese. Sprinkle with bread crumbs and chili powder if desired. Bake 10 minutes, until hot dogs are heated through. Transfer each hot dog to plates with a spatula. Serve with remaining mac and cheese. Makes 8 servings.
EACH SERVING *469 cal, 25 g fat, 58 mg chol, 1,015 mg sodium, 40 g carb, 1 g fiber, 19 g pro.*

MAC AND CHEESE
DOGS

BARBECUE
POTATO CHIP
CRUNCH DOGS

LIME BEER-
BRAISED SALSA
DOGS

KID FRIENDLY | FAST
Double Vanilla Shakes
START TO FINISH 10 min.

1   quart vanilla ice cream
1   cup half-and-half or whole milk
1   vanilla bean, halved lengthwise
4   purchased meringue cookies
    (optional)

In blender combine ice cream and half-and-half. With knife tip, scrape vanilla bean seeds into blender. Blend until smooth. Divide among four glasses; top with meringue cookies if desired. Makes 4 (1¼ cup) servings.

EACH SERVING 409 cal, 23 g fat, 86 mg chol, 145 mg sodium, 44 g carb, 1 g fiber, 7 g pro.

FAST
Grapefruit-Gin Cocktail Shakes
START TO FINISH 10 min.

1   pint raspberry sorbet
⅓   to ⅔ cup pink grapefruit juice, chilled
1   pint vanilla ice cream
¼   cup gin or pink grapefruit juice
    Lemon slices

In blender combine sorbet and ⅓ cup grapefruit juice; cover and blend until smooth. Blend in ice cream and gin. If necessary, blend in additional juice. Divide among four tall glasses. Garnish with lemon slices. Makes 4 servings.

EACH SERVING 312 cal, 8 g fat, 32 mg chol, 58 mg sodium, 50 g carb, 3 g fiber, 3 g pro.

KID FRIENDLY | FAST
Peach Pie Shakes
START TO FINISH 10 min.

⅓   9-inch bakery double-crust peach pie
2   cups frozen sliced peaches
⅓   to ½ cup milk
1   pint vanilla ice cream

Cut 4 very small wedges from the ⅓ pie; set aside. In blender combine the remaining wedge of pie, peaches, and ⅓ cup milk. Blend until nearly smooth. Blend in ice cream, a scoop or two at a time. If necessary, add milk. Divide among four tall glasses. Top with reserved pie wedges. Makes 4 servings.

EACH SERVING 382 cal, 15 g fat, 33 mg chol, 195 mg sodium, 59 g carb, 2 g fiber, 4 g pro.

GRAPEFRUIT-GIN
COCKTAIL SHAKE

DOUBLE
VANILLA
SHAKE

PEACH PIE
SHAKE

KID FRIENDLY | **FAST**

Coconut-Doughnut Shakes

START TO FINISH 15 min.

4 miniature frosted cake doughnuts
3 cups vanilla ice cream
⅔ to ¾ cup milk
3 Tbsp. cream of coconut
4 miniature frosted cake doughnuts (optional)

Coarsely crumble 4 doughnuts; set aside. In blender combine ice cream, milk, and cream of coconut until smooth. Add crumbled doughnuts; pulse just until blended. Divide among four tall glasses; top each with mini doughnut if desired. Makes 4 (¾ cup) servings.

EACH SERVING 344 cal, 20 g fat, 55 mg chol, 154 mg sodium, 35 g carb, 1 g fiber, 6 g pro.

KID FRIENDLY

Red, White, and Blue Shakes

PREP 20 min. FREEZE 30 min.

2 cups strawberry ice cream
⅔ cup whole milk
1 cup strawberries, cut up
3 cups vanilla ice cream
⅓ cup bottled blueberry smoothie or blueberry juice blend
1 cup blueberries

1. For strawberry layer, in blender combine strawberry ice cream and ⅓ cup milk until smooth. Blend in strawberries until coarsely chopped. Scoop into bowl; cover and freeze 30 to 60 minutes. Wash and rinse blender.

2. For vanilla layer, blend half the vanilla ice cream and remaining milk until smooth. Scoop into separate bowl; cover and freeze 30 to 60 minutes. Wash and rinse blender.

3. For blueberry layer, blend remaining vanilla ice cream and blueberry smoothie until smooth. Blend in ¾ cup blueberries until coarsely chopped. Scoop into separate bowl; cover and freeze 30 to 60 minutes.

4. Scoop layers of strawberry, vanilla, and blueberry among four tall gasses. Top with remaining blueberries. Makes 4 servings.

EACH SERVING 422 cal, 19 g fat, 71 mg chol, 145 mg sodium, 57 g carb, 3 g fiber, 7 g pro.

RED, WHITE, AND BLUE SHAKE

COCONUT-DOUGHNUT SHAKE

Home Cooking

CORN GETS FRESH Summer's most iconic vegetable is more versatile than it gets credit for. Chef Scott Peacock shows four new ways to use it.

Boiled-in-the-Husk Corn on the Cob

"I like to put out thick napkins so everyone can peel the husks back, wrap a napkin around them, and use this as a handle when eating," Scott says.
PREP 30 min. COOK 10 min.

1   recipe Flavored Butter
6   ears fresh corn in the husk

1. Prepare Flavored Butter. Peel husks from tip of each cob to base, but do not detach from cob. Remove and discard any damaged or discolored outer husks. Thoroughly remove all silks from each ear of corn (a nubby kitchen towel rubbed briskly between rows of kernels makes easy work of this, Scott says). Pull husks back up over the corn and tie ends with strips of husks or 100-percent-cotton kitchen string.

2. In large kettle bring 6 quarts water to boiling and add 3 Tbsp. kosher salt. Add corn. Cook 10 minutes. Using tongs, remove corn and let drain briefly. Serve with Flavored Butter. Makes 6 servings.
Flavored Butter In small bowl stir together 6 Tbsp. unsalted butter, softened, ½ tsp. sea salt* or kosher salt, 2 tsp. crushed Aleppo pepper,** and ⅛ tsp. cayenne pepper. Cover and allow to stand at room temperature 3 hours to allow flavors to meld or refrigerate up to 24 hours. Bring to room temperature before serving.
* Scott prefers Maldon sea salt, which is available at specialty food and grocery stores.
** ½ tsp. cayenne pepper can be substituted for the Aleppo pepper.
EACH SERVING *182 cal, 13 g fat, 31 mg chol, 208 mg sodium, 17 g carb, 2 g fiber, 3 g pro.*

PREPPING
Tying the husks back up after removing the silks ensures even cooking as the corn boils. Corn can be cleaned and tied back together a few hours ahead.

BOILED "Boiling in the husks keeps the flavor in the kernels and protects the corn from overcooking. Serving the ears still in the husks adds a little bit of drama to the meal too."

BOILING
The simpler the technique, the more important the details become. Here it's all about the right ratio of salt to water, which results in properly seasoned corn.

RAW "Timing is everything. Wait until the very last minute to cut the corn from the cobs for this salad—that way, the corn stays as sweet and crisp as possible."

CUTTING
Trim base of corn flat and stand it upright on a stable surface. With a sharp knife use a sawing motion to slice kernels from ears.

LOW FAT

Fresh Corn Salad

"If corn is less than sparkling and perfect, refresh it," Scott says. Blanch 1 minute in boiling salted water, then transfer to salted ice water to stop cooking.
START TO FINISH **35 minutes**

½   cup cider vinegar
¼   to ⅓ cup sugar
1   tsp. kosher salt
½   tsp. coarsely ground black pepper
4   ears fresh corn
½   cup finely diced red onion (cut to same size as the corn kernels), soaked in ice water for 20 minutes and patted dry
½   cup cucumber, seeded but not peeled (if unwaxed), diced to same size as onions
½   cup red or orange sweet pepper, diced to same size as onions
½   cup cherry or pear tomatoes, halved or quartered
3   Tbsp. parsley, finely torn
1   Tbsp. basil leaves or buds, pulled apart
1   Tbsp. fresh jalapeño, seeds and veins removed, very finely diced (see note, page 69)
½   tsp. sea salt or kosher salt
1   to 2 cups small arugula leaves

1. For dressing, in glass bowl whisk together vinegar, sugar, the 1 tsp. kosher salt, and black pepper until sugar is dissolved. Allow dressing to stand while preparing salad.
2. For salad, cut corn kernels from cobs. In large bowl toss corn and remaining ingredients except sea salt and arugula leaves.
3. At serving time, transfer corn mixture to serving bowl. Season with the ½ tsp. sea salt. Add the dressing; gently thread in arugula leaves. Serve immediately. (The cucumbers and tomatoes will begin to break down.) Makes 8 servings.
EACH SERVING *77 cal, 1 g fat, 0 g chol, 401 mg sodium, 17 g carb, 2 g fiber, 2 g pro.*

BROWNED "Cooking fresh corn in a hot skillet with a little oil gives it a rich nutty flavor. Resist the urge to stir too soon."

LOW FAT   FAST

Skillet Corn Griddle Cakes

"The savory toppers are delicious and colorful," Scott says. "Another time around, you can serve these versatile cakes with butter and maple syrup."

PREP 15 min.   COOK 16 min. plus 2 min. per batch

1   Tbsp. vegetable or olive oil
1¼ cups corn kernels, freshly cut from the cob
¼   cup all-purpose flour
¼   cup coarse ground yellow cornmeal
¼   tsp. kosher salt
1   tsp. baking powder
½   cup milk, plus additional for thinning batter
1   egg, lightly beaten
1   Tbsp. vegetable oil
1   Tbsp. finely chopped onion
½   cup sour cream (optional)
½   cup chopped fresh tomato
¼   cup sliced green onion
¼   cup crumbled ricotta salata or feta cheese

1. In a 12-inch nonstick skillet heat 1 Tbsp. vegetable or olive oil over medium heat. Add the corn kernels in an even layer; sprinkle generously with salt. Cook, without stirring, for 3 to 4 minutes until the corn kernels are sizzling. Give the pan a shake and continue cooking about 16 minutes total, until kernels are browned. Reserve 2 Tbsp. of the browned corn for garnish.

2. Meanwhile, in medium bowl whisk together flour, cornmeal, ¼ tsp. salt, and baking powder. Whisk in milk, egg, and the 1 Tbsp. vegetable oil, mixing just until batter is smooth. Stir in chopped onion and remaining browned corn.

3. Wipe out skillet with a lightly oiled paper towel and heat over medium heat. Drop batter by 1 or 2 Tbsp. measures; cook until browned on one side and batter appears set, about 1 minute. Turn and cook 1 additional minute or less. Repeat with remaining batter. Set aside and keep warm.

4. Top each griddle cake with sour cream if desired, chopped tomato, reserved browned corn kernels, sliced green onion, and the ricotta salata. Makes 6 side-dish servings.

EACH SERVING *154 cal, 5 g fat, 38 mg chol, 341 mg sodium, 18 g carb, 1 g fiber, 5 g pro.*

BROWNING
Allow corn to cook undisturbed until well browned on one side, then turn. As corn gets close to doneness, kernels may pop and leap. If that happens, cover pan loosely with lid.

PUREED "The blender does most of the work in this recipe, but you have to blend the corn longer than other vegetables to get it smooth."

Fresh Corn Soup

"This soup is quickly made from just a few ingredients—the starch in the corn is a natural thickener," Scott says. Starch levels in corn can vary dramatically, so if the soup is too thick, add additional hot milk.

START TO FINISH 35 min.

4	Tbsp. unsalted butter
½	cup coarsely chopped Vidalia or other sweet onion
4	cups corn, freshly cut from the cob
1	to 2 Tbsp. sugar
2	to 3 cups milk
1	cup half-and-half
¼	tsp. freshly grated nutmeg, plus additional for grating over servings

1. In a medium saucepan over medium-low heat melt butter. Add onion and cook gently for 3 to 5 minutes until tender; do not let onion brown. Add 3½ cups of the corn and sprinkle generously with kosher salt. "Good seasoning at this stage really draws out the flavor of the corn," Scott says. Stir well and cook 5 to 7 minutes; again, do not let onions or corn brown. Stir in 1 Tbsp. of the sugar.

2. In a medium saucepan combine 2 cups of the milk and the half-and-half, and warm over medium-low heat until heated through. Pour the corn mixture over the heated milk and over medium heat, stirring often, bring just to a simmer. Remove from heat. Cool slightly.

3. Puree soup in batches, one-third at a time, until very smooth. Pour into a fine-wire strainer set over a bowl. Allow soup to drain through. Transfer soup back to pan. Reheat over medium heat; whisk in grated nutmeg. If thinner soup is desired, heat the remaining 1 cup milk over medium heat; gradually stir into soup to desired consistency. Taste for seasoning, adding more salt and some of remaining 1 Tbsp. sugar. To serve, divide among bowls; top each with some of the remaining ½ cup corn and dusting of additional nutmeg. Makes 4 to 6 servings.
EACH SERVING *395 cal, 23 g fat, 63 mg chol, 600 mg sodium, 42 g carb, 3 g fiber, 11 g pro.*

STRAINING
After pureeing, strain the soup. Use a sweeping motion with the back of a wooden spoon to break down any bits of pulp the blender might have missed.

Delicious on a Dollar

Stack up the savings with this fresh vegetable salad that you can make hours ahead.

Stacked Summer Vegetable Salad

PREP 50 min. CHILL 1 hr.

3 medium yellow or green zucchini
  Kosher salt
4 medium carrots
¼ small red onion
1 cup torn leaf lettuce
3 Tbsp. lemon juice
¼ cup olive oil or canola oil
1 Tbsp. snipped fresh dill
  Freshly ground black pepper

1. With a vegetable peeler or mandoline shave zucchini in thin strips. Salt lightly, then transfer to colander to drain, about 15 minutes. Meanwhile, shave carrots in strips lengthwise and thinly slice onion.
2. Rinse zucchini and allow to drain in colander. To assemble salad, in a 2-quart square dish layer one-third each of the vegetables and onion. For dressing, in a glass measuring cup whisk together lemon juice and oil. Drizzle some of the dressing on layered vegetables. Repeat layering and dressing twice. Cover and refrigerate 1 hour or up to 12 hours before serving.
3. To serve, sprinkle salad with fresh dill and pepper. Cut salad in rectangles with a sharp knife; lift out with a spatula. Makes 6 to 8 servings.

EACH SERVING 117 cal, 9 g fat, 0 g chol, 202 mg sodium, 8 g carb, 2 g fiber, 2 g pro.

STACKED SUMMER VEGETABLE SALAD

GARDEN
VEGETABLE
TART

august

SUMMER TIME Keep your cool with frosty ice cream treats. And let the produce shine with fresh vegetables from the garden.

187

196

199

Keep It Cool

The best thing about this no-bake dessert? It can be made ahead and served straight from the fridge. Delight friends with a slice of this light and lemony pie—a refreshing finish to a hot summer night.

KID FRIENDLY

Lemon Icebox Pie

PREP 45 min. STAND 20 min.
CHILL Overnight

1⅓ cups crushed shortbread cookies
3 Tbsp. lemon drops, finely crushed
¼ cup butter, melted
1 cup sugar
1 envelope unflavored gelatin
2 Tbsp. cornstarch
1 Tbsp. finely shredded lemon peel
6 Tbsp. lemon juice
6 Tbsp. water
6 egg yolks, lightly beaten
¼ cup butter, cut up
1 32-oz. carton vanilla Greek yogurt
½ cup whipping cream
1 Tbsp. lemon drops, finely crushed
  Candied Lemon Slices (optional)
  Fresh mint leaves (optional)

1. For crust, in a medium bowl combine cookie crumbs, the 3 Tbsp. crushed lemon drops, and melted butter. Press into bottom of a 9- or 10-inch pie plate or an 8- or 9-inch springform pan. Set aside.*
2. For filling, in a medium saucepan combine sugar, gelatin, and cornstarch. Add lemon peel, lemon juice, and the water. Cook and stir over medium heat until thickened and bubbly.
3. Stir half of the lemon mixture into the egg yolks. Return egg mixture to saucepan. Cook, stirring constantly, over medium heat until mixture comes to a gentle boil. Cook and stir 2 minutes more. Remove from heat. Add cut-up butter, stirring until melted. Transfer to a bowl; cover with plastic wrap. Cool 20 minutes.
4. Place yogurt in a large bowl; gradually stir in lemon mixture. Carefully spoon into crust-lined pan. Cover and chill overnight.
5. For topping, in chilled medium bowl beat whipping cream to soft peaks; fold in 1 Tbsp. crushed lemon drops. To serve, carefully loosen and remove sides of springform pan, if using. Top pie with whipped cream mixture and Candied Lemon Slices and fresh mint, if desired. Makes 12 servings.

Candied Lemon Slices In a large skillet combine 1 cup sugar and 1 cup water. Cook and stir over medium heat until sugar is dissolved. Bring mixture to a boil; reduce heat. Add lemon slices. Cook for 1 minute, turning once. Transfer to waxed paper to cool.**
*Tip For a crispier crust, bake in a 375°F oven for 5 minutes; cool.
**Tip Cover and chill the leftover syrup up to 2 weeks. Use for sweetening iced tea or toss with fresh berries for a quick dessert.
EACH SERVING *335 cal, 17 g fat, 129 mg chol, 165 mg sodium, 37 g carb, 10 g pro.*

BLISTERED GREEN
BEANS

Growing Season

Summer means beans, zucchini, tomatoes, beets, and more—all in abundance. Cookbook author Ian Knauer makes the most of his garden's bounty with a meal that puts fresh vegetables first. Since planting the garden, Ian says he's never eaten so well or learned so much. "I've grown closer to my family, the place, the garden, and the beautiful yet sometimes difficult lessons they taught me," he says. "It gives back to me what I've given to it."

Blistered Green Beans

"This method for cooking green beans is inspired by high-heat Chinese wok cooking," Ian says. "Blistering, or charring, the beans adds real depth of flavor, and the beans keep a nice crunch."

PREP 20 min. COOK 15 min.

⅓ cup apple cider vinegar
¼ cup water
2 shallots, sliced
2 tsp. sugar
1½ tsp. fine sea salt
¼ lb. bacon, chopped (about 4 slices)
2 Tbsp. extra virgin olive oil

2 lb. green beans, trimmed
½ tsp. ground black pepper
4 cloves garlic, thinly sliced
½ cup fresh cilantro leaves
1 fresh jalapeño pepper, thinly sliced (see note, page 69)

1. For pickled shallots, in small saucepan bring vinegar, the water, shallots, sugar, and 1 tsp. of the salt to a simmer. Remove from heat and let stand until ready to use.
2. In a very large skillet cook bacon over medium heat 6 to 8 minutes until browned and crisp. Transfer to paper towels to drain, leaving fat in skillet. Add oil to skillet and increase heat to high. Add beans, the remaining ½ tsp. salt, and the black pepper. Cook, stirring occasionally, 8 to 10 minutes until beans are blistered and crisp tender. Stir in garlic and cook 1 to 2 minutes, stirring until garlic is browned. Season with salt and pepper to taste. Transfer beans to a serving platter and top with cilantro, jalapeño, bacon, and drained pickled shallots. Makes 10 servings.

EACH SERVING 114 cal, 8 g fat, 8 mg chol, 432 mg sodium, 9 g carb, 3 g fiber, 3 g pro.

Ian loves discovering a perfectly ripe tomato on the vine. "The tomatoes explode in your mouth when you bite into these rolls," he says.

Tomato Pizza Rolls

"I love to bake bread, and I also love pizza," Ian says. "So wrapping the flavors of pizza together in a neat little dough package brings in the best of both."

PREP 45 min. RISE 1 hour
BAKE 25 min. OVEN 425°F

2	cups warm water (105°F–115°F)
2	packages active dry yeast
6	cups bread flour or all-purpose flour
2½	tsp. fine sea salt
1	large garlic clove
3	cups cherry tomatoes, halved and/or quartered
½	cup finely grated Parmesan cheese
¼	cup extra virgin olive oil
1	tsp. finely shredded lemon peel
½	tsp. finely ground black pepper
2	to 4 oz. thinly sliced prosciutto
1	cup basil leaves
	Olive oil
	Snipped fresh basil

1. In a large bowl combine the water and yeast; let stand for 5 minutes. Add flour and 2 tsp. of the salt, stirring to combine. Turn out onto a lightly floured surface. Knead 6 to 8 minutes to make a moderately stiff dough that is smooth and elastic. Shape dough in a ball. Place in a lightly greased bowl; turn once to grease surface of dough. Cover with a kitchen towel. Let rise at warm room temperature 1 to 2 hours until doubled in size.

2. For sauce, while dough rises, mince and mash garlic with a large pinch of salt to a paste. Stir together with tomatoes, Parmesan, ¼ cup oil, lemon peel, pepper, and remaining ½ tsp. salt.

3. Position racks in the upper and lower thirds of oven and preheat to 425°F.

4. Place raised dough on a well-floured work surface. Stretch or roll dough to a 22×14-inch rectangle. Scatter prosciutto and basil leaves on dough. Place tomato sauce along the lengthwise center of dough. Fold bottom third of dough over tomato sauce, then fold over top third of dough. Cut dough crosswise in 10 pieces. Transfer rolls cut sides up to two baking sheets, gently pressing dough to expose some of the filling. Space about 2 inches apart.

5. Bake rolls 25 to 35 minutes, switching baking sheet positions midway through baking time, until crust is golden and hollow-sounding. To serve, drizzle with olive oil and sprinkle with snipped fresh basil. Makes 10 servings.

EACH SERVING 409 cal, 12 g fat, 7 mg chol, 770 mg sodium, 60 g carb, 3 g fiber, 15 g pro.

**TOMATO PIZZA
ROLLS**

In late August, when the warm ground swells with sun-ripened produce, Ian Knauer heads to his family's Pennsylvania farm to get his hands dirty.

ZUCCHINI STEAKS
WITH HERB GARDEN
CHIMICHURRI

Zucchini Steaks with Herb Garden Chimichurri

Chimichurri—a mix of herbs, garlic, and oil spiked with tangy vinegar—boosts the fresh flavor of grilled zucchini. "Chimichurri is traditionally served with a grilled skirt steak, so when I serve meat alongside this dish, I go for that cut," Ian says.

PREP **15 min.** GRILL **20 min.**
STAND **20 min.**

2	to 3 red sweet peppers
3	cloves garlic
1	tsp. fine sea salt
¾	cup extra virgin olive oil
2	Tbsp. cider vinegar
¾	tsp. ground black pepper
6	medium zucchini (about 2½ lbs.)
1½	cups chopped mixed fresh herbs, such as parsley, cilantro, basil, dill, or oregano

1. For a gas or charcoal grill, place peppers on the rack directly over medium heat. Cover and cook 12 minutes or until blackened and blistered, turning occasionally. Transfer to a bowl. Cover bowl with a plate or plastic wrap. Let peppers stand 20 minutes. Discard skins, seeds, and cores, and slice peppers thinly. Set aside.

2. Using a chef's knife, mince and mash garlic with ¼ tsp. of the salt to a paste. Transfer to a large bowl. Add ¼ cup of the oil, 1 Tbsp. of the vinegar, ½ tsp. of the salt, and ½ tsp. of the pepper; whisk to combine. Halve zucchini lengthwise, then coat with marinade in bowl. Transfer zucchini to grill rack (do not wash bowl). Grill, covered, 8 to 10 minutes or until tender, turning occasionally. Transfer zucchini to serving platter.

3. For chimichurri, in marinade bowl stir together reserved peppers, herbs, the remaining ½ cup oil, remaining 1 Tbsp. vinegar, and remaining ¼ tsp. each salt and pepper. Spoon chimichurri over zucchini. Makes 6 main-dish or 12 side-dish servings.

EACH SERVING *146 cal, 14 g fat, 197 mg sodium, 5 g carb, 2 g fiber, 2 g pro.*

SHREDDED SWISS CHARD SALAD

Shredded Swiss Chard Salad

"This is one of my favorite salads, good with eggs for breakfast, pizza for lunch, or a summer barbecue for dinner," Ian says. "It's unusual to serve chard raw, but the leaves have a wonderful freshness and they're easy to eat when sliced into very thin strands. Creamy mozzarella balances the nicely bitter chard."

START TO FINISH **15 min.**

1	large bunch rainbow chard (12 oz.)
½	clove garlic
	Kosher salt
2	Tbsp. extra virgin olive oil
1	Tbsp. apple cider vinegar
1	Tbsp. finely chopped shallot
1	fresh hot chile pepper, very thinly sliced (see note, page 69)
¼	tsp. ground black pepper
5	oz. fresh mozzarella cheese, coarsely shredded (1½ cups)

1. Wash and dry the chard leaves. Remove the stems. Stack the leaves in a pile, roll them up tightly, like a cigar, and thinly slice crosswise into very fine strands.

2. For vinaigrette, mash the garlic with a pinch of salt to a paste. In a large bowl whisk garlic paste with the oil, vinegar, shallot, chile pepper, ½ tsp. salt, and ¼ tsp. pepper. Toss the chard in the vinaigrette. Sprinkle with the mozzarella and season with salt and pepper to taste. Makes 6 servings.

EACH SERVING *120 cal, 10 g fat, 17 mg chol, 377 mg sodium, 3 g carb, 1 g fiber, 5 g pro.*

Beets pulled from the garden pair deliciously with blue cheese, crunchy almonds, and a shredded beet-and-lemon dressing, while just-picked carrots star in a simple, beautiful salad that includes golden raisins and green onions.

KID FRIENDLY LOW FAT
Carrot Ribbon Salad

"This salad is a new version of what used to be called copper penny salad, and it's all about freshness," Ian says. "Raw carrots are tossed with raisins and green onions in a simple lemon dressing. The thinly shaved carrot ribbons soak up the dressing—and they are pretty too."

PREP 30 min. STAND 10 min.

6	Tbsp. mayonnaise
2	tsp. finely shredded lemon peel
5	Tbsp. fresh lemon juice
1	Tbsp. sugar
1	tsp. fine sea salt
¾	tsp. finely ground black pepper
3	lb. carrots
½	cup raisins
1	small bunch green onions, sliced

1. For dressing, in a large bowl whisk together the mayonnaise, lemon peel, lemon juice, sugar, salt, and pepper.
2. Using a vegetable peeler, shave carrots into ribbons. Toss carrots with dressing, raisins, and green onions. Season with salt to taste. Let salad stand 10 minutes or until carrots slightly wilt before serving. Toss frequently when serving to distribute dressing. Salad can be covered and chilled up to 4 hours before serving. Toss well before serving. Makes 10 servings.

EACH SERVING *142 cal, 6 g fat, 3 mg chol, 371 mg sodium, 21 g carb, 4 g fiber, 2 g pro.*

Beet, Blue Cheese, and Almond Salad

Ian uses both cooked and grated raw beets in this salad. "The sweetness of beets comes forward when they're cooked," he says. "And raw beets have a nice earthiness. Combining the two takes full advantage of the beet and adds a nice texture component."

PREP 25 min. COOL 1 hour COOK 20 min.

7	medium beets (2½ lb.)
1	small clove garlic
	Kosher salt
3	Tbsp. extra virgin olive oil
2	Tbsp. lemon juice
¾	tsp. ground black pepper
8	oz. creamy blue cheese
2	oz. Marcona almonds
1	Tbsp. chopped fresh flat-leaf Italian parsley

1. Trim and peel the beets. Cut 6 beets in bite-size pieces. Place in a steamer rack over a pot of boiling water. Cover the pot and steam 20 to 25 minutes, until tender.
2. Coarsely grate the remaining beet; place in a large bowl. For dressing, mash the garlic with a pinch of salt to a paste; add to grated beet along with the oil, lemon juice, 1 tsp. salt, and the pepper. When the beets are cooked, toss them with the dressing. Cool to room temperature.
3. Crumble blue cheese over the salad and sprinkle with almonds and parsley. Makes 6 servings.

EACH SERVING *333 cal, 23 g fat, 28 mg chol, 1,005 mg sodium, 21 g carb, 6 g fiber, 13 g pro.*

MAKING A GARLIC PASTE
Many of Ian's recipes call for mashing garlic into a paste. This method is often used in recipes—such as vinaigrettes and marinades—that call for serving garlic raw, or any time you want to diffuse the sharp garlic flavor. To make a smooth paste, first mince the garlic, then sprinkle with a pinch of salt. Drag the flat, broad side of the knife across the garlic at a 20-degree angle in one direction and then the other until smooth. It's easy! Go to BHG.com/GarlicPaste to watch our quick how-to video.

BEET, BLUE CHEESE,
AND ALMOND SALAD

CARROT RIBBON
SALAD

CORN AND POTATO SALAD

Friends and family gather around the table for a simple meal at the end of the day. "This is the way I watched my grandparents eat— from the garden to the table," Ian says. "I am so grateful to get to repeat history."

Corn and Potato Salad

"The key to success for this potato salad is smashing the potatoes to break the skins," Ian says. "The potato flesh is like a flavor sponge; it sucks the olive oil and vinegar dressing right up."

PREP 30 min. COOK 17 min.
STAND 2 hr.

3	ears corn
2	lb. small waxy potatoes, such as Yukon gold or red bliss
	Kosher salt
1	medium red onion
3	Tbsp. apple cider vinegar
	Black pepper
¼	cup extra virgin olive oil
½	cup finely chopped fresh basil
½	cup finely chopped cilantro

1. Shuck corn, then place the ears in a large pot with the potatoes. Add water and 1 Tbsp. salt to cover by 2 inches; bring to boiling. Boil, covered, for 2 to 4 minutes until corn is tender. Remove corn. Continue to boil potatoes 15 to 20 minutes until very tender.

2. While the potatoes cook, finely chop onion. In a large bowl combine onion with the vinegar, 1 tsp. salt, and ½ tsp. pepper. Cut kernels from ears of corn and add to the onion in the bowl.

3. When potatoes are very tender, drain in a colander. Cool enough to handle. Place them on a board and press with hands or a potato masher to break up. Add them to the bowl with the onion and corn. Add the oil and gently stir to combine. Let the potato salad come to room temperature, then add the herbs and season with salt and pepper to taste. If desired, cover and chill up to 24 hours. Let stand at room temperature at least 1 hour. If needed, toss with additional olive oil and vinegar before serving. Makes 8 to 10 servings.
EACH SERVING *174 cal, 7 g fat, 0 g chol, 396 mg sodium, 26 g carb, 3 g fiber, 3 g pro.*

In his book, *The Farm: Rustic Recipes for a Year of Incredible Food* (Houghton Mifflin Harcourt, $30), Ian shares more than 150 simple, delicious recipes to help you make the most of fresh produce. Each one delivers a nourishing dish that highlights ingredients at their peak. Reprinted with permission from Houghton Mifflin Harcourt. ©Copyright 2012. All rights reserved.

Home Cooking

TASTY FREEZES Learn to make the best-ever classic vanilla ice cream, then go a little crazy with mix-ins, toppings, and sundae possibilities.

What should vanilla ice cream taste like? Well, vanilla. That's the view of pastry chefs (below, from left) Kris Hoogerhyde and Anne Walker, of San Francisco's hugely popular Bi-Rite Creamery. "Early on, we became obsessed with making the most intensely flavored ice cream possible," Kris says. "We felt that, all too often, ice cream didn't taste enough of what it was supposed to be." If the long line outside their little ice cream shop, across the street from the legendary Bi-Rite Market, is any indication, they're doing something right.

Kris and Anne care deeply about their ingredients, sourcing them as close to home as possible and staying true to the season. They bring that passion to every ice cream they make, including this luscious vanilla, opposite, and to every sauce, mix-in, and topping that they add. And now you can take home their secrets to ice cream success.

KID FRIENDLY

Classic Vanilla Ice Cream

PREP **20 min.** STAND **30 min.**
CHILL **2 hr.**

1¾ cups heavy cream
¾ cup milk
½ cup sugar
¼ tsp. kosher salt
1 whole vanilla bean
5 large egg yolks
2 tsp. pure vanilla extract

1. In heavy saucepan stir together cream, milk, ¼ cup of the sugar, and the salt. With a small knife split vanilla bean lengthwise and scrape seeds from bean. Add seeds and split bean to pan. Heat over medium-high heat. When mixture just begins to bubble around edges, remove from heat; cover. Let seeds and split bean soak for 30 minutes to infuse the liquid. Remove and discard vanilla bean.
2. Place egg yolks in a medium heatproof bowl and whisk just enough to break up yolks. Whisk in remaining sugar until smooth. (The sugar dilutes the eggs a bit and prevents them from scrambling when the hot cream is added.) Set aside. Uncover cream mixture and heat over medium-high heat until almost simmering. Reduce heat to medium.

3. Using a ladle, carefully scoop out about ½ cup of the hot cream; whisking constantly, pour into yolks. Repeat. (This step, known as tempering, gradually heats the yolks to reduce the risk of overcooking.) Stirring constantly with a wooden spoon, slowly pour yolk mixture into hot cream in saucepan. Continue to cook on medium, stirring constantly in a figure eight to cover entire bottom of pan. Pay close attention as the consistency can change quickly. Cook until mixture goes from the consistency of heavy cream to that of a thin puree, but no thicker. You'll notice the mixture thickening slightly and feel a little more resistance as you stir.

4. To test the readiness of the custard, remove the spoon from the saucepan and drag your finger across it. If the base coats the back of the spoon and the path made by your finger holds for a second or two, it's ready. Remove the pan from heat and immediately pour through a fine-mesh sieve into a measuring cup or small bowl.
5. Set the bowl in a larger bowl of ice water and stir frequently with a clean spatula until cool. Remove and cover with plastic wrap. Refrigerate for at least 2 hours until completely cold. Stir in vanilla extract just before churning and freezing the ice cream. Makes 8 servings.
EACH SERVING *279 cal, 23 g fat, 188 mg chol, 97 mg sodium, 16 g carb, 0 g fiber, 4 g pro.*

"A custard-based ice cream has the most flavor, along with the best body and texture," Kris says. "Once you've got this basic recipe down, you can add mix-ins, toppings, and sauces."

CHURNING AND FREEZING "When churning the ice cream, keep an eye on it," Anne says. "Once the swirls made by the dasher hold their shape, it's ready. You want it to have the consistency of soft-serve ice cream before it goes into the freezer."

Ice cream FAQs

To get the best results, start by following the manufacturer's instructions for freezing ice cream in your machine. The exact timing might vary from one machine to the next. Get the scoop from Kris and Anne on other common questions about making ice cream:

Can ice cream be overchurned? If it is overchurned, can I fix it?

Yes, ice cream can be overchurned. That causes the butterfat to separate out—basically turning the cream to butter and producing an unpleasant texture. There is no way to fix overchurned ice cream, so be watchful as it approaches the finished stage.

When do I add stir-ins?

If using mix-ins such as chopped nuts, grated chocolate, or crumbled cookies, add them during the last few minutes of churning. If you miss that window, fold them in by hand once the machine is off. Work quickly so the ice cream doesn't melt.

How long can I store ice cream?

Enjoy homemade ice cream right away as soft-serve or transfer it to a chilled container and freeze it to firm and ripen, further developing the flavors. The colder the freezer, the better. Store homemade ice cream in the freezer up to one week. Any longer and flavor will diminish.

Cinnamon and snickerdoodles

The combo of cinnamon-sugar cookie crumbles and a hefty sprinkling of cinnamon adds texture and homey flavor to vanilla ice cream. Stir them in, then top with sautéed apples or a drizzle of caramel sauce.

Lavender and honey

Honey creates a sweet base for delicate culinary lavender. When making the ice cream base, add ¼ cup honey and 2 Tbsp. dried lavender to the cream instead of the vanilla bean; cover and steep for 15 minutes instead of 30. Strain and continue as in basic recipe.

Strawberries and balsamic vinegar

Balsamic gives sweet berries spark. Before stirring the fruit into the ice cream, chop and cook the berries with a little sugar to remove excess water. Cool, puree, then stir into ice cream with a few dashes of balsamic for bright flavor.

Double chocolate

Before starting Step 1, stir together ¼ cup Dutch cocoa powder and half the sugar. Whisk in a little of the cream to make a paste. Then whisk in remaining cream, milk, and salt. Proceed with basic recipe. Stir in chopped chocolate after churning.

MIX-INS AND FLAVORS "Choose an ingredient and let it shine," Kris says, "whether it's an intense single flavor or a pair, where one taste makes the other pop."

TOPPINGS AND SAUCES "The key to choosing toppings is balance," Anne says. "Add a sauce and something for crunch to complement the creamy ice cream. Never go overboard—you want the flavor of the ice cream to be enhanced, not overwhelmed."

Blueberry-lemon pie sundae

Start with a sweet blueberry sauce made by cooking the berries with sugar and a squeeze of lemon until thickened. Pour over ice cream; finish with crumbled gingersnaps or graham crackers.

Citrus olive oil and sea salt sundae

Drizzle ice cream with bergamot olive oil (bergamot is the citrus fruit that gives Earl Grey tea its hint of orange—find it at health food stores). Meyer lemon- or orange-flavor oil will add the same brightness. Top with a dollop of whipped cream and crunchy coarse sea salt flakes.

Caramelized banana sundae

Melt butter and brown sugar in a skillet. Add a couple of split bananas; cook until caramelized. If desired, add a little rum and cook and stir a few minutes more. Spoon over ice cream. Top with whipped cream and toasted chopped pecans.

Delicious on a Dollar

Complement the natural sweetness of seasonal fruit—with bacon.

Bacon-and-Crumb-Topped Plum Crisp

A bit of bacon seems to show up in nearly every food these days, and this ideal dessert—or breakfast treat—is no exception. Contrasts of sweet and salty mingle with mouthwatering fresh fruit to tickle taste buds. For variety, as fruits come and go at the market, substitute peaches, apricots, or nectarines for the plums. With or without the bacon, the warm, ripe fruit with light crisp topping has a delectable flavor and crunch.

PREP **20 min.** BAKE **30 min.**
OVEN **375°F**

2   to 4 Tbsp. granulated sugar
1   Tbsp. all-purpose flour
5   cups sliced, pitted plums
⅓   cup quick-cooking or regular oats
⅓   cup packed brown sugar
2   Tbsp. all-purpose flour
¼   tsp. ground spice, such as nutmeg, ginger, or cinnamon
3   Tbsp. canola or vegetable oil
3   slices bacon, crisp-cooked and finely chopped
    Vanilla ice cream (optional)

1. Preheat oven to 375°F. In a large bowl combine granulated sugar and 1 Tbsp. flour. Stir in fruit. Divide fruit among six 6-oz. custard cups or ramekins. Place custard cups on a 15×10×1-inch baking pan.
2. For topping, in a small bowl combine oats, brown sugar, 2 Tbsp. flour, and spice. Stir in oil until topping resembles coarse crumbs. Stir in bacon. Evenly sprinkle topping over fruit in cups.
3. Bake for 30 to 35 minutes, just until fruit is tender and topping is crisp and golden brown. Serve warm with ice cream for dessert or without ice cream for breakfast. Makes 6 servings.

EACH SERVING *236 cal, 9 g fat, 4 mg chol, 81 mg sodium, 38 g carb, 2 g fiber, 3 g pro.*

BACON-AND-CRUMB-TOPPED PLUM CRISP

GRILLED CHICKEN AND
PEACHES WITH GREEN
BEANS AND ORZO

Everyday Easy

Unexpected pairings and kicky spices help
summer produce bust out of its stereotypes.

FAST

Grilled Chicken and Peaches with Green Beans and Orzo

START TO FINISH 30 min.
BUDGET $3.29 per serving

- 8 oz. dried orzo (1⅓ cups)
- 8 oz. green beans, trimmed (about 2½ cups)
- 1 lb. chicken tenders
- 2 peaches, cut in wedges
- 2 Tbsp. olive oil
- 4 oz. herb-flavor feta cheese (garlic and herb or peppercorn), crumbled Fresh thyme (optional)

1. In large saucepan or Dutch oven cook orzo according to package directions. Add green beans during last 5 minutes of cooking time. Drain; do not rinse.
2. Meanwhile, lightly brush chicken and peaches with some of the oil; season with salt and pepper. Grill over medium heat for 4 to 6 minutes, until no pink remains in chicken and peaches are tender and grill-marked.
3. In large bowl combine orzo, beans, grilled chicken and peaches (chopped, if desired), and feta. Drizzle with remaining olive oil; season with salt and pepper. Sprinkle with thyme, if desired. Makes 4 servings.

EACH SERVING 526 cal, 17 g fat, 93 mg chol, 604 mg sodium, 55 g carb, 5 g fiber, 38 g pro.

MEATBALLS WITH CUCUMBER
SAUCE ON FLATBREADS

PINEAPPLE-GLAZED
SALMON

Meatballs with Cucumber Sauce on Flatbreads

START TO FINISH 27 min.
BUDGET $2.98 per serving

1   medium seedless cucumber
1   5- to 6-oz. carton plain Greek yogurt
2   Tbsp. snipped fresh mint (optional)
1   16-oz. pkg. frozen fully cooked
    meatballs, thawed
2   tsp. Greek seasoning blend (or
    ½ tsp. each sesame seeds, garlic
    powder, crushed red pepper, and
    dried oregano)
4   flatbreads or naan, garlic or plain
    Thinly sliced red onion, snipped
    mint leaves, and/or orange or lemon
    wedges (optional)

1. Preheat broiler. For sauce, coarsely
shred half the cucumber. Thinly slice
remaining cucumber; set aside. In a bowl
combine shredded cucumber, yogurt, and
if desired, mint. Cover and refrigerate.
2. Thread meatballs on bamboo or metal
skewers. Sprinkle Greek seasoning on
meatballs. Broil on broiler pan 4 to
5 inches from heat for 8 to 10 minutes,
turning occasionally, to heat through.
During last 2 minutes, warm flatbreads
on pan.
3. Serve sauce, sliced cucumber, onion,
mint, and meatball kabobs on warm
flatbreads. Serve with citrus wedges if
desired. Makes 4 servings.
EACH SERVING 575 cal, 33 g fat, 48 mg
chol, 1,562 mg sodium, 45 g carb, 4 g fiber,
25 g pro.

Pineapple-Glazed Salmon

START TO FINISH 30 min.
BUDGET $3.14 per serving

½   cup frozen pineapple juice
    concentrate, thawed
¼   cup water
2   Tbsp. reduced-sodium soy sauce
2   tsp. packed brown sugar
2   tsp. cornstarch
2   tsp. toasted sesame oil
¼   tsp. crushed red pepper
4   5-oz. fresh or frozen salmon fillets,
    thawed
½   tsp. cracked black pepper

1. For glaze, in small saucepan combine
pineapple juice, the water, soy sauce,
brown sugar, cornstarch, sesame oil, and
red pepper. Cook and stir over medium
heat until thickened and bubbly. Cook and
stir 2 minutes more.
2. Preheat broiler. Line baking sheet
with foil; lightly coat with nonstick
cooking spray. Rinse salmon and pat
dry. Place fillets, skin sides down, on
prepared sheet. Drizzle salmon with a
few tablespoons glaze; sprinkle with
black pepper. Broil 4 inches from heat for
10 to 12 minutes, until fish flakes easily
when tested with a fork. Drizzle with
remaining glaze. Makes 4 servings.
EACH SERVING 305 cal, 11 g fat, 78 mg
chol, 352 mg sodium, 20 g carb, 29 g pro.

GARDEN
VEGETABLE
TART

PORK TACOS WITH SPICY WATERMELON SALSA

FAST

Garden Vegetable Tart
START TO FINISH 34 min.
BUDGET $2.93 per serving

1   frozen puff pastry sheet (half a 17.3-oz. package)
2   ears of fresh sweet corn
1   medium zucchini, thinly sliced lengthwise
1   pint cherry tomatoes
1   Tbsp. extra virgin olive oil
¼   cup tomato paste
¼   cup water
4   oz. fresh mozzarella, thinly sliced
    Crushed red pepper and dried basil (optional)

1. Preheat oven to 425°F. On a lightly floured surface roll puff pastry to a 14×10-inch rectangle; transfer to a 15×10×1-inch baking pan. Prick pastry all over with a fork. Bake 10 minutes, until center is set. Remove from oven; lightly press center with a spatula.
2. Meanwhile, wrap cleaned corn in waxed paper. Microcook on 100 percent power (high) for 2 minutes. Brush zucchini, tomatoes, and corn with 1 Tbsp. olive oil; sprinkle with ½ tsp. salt. Preheat an indoor grill pan over medium-high heat. Grill vegetables until tender, 5 to 7 minutes, turning occasionally. Transfer to platter; cover and keep warm.
3. In small bowl whisk together tomato paste and the water; spread on puff pastry. Cut corn from cobs. Top pastry with cheese and vegetables. Bake tart 10 minutes, until pastry is golden and cheese is melted. Top with red pepper and basil, if desired. Makes 4 servings.
EACH SERVING 454 cal, 29 g fat, 20 mg chol, 750 mg sodium, 38 g carb, 3 g fiber, 11 g pro.

FAST

Pork Tacos with Spicy Watermelon Salsa
START TO FINISH 20 min.
BUDGET $1.91 per serving

1½ cups chopped seeded watermelon
1   or 2 fresh banana or Anaheim peppers, finely chopped (see note, page 69)
¼   cup snipped fresh cilantro
½   tsp. each salt, sugar, garlic powder, and ground chipotle chile pepper or chili powder (or 2 tsp. Southwestern smoky blend chipotle seasoning)
4   boneless pork country-style ribs (1¼ lb.)
24 extra-thin or 12 typical corn tortillas

1. For salsa, in medium bowl combine melon, chopped pepper(s), and cilantro. Set aside.
2. For rub, in small bowl combine salt, sugar, garlic powder, and ground chile or chili powder. Rub on ribs to coat. Grill, covered, directly over medium heat for 10 to 12 minutes, until 145°F (test with instant-read thermometer), turning once. Meanwhile, wrap tortillas in foil. Warm on grill during last 5 minutes of cooking time for ribs, turning once.
3. Transfer ribs to cutting board; let rest 2 minutes. Slice meat. Serve with tortillas and watermelon salsa. Makes four 3-taco servings.
EACH SERVING 449 cal, 19 g fat, 105 mg chol, 420 mg sodium, 38 g carb, 5 g fiber, 32 g pro.

PEPPERED STEAKS
WITH ROASTED
BEETS

september

FOOD, FAMILY, AND FRIENDS Guy Fieri serves his signature fun-style foods, and Sarah Copeland shares her secret for easy pan sauces that give plain pasta a boost for a quick dinner.

211

216

229

ROSEMARY GARLIC
FLATBREAD WITH
SPICY TUNA SALAD

Family Style, Fieri Style

When the Food Network star has a backyard bash, it's as laid-back, off-the-cuff, and fun-loving as he is.

For Guy Fieri, it's all about food, family, and friends. "My whole life, all I've thought about was food," he says. "I feed people their favorite foods. That's the way I want to eat. I do what feels good, and I want my friends and family to feel good when they're at my house too."

Guy's house often becomes the spot for casual, stop-on-by gatherings. Standbys such as his homemade pizza dough, page 212, can be turned into spicy or sweet pizzas on the fly. "If you don't want to make your own dough, go to your favorite pizzeria, bribe them, buy some dough, then go home and knock out a pizza," he says.

Other favorites like a spice-rubbed beef roast, page 208, can be grilled ahead, then sliced for sandwiches at a moment's notice. And friends get the sushi they crave in a Guy-style spicy tuna salad piled on crispy flatbread.

When he's not hanging out with friends and family, Guy is the host of Food Network's *Diners, Drive-Ins, and Dives*. He's also a cookbook author and owner of several restaurants that serve his signature-style fun foods. "I feel so blessed to be where we are," Guy says. "I couldn't possibly love life more." Learn more about him at guyfieri.com.

Rosemary Garlic Flatbread with Spicy Tuna Salad

"Super fresh sushi-grade tuna folded into a spicy mayo makes this a whole new take on flatbread," Guy says.

PREP 35 min. BAKE 2 min. OVEN 500°F

Flatbread
1 recipe Pizza Dough, page 212, or one 1-lb. ball purchased pizza dough
   All-purpose flour (for dusting)
¼ cup extra virgin olive oil
3 cloves garlic, finely shaved lengthwise
2 Tbsp. fresh rosemary leaves
   Flaked sea salt
   Freshly cracked black pepper

Spicy Tuna Salad
2 Tbsp. mayonnaise
2 Tbsp. sour cream
1 tsp. Sriracha (Asian hot sauce)
1 tsp. lemon juice
½ tsp. toasted sesame oil
   Flaked sea salt
1 lb. maguro (sushi-grade tuna), ¼- to ½-inch dice
   Micro greens or radish sprouts
   Good-quality aged balsamic vinegar

1. Preheat oven with pizza stone to 500°F (or see "No Pizza Stone? No Problem," page 212).

2. For Flatbread, evenly divide dough in 3 pieces. Stretch each piece thinly, dusting with flour. Roll out each to wafer thin. Drizzle dough with olive oil, smearing evenly. Top with shaved garlic, rosemary, sea salt, and pepper. Bake 2 to 4 minutes each, until crispy, golden, and bubbled up around edges.

3. For Spicy Tuna Salad, mix mayonnaise, sour cream, Sriracha, lemon juice, sesame oil, and salt. Fold in tuna.

4. To serve, break crisp flatbreads in pieces. Top pieces with a spoonful of salad and some greens. Drizzle with a few drops of balsamic vinegar. Makes 3 flatbreads (about 12 servings).

EACH SERVING *244 cal, 10 g fat, 17 mg chol, 499 mg sodium, 24 g carb, 1 g fiber, 13 g pro.*

BAKED POTATO
PIZZA

WAKA WAKA SALAD

KID FRIENDLY

Baked Potato Pizza

"Baked potatoes are all-American. You've had them so many different ways. I decided to put them on pizza," Guy says. This potato pizza includes all the fixings—bacon, cheese, sour cream, and chives.

PREP 30 min. BAKE 8 min. OVEN 500°F

Pizza

1   recipe Pizza Dough, page 212, or one 1-lb. ball purchased pizza dough
    All-purpose flour (for dusting)
4   medium-size Yukon gold potatoes, skin on (1¼ lb.)
2   cloves garlic, minced
½   cup very finely sliced sweet onion
6   slices applewood-smoked bacon, crisp-cooked and crumbled
1   Tbsp. chopped fresh thyme leaves
    Extra virgin olive oil
1   tsp. flaked sea salt
    Freshly cracked black pepper
⅓   cup shredded Monterey Jack cheese
⅓   cup shredded sharp white cheddar cheese
¼   cup finely grated Parmigiano-Reggiano

Toppings

1½ cups sour cream
4   Roma tomatoes, diced
¼   cup finely chopped chives

1. Preheat oven with pizza stone to 500°F (or see "No Pizza Stone? No Problem," page 208).

2. For Pizza, evenly divide dough in two pieces. Thinly stretch or roll each piece, dusting with flour.

3. Fill a large bowl with cold water. Using a mandoline (or very sharp knife), slice potatoes paper-thin. Place slices in water; swirl to remove excess starch and prevent potatoes from turning brown. Drain off water; lightly pat potatoes dry with paper towels. Add garlic, onion, bacon, and thyme to potatoes in bowl. Drizzle with a little olive oil. Season with some sea salt and pepper. Mix well.

4. Combine Monterey Jack and cheddar cheeses. Divide cheeses between pizza dough, spreading evenly. Divide potato mixture and spread evenly on cheeses. Drizzle each pizza with olive oil. Top with some sea salt, a little cracked black pepper, and a sprinkle of Parmigiano-Reggiano.

5. Bake pizzas 8 to 10 minutes, until crust is golden brown, potato edges are lightly curled, and cheese is bubbly.

6. To serve, cut pizzas into squares. Top with a dollop of sour cream, diced tomatoes, and chopped chives. Makes 2 pizzas (about 12 servings).
EACH SERVING 282 cal, 13 g fat, 25 mg chol, 547 mg sodium, 33 g carb, 3 g fiber, 9 g pro.

KID FRIENDLY | FAST

Waka Waka Salad

"I like to use napa cabbage in this salad because it's nice and tender," Guy says. "If napa cabbage isn't in your local grocery store, then go ahead and use regular green cabbage."

START TO FINISH 25 min.

1   cup canola oil
1   cup red wine vinegar
1   to 2 tsp. minced garlic
1   to 2 tsp. minced fresh ginger
2   to 3 ramen noodle packages
    Pinch salt and freshly ground black pepper
½   head napa cabbage, sliced ⅛ inch thick (about 10 cups)
¼   head red cabbage, sliced ⅛ inch thick (about 4 cups)
2   red onions, thinly sliced
2   carrots, shredded
2   to 4 Tbsp. chopped cilantro leaves
¾   cup Spanish peanuts, finely chopped
24 wonton skins, fried*

1. In a bowl combine oil, vinegar, garlic, ginger, 1 tsp. ramen Oriental seasoning (½ packet), salt, and pepper. Set aside.

2. In a large bowl mix cabbages, onions, carrots, and cilantro. Whisk the dressing, then pour over salad. Toss thoroughly. (Dress the salad no more than 10 minutes prior to serving.)

3. Top with ramen noodles, broken in small pieces, and peanuts. Serve immediately with wonton skins. Makes 18 cups (about thirty-six ½-cup servings).

* To fry wonton skins, in a large saucepan heat 2 inches of oil to 350°F. Fry, a few skins at a time, 1 minute or until crisp and lightly browned; drain.
EACH ½-CUP SERVING 132 cal, 10 g fat, 0 mg chol, 75 mg sodium, 9 g carb, 1 g fiber, 2 g pro.

"If you're having fun and enjoying life and can get away with it, that's style," Guy says.

Pit Beef Sandwiches

These sandwiches feed a crowd and are gone quickly at Guy's house. For a big boost of flavor, the beef is marinated in spice rub 1 or 2 days. "If you can't wait for beef to marinate, just go with it. It won't be over-the-top, but it will be really good," Guy says.

PREP **20 min.** MARINATE **24 hr.**
STAND **20 min.** GRILL **10 min.**
REST **5 min.**

Spiced Beef

1   Tbsp. fine sea salt
    Freshly ground black pepper
1   Tbsp. onion powder
1   Tbsp. garlic powder
1   Tbsp. paprika
2   tsp. dried oregano
1   tsp. chili powder
2   lb. beef top round, cut in 2 equal
    pieces

Horseradish Cream

½   cup sour cream
½   cup mayonnaise
1   tsp. fresh lemon juice
½   cup prepared hot horseradish
1   tsp. minced garlic
½   tsp. fine sea salt
    Freshly ground black pepper

Sandwiches

16 slices rye bread, lightly toasted
2   white onions, sliced paper-thin

1. For the Spiced Beef, combine spices for the meat in a resealable 1-gallon plastic bag and shake to mix thoroughly. Add 1 piece of meat, shake it around in the bag, remove it, and repeat with the second piece of meat. Return the first piece to the bag, seal and marinate both pieces as long as you can in the refrigerator (24 to 48 hours is recommended).

2. For Horseradish Cream, in a medium bowl combine the sour cream, mayonnaise, lemon juice, horseradish, garlic, sea salt, and pepper to taste. Mix thoroughly; refrigerate at least 4 hours.

3. About 20 minutes before you plan to grill, remove the meat from the refrigerator and let sit at room temperature. Preheat a grill or a large grill pan to high.

4. Grill the meat for 10 to 15 minutes (7½ minutes per side), or until desired doneness. (It's best at medium-rare, about 145°F.) Set the meat aside; cover and let rest for 5 to 10 minutes.

5. Slice the meat paper-thin with a long, sharp slicing knife or a countertop deli slicer. Divide the meat among 8 bread slices, spread some Horseradish Cream on each stack, then add a few rings of onion slices and top with remaining bread. Makes 8 sandwiches (about 16 servings).

EACH ½-SANDWICH SERVING *231 cal, 10 g fat, 35 mg chol, 762 mg sodium, 19 g carb, 3 g fiber, 16 g pro.*

PIT BEEF
SANDWICHES

When a party takes shape, Guy wants to be inspired by what's growing and by what he and his guests are craving: "It's not uncommon for us to have Chinese food, barbecue, and Italian all in the same meal. Nobody goes away hungry or bored."

Spring Rolls with Lime Aïoli

"Sambal oelek—a spicy-sweet red chile paste—gives these light vegetable spring rolls a kick."

PREP 1 hr.   CHILL 1 hr.

Spring Roll Filling

½ medium head napa cabbage, cored and shredded in ribbons
1 Tbsp. kosher salt
½ cup water
¼ cup tamari soy sauce
¼ cup seasoned rice vinegar
2 Tbsp. mirin (rice wine)
2 Tbsp. minced garlic
1 Tbsp. sugar
1 Tbsp. sambal oelek red chile paste
½ cup carrot, cut in thin strips
½ cup English cucumber, cut in thin strips
¼ cup zucchini, cut in thin strips
3 green onions, bias-sliced

Lime Aïoli

1 cup mayonnaise
1 Tbsp. sambal oelek red chile paste
1 Tbsp. fresh lime juice
½ tsp. honey
   Kosher salt, to taste
   Cracked black pepper, to taste
½ cup fresh cilantro
¼ cup Thai basil or basil
12 to 15 round spring roll wrappers, soaked in water to soften

1. For Spring Roll Filling, in a colander in the sink sprinkle cabbage with salt; toss to combine. Let stand about 1 hour to wilt. Rinse several times with cold water; drain well. Squeeze out any excess water.
2. In a large bowl whisk together the ½ cup water, tamari, rice vinegar, mirin, garlic, sugar, and chile paste. Add cabbage, carrot, cucumber, zucchini, and green onions. Transfer to glass jar or bowl, pouring liquid over vegetables. Place in refrigerator or cool, dark place for at least 1 hour (24 hours is optimal).
3. For Lime Aïoli, in bowl mix together mayonnaise, chile paste, lime juice, honey, salt, and pepper. Cover and refrigerate.
4. For Spring Rolls, drain pickled vegetables well. Place 2 or 3 pieces cilantro and basil in center of each softened wrapper. Place a line of pickled vegetables. Tightly roll each wrapper, tucking in edges to seal completely. Bias-slice rolls and serve with aïoli. Makes 12 to 15 spring rolls (about 12 servings).
EACH SERVING *201 cal, 15 g fat, 7 mg chol, 1,073 mg sodium, 16 g carb, 1 g fiber, 2 g pro.*

Guy's priority is cultivating a sense of fun and surprise. "I cook the way I want to eat," Guy says, "and I do things that feel good."

KID FRIENDLY

Candied Apple Pizza

"This is like the state fair on a pizza," Guy says. "As soon as it comes out of the oven, it's doused in caramel sauce and sprinkled with coarse salt."

PREP 30 min. BAKE 16 min. OVEN 500°F

Pizza

1	recipe Pizza Dough, right, or one 1-lb. ball purchased pizza dough
	All-purpose flour (for dusting)
1½	cups mascarpone
1½	Tbsp. powdered sugar
¼	tsp. vanilla bean paste or pure vanilla extract
4	medium green apples
2	Tbsp. lemon juice

Streusel Topping

3	Tbsp. all-purpose flour
⅓	cup packed brown sugar
1½	tsp. ground cinnamon
¼	tsp. salt
3	Tbsp. unsalted butter
¾	cup chopped pecans (optional)
	Purchased caramel sauce
	Pinch flaked sea salt
	Powdered sugar, for finishing

1. Preheat oven with pizza stone to 500°F (or see "No Pizza Stone? No Problem," right).
2. For Pizza, evenly divide dough in 2 pieces. Stretch each piece thin and dust with flour. Bake crusts 6 to 8 minutes or until firm with no browning. Let crusts stand to cool.
3. In a small bowl mix mascarpone with powdered sugar and vanilla paste. Divide between 2 crusts; smear evenly to edges.
4. Core and finely slice apples. Place slices in large bowl. Sprinkle with lemon juice; toss to coat.

5. For Streusel Topping, in medium bowl combine flour, brown sugar, cinnamon, and salt. Cut in butter until crumbly. Stir in pecans. Evenly spread apples then topping on cheese layer. Bake each pizza for 10 to 12 minutes.
6. Combine caramel sauce with a pinch of sea salt. Remove pizzas from oven. Drizzle with caramel sauce. Generously sprinkle with powdered sugar. Makes 2 pizzas (about 16 servings).
EACH SERVING 296 cal, 14 g fat, 33 mg chol, 263 mg sodium, 40 g carb, 2 g fiber, 7 g pro.

KID FRIENDLY | **LOW FAT**

Pizza Dough

"Good pizza starts with good dough. This is easy to make, but if you are not into dough making, find a good purchased dough and use that."

PREP 20 min. STAND 10 min.
RISE 1 hr. 30 min.

1	tsp. sugar
1	cup warm water (113°F)
1	Tbsp. active dry yeast (or 2 packets)
2	Tbsp. olive oil, plus more to grease bowl
1	tsp. fine sea salt
2½	cups all-purpose flour, plus more for dusting

1. In the bowl of a stand mixer, dissolve the sugar in the warm water. Sprinkle yeast on top. Let stand for 10 minutes or until foamy.

2. Add olive oil and salt to yeast mixture, then use the dough hook to mix in the all-purpose flour. Mix until dough comes together. Add more flour as needed and allow machine to knead the dough until smooth.
3. Turn the dough onto a floured surface and knead about 2 minutes more (dough will no longer be sticky). Place dough in an oiled bowl and turn to coat surface. Cover bowl with plastic wrap; let stand in a warm place about 1 hour, until doubled in size.
4. Turn out dough onto a floured surface. Divide in half. Form into smooth, tight balls. Cover loosely with a floured kitchen towel and set in a warm place to rise again for 30 to 45 minutes.
5. When ready to use, press dough with fingers to flatten as much as possible. Drape dough over hands, stretching to desired size and thickness. Place dough on a floured pizza peel. Top and bake as directed in recipes. Makes 2 (12-oz.) portions.

NO PIZZA STONE? NO PROBLEM
If you don't have a pizza stone, place a large sturdy baking sheet upside down on an oven rack. Preheat in the oven. To transfer pizza to the baking sheet, dust a baking peel or a second baking sheet with flour or cornmeal. Place pizza on the baking peel or baking sheet. Gently shimmy the pizza onto the baking stone or preheated baking sheet.

Get more than 150 recipes, benefit from Guy's cooking wisdom, and peek into his kitchen in *Guy Fieri Food: Cookin' It, Livin' It, Lovin' It* (HarperCollins, $30).

CANDIED APPLE
PIZZA

Home Cooking

PASTA PERFECT Cookbook author Sarah Copeland whips up easy, flavorful pan sauces to put a fresh spin on everyday. The best part? All are ready in less than half an hour.

PAN SAUCE HOW-TO Sarah's pan sauces are more than just sauce—they're quick sautés of fresh, crunchy and colorful ingredients that give plain old pasta a boost. "They're light and healthful yet create a filling and satisfying dish when tossed with your favorite pasta," Sarah says. Use these tips—plus the four recipes that follow—to create a fresh take on a quick dinner.

1. Start with flavorful oil and aromatics.

"The first step to building a delicious sauce is to use extra virgin olive oil," Sarah says. "If you can, taste the oil first. If you like its flavor, then you'll like it in a sauce. Look for one that is flavorful and affordable so you can be lavish with it. Next, add aromatics like onions, shallots, garlic, or leeks for warmth and depth."

2. Spice it up.

A hallmark of Sarah's sauces is a touch of spice. "Crushed red pepper is a go-to because it's always on hand," she says. "I've also used hot paprika, fresh chiles, or even spicy sausage to add a nice kick."

3. Stir in fresh veggies.

"Flavorful and colorful tomatoes get really saucy when cooked, adding moisture and healthfulness to the dish. Other vegetables like mixed greens, thinly sliced peppers, or shaved corn add crunch and color to the sauce."

4. Drizzle on liquid.

"Adding a little liquid makes the sauce saucier. The pasta cooking water is a great way to use what is already on hand, and the starch from the pasta will help pull the sauce together. You can also use chicken broth."

5. Finish with a bit of cheese.

"Give the sauce a luxe finish with a delicious cheese. Fresh ricotta or mozzarella melts into the sauce and adds richness; Parmesan or feta gives a nice touch of salty flavor. Now all that's left is to add the cooked pasta—toss it in and let it meld with the flavors of the sauce."

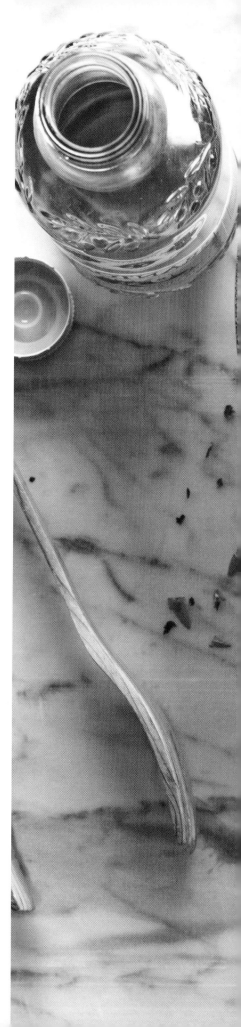

"This dish gets so much flavor from just a few ingredients. Juicy tomatoes soften into a light sauce, basil brings a boost of bright freshness, and crumbled feta adds the right salty flourish at the finish."

FAST

Bucatini with Shrimp and Spicy Cherry Tomato Pan Sauce

START TO FINISH 30 min.

¾ lb. bucatini or other fat spaghetti noodle
2 Tbsp. extra virgin olive oil
2 cloves garlic, minced
2 pints red and/or yellow cherry tomatoes, halved
¾ lb. wild Patagonian or Gulf shrimp, peeled and deveined
 Generous pinch crushed red pepper
6 oz. aged feta cheese, broken in pieces
1 handful basil, thinly sliced (about 1 cup)
 Extra virgin olive oil (optional)
 Aged feta cheese (optional)

1. Bring a large pot of generously salted water to boiling. Add the bucatini and cook until al dente, about 9 minutes. Drain, reserving ⅓ cup of the pasta cooking liquid to use in the sauce.
2. Meanwhile, in a large skillet heat oil over medium-high heat. Add the garlic and tomatoes. Cook, stirring occasionally, until tomatoes soften and the juices begin to bubble, about 3 minutes. If the cherry tomatoes don't give out a lot of juice, add 1 Tbsp. water and a splash (about ½ tsp.) of red wine vinegar for acidity. Add the shrimp and a large pinch of crushed red pepper, then toss just until the shrimp are cooked through, about 2 minutes.

3. Add the pasta with the reserved pasta cooking liquid. Toss together over low heat. Remove from heat. Stir in the feta and basil; toss with tongs, adding up to 1 Tbsp. more oil and additional feta to taste. Divide among four bowls. Serve warm. Makes 4 servings.
EACH SERVING *585 cal, 18 g fat, 145 mg chol, 971 mg sodium, 74 g carb, 5 g fiber, 31 g pro.*

BUCATINI
This long, thin tube pasta is a hearty choice that pairs equally well with a light sauce or a rich, meaty one. Look for it in large or Italian markets. In a pinch, substitute spaghetti.

"I love this combination of creamy ricotta with the chew and slight bitterness of chard. The hint of crushed red pepper adds satisfying spice that lingers."

FAST

Orecchiette with Ricotta and Chard Pan Sauce

START TO FINISH 25 min.

1   large bunch organic green or rainbow Swiss chard
¾   lb. dried orecchiette
2   Tbsp. extra virgin olive oil
2   Tbsp. butter
    Crushed red pepper (optional)
2   oz. ricotta salata, Asiago, or pecorino cheese
    Cracked black pepper
    Nutmeg
¼   cup fresh, whole-milk ricotta cheese
    Sea salt and cracked black pepper
    Freshly grated ricotta salata, Asiago, or pecorino cheese

1. Bring large pot of generously salted water to boiling. Separate chard stems from leaves; cut both into bite-size pieces. Add orecchiette to boiling water. Set timer for 10 minutes.
2. Meanwhile, for pan sauce, in large skillet heat oil over medium-high heat. Add chard stems; cook 3 to 5 minutes, until crisp-tender.
3. After 10 minutes, add chard leaves to cooked pasta; cook 2 minutes more. Drain, reserving about ¼ cup of cooking liquid. Return pasta and chard to pot; place over lowest heat setting. Add chard stems and any residual oil to pasta, along with butter, crushed red pepper (if using), and reserved cooking liquid. Grate in ricotta salata; toss. Season with black pepper and nutmeg. Divide among bowls. Top each with about 1 Tbsp. ricotta. Add sea salt, pepper, and additional ricotta salata to taste. Makes 4 servings.
EACH SERVING *530 cal, 21 g fat, 42 mg chol, 850 mg sodium, 70 g carb, 4 g fiber, 16 g pro.*

ORECCHIETTE
This oval pasta has a slight bowl shape that will hold little splashes of sauce or cheese. The edges are thicker than the center for a contrast of texture. Cavatelli or other bite-size pasta can be substituted.

"Juicy tomatoes, crunchy sweet corn, and a burst of pungent arugula make a healthful, satisfying sauce for pillowy stuffed pasta. It's like a dreamy restaurant dish made right at home."

KID FRIENDLY | **FAST**

Mushroom Agnolotti with Corn, Tomatoes, and Arugula Pan Sauce

START TO FINISH 30 min.

2	ears sweet corn on the cob
18	oz. wild mushroom agnolotti or ravioli (two 9-oz. pkgs.)
2	Tbsp. extra virgin olive oil
1	small onion, thinly sliced
1	clove garlic, thinly sliced
2	medium tomatoes, cored and chopped
2	Tbsp. unsalted butter
5	oz. baby arugula (6 cups)
2	oz. Parmigiano-Reggiano or pecorino cheese, finely shredded

1. Bring a large pot of generously salted water to a boil. Shave corn off the ears with a serrated knife and reserve. Add the cobs (to release corn starches and add richness) and agnolotti to water; set timer for 6 minutes.

2. Meanwhile, for pan sauce, heat oil in a large skillet over medium-high heat. Add onion and garlic; cook until fragrant, about 2 minutes.

3. Add corn kernels to skillet; cook over medium-high heat until bright and crisp-tender, 1 minute. Add the tomatoes and toss until they begin to release some juices, about 2 minutes more.

4. Drain the pasta, reserving ¼ cup cooking liquid; discard cobs. Add pasta back to the pot with the reserved cooking water, corn mixture, and butter. Gently toss over low heat to melt butter. Stir in arugula and toss until just wilted. Divide among four bowls and top with finely grated cheese. Makes 4 servings.

EACH SERVING *566 cal, 31 g fat, 102 mg chol, 1,075 mg sodium, 55 g carb, 6 g fiber, 23 g pro.*

AGNOLOTTI

Crescent-shape agnolotti are similar to ravioli and can be stuffed with a variety of fillings such as cheese, meat, and/or vegetables. Ravioli or tortellini can be used in dishes that call for agnolotti.

"This simple, oh-so-satisfying egg sauce thickens as it's swirled into leggy linguine. Flavorful sausage adds an aromatic, spicy punch—the perfect match for a bright green burst of mustard greens."

FAST

Linguine with Sausage, Greens, and Egg Pan Sauce

START TO FINISH 23 min.

- 12 oz. fresh or 8 oz. dried linguine pasta
- 4 uncooked organic sweet or spicy Italian sausage links, skins removed (1 lb.)
- 1 clove garlic, finely chopped
- 4 egg yolks
- ½ cup whole milk, half-and-half, or light cream
- ½ cup freshly grated Parmigiano-Reggiano cheese (about 3 oz.)
- 2 tsp. finely shredded lemon peel (from 1 lemon)
- ¼ tsp. sea salt
- ¼ tsp. freshly ground black pepper
- 2 cups coarsely chopped mustard greens or turnip tops
  Handful fresh flat-leaf Italian parsley leaves
- ¼ cup shaved Parmigiano-Reggiano

1. Bring a large pot of generously salted water to a boil. Cook linguine according to package directions. Drain, reserving ½ cup cooking liquid. Return to pot; cover to keep warm.

2. Meanwhile, for pan sauce, cut sausage into little blunt-edged meatballs. In a large skillet cook sausage over medium-high heat until golden brown all over, about 5 minutes, adding garlic for the last minute of cooking. Set aside.

3. In a medium bowl whisk together the egg yolks, milk, ½ cup grated cheese, the lemon peel, salt, and pepper. Add to the pot with the pasta. Add the hot sausage and chopped greens. Toss it all together, and let the heat from the pot and the linguine cook and thicken the egg to a silky sauce. Add ¼ to ½ cup reserved pasta water to loosen. Toss with the parsley and shaved cheese. Serve immediately in shallow bowls or plates. Makes 4 servings.

EACH SERVING *828 cal, 51 g fat, 343 mg chol, 1,433 mg sodium, 51 g carb, 3 g fiber, 41 g pro.*

LINGUINE

This thin ribbon pasta is flat and narrow. Its shape makes it easy to toss in a light creamy sauce. Other long thin pasta such as spaghetti or vermicelli can be swapped for linguine in recipes.

GARLIC PORK AND
SWEET POTATO
HASH

Everyday Easy

On a hectic night, you can put a hearty
meal on the table in a half hour or less.

Garlic Pork and
Sweet Potato Hash

START TO FINISH 30 min.
BUDGET $2.89 per serving

3   small sweet potatoes, scrubbed and
      chopped (4 cups)
1½   lb. pork tenderloin, cut into 1-inch
      slices
2   Tbsp. reduced-sodium soy sauce
8   cloves garlic, peeled and thinly sliced
3   Tbsp. cooking oil
2   green onions, sliced
2   Tbsp. honey

1. In a microwave-safe bowl microcook
potatoes, covered with vented plastic
wrap, 8 minutes on high. Carefully
uncover; stir once. Meanwhile, to
butterfly pork slices, cut three-quarters
through each; open and flatten slightly.
Brush with some soy sauce and lightly
sprinkle with black pepper.
2. In a 12-inch skillet cook garlic in hot
oil over medium-high heat just until it
begins to turn golden brown. Remove and
set aside. Cook pork in the same skillet
2 to 3 minutes each side until 160°F when
tested with an instant-read thermometer.
Transfer to platter; cover. Add potatoes
to skillet. Cook, stirring occasionally,
until beginning to crisp. Add onions; cook
1 minute. Spoon onto individual plates;
top with pork and garlic.
3. For sauce, in a hot skillet whisk
together honey, 2 Tbsp. water, and
remaining soy sauce until bubbly. Drizzle
over pork. Makes 4 servings.
EACH SERVING *450 cal, 16 g fat, 107 mg chol,
449 mg sodium, 39 g carb, 4 g fiber, 37 g pro.*

TURKEY-VEGETABLE CASSEROLES

BACON-WRAPPED SALMON WITH FRUIT CHUTNEY

KID FRIENDLY | **LOW FAT** | **FAST**

Turkey-Vegetable Casseroles

START TO FINISH 25 min.
BUDGET $2.89 per serving

- 1 16-oz. bag frozen stew vegetables (potatoes, carrots, onion, celery)
- 1 18-oz. jar home-style gravy (1¾ cups)
- 1 tsp. finely snipped fresh sage or ½ tsp. ground sage
- 2 cups cooked turkey or chicken, cut into slices
- ¼ tsp. each black pepper and nutmeg
- 1 cooking apple, thinly sliced
  Fresh sage leaves (optional)
- 2 Tbsp. butter, melted

1. Preheat oven to 450°F. In a large microwave-safe bowl combine vegetables, gravy, and sage. Cover with vented plastic wrap; microcook on high for 5 minutes. Add the turkey; cover and microcook for 4 to 6 minutes or until stew is heated through and vegetables are tender, stirring

occasionally. In a small bowl combine the pepper and nutmeg; set aside.
2. Spoon stew into four 14- to 16-oz. casseroles. Top with apple and, if desired, fresh sage. Drizzle with melted butter and sprinkle with nutmeg mixture. Bake, uncovered, 10 minutes or until bubbly and apple slices begin to brown. Makes 4 servings.

EACH SERVING *297 cal, 12 g fat, 70 mg chol, 753 mg sodium, 23 g carb, 3 g fiber, 24 g pro.*

FAST

Bacon-Wrapped Salmon with Fruit Chutney

START TO FINISH 21 min.
BUDGET $3.53

- 8 slices center-cut bacon
- 4 4-oz. skinless salmon fillets, ½ inch thick
  Salt and ground black pepper
- 1 tsp. olive oil
- ⅓ cup apricot jam
- ½ cup fresh or frozen cranberries, coarsely chopped
- 1 tsp. fresh thyme leaves

1. On a microwave-safe plate lined with paper towels, microcook 4 slices of bacon at a time for 1½ minutes. Meanwhile, rinse salmon, pat dry; lightly sprinkle with salt and pepper. Wrap 2 bacon strips around each fillet. In a 12-inch skillet heat oil over medium-high heat. Cook fish, bacon seam side down first, for 3 to 4 minutes per side (longer for thicker fillets) or until bacon is crisp and fish flakes easily with a fork.
2. For chutney, in a small saucepan combine jam and cranberries. Cook, stirring occasionally, over medium heat until heated through. Serve salmon with chutney and thyme. Makes 4 servings.

EACH SERVING *341 cal, 15 g fat, 80 mg chol, 706 mg sodium, 20 g carb, 1 g fiber, 28 g pro.*

**BEANS AND GREENS
WITH CORN BREAD
CROUTONS**

PEPPERED STEAKS WITH ROASTED BEETS

FAST

Beans and Greens with Corn Bread Croutons

START TO FINISH 25 min.

BUDGET $1.30 per serving

12	oz. purchased or prepared corn bread
2	Tbsp. finely shredded Parmesan cheese
3	Tbsp. olive oil
1	red onion, thinly sliced
3	Tbsp. red wine vinegar or balsamic vinegar
1	15-oz. can no-salt-added cannellini beans, rinsed and drained
2	1-lb. pkgs. collard greens (torn), curly endive (torn), or baby spinach
	Finely shredded Parmesan cheese (optional)
	Crushed red pepper (optional)

1. Preheat oven to 400°F. Cut corn bread in 1-inch cubes (about 4½ cups); place in a 15×10×1-inch baking pan. Lightly coat with nonstick cooking spray. Heat for 10 minutes or until crisp and golden. Remove from oven; sprinkle with the 2 Tbsp. Parmesan cheese.

2. In a 12-inch skillet heat 1 Tbsp. of the olive oil over medium heat. Cook onion for 4 to 5 minutes, until tender. Stir in 2 Tbsp. of the vinegar. Add cannellini beans; heat through. Transfer to a bowl; cover to keep warm.

3. In the same skillet heat remaining oil. Cook and stir greens, in batches if necessary, just until wilted. Sprinkle with ¼ tsp. salt and ½ tsp. black pepper; drizzle with remaining vinegar. To serve, top with additional cheese and red pepper, if desired. Makes 4 servings.

EACH SERVING *490 cal, 19 g fat, 36 mg chol, 827 mg sodium, 67 g carb, 15 g fiber, 17 g pro.*

FAST

Peppered Steaks with Roasted Beets

START TO FINISH 30 min.

BUDGET $3.50 per serving

2	lb. small golden and/or red beets with tops
	Olive oil
1	lb. boneless beef sirloin steak, 1 inch thick
1	Tbsp. deli-style mustard
1	tsp. packed brown sugar
½	8-oz. pkg. cream cheese, softened
½	tsp. dried Italian seasoning

1. Trim and reserve beet greens; set aside. Peel beets; cut in wedges. Place in a 1½-quart microwave-safe dish. Cover with vented plastic wrap. Microcook on high 9 to 12 minutes or until tender, stirring once. Rinse and drain greens; tear to measure 1 cup; set aside. Carefully uncover and drain beets. Toss with 1 Tbsp. olive oil, ⅛ tsp. each salt and black pepper, and torn greens.

2. Meanwhile, season both sides of steak with ¼ tsp. salt and 1 tsp. cracked black pepper. Lightly coat grill pan or cast-iron skillet with nonstick cooking spray. Heat over medium-high heat. Cook steak 5 minutes per side or to desired doneness. For sauce, in a small saucepan stir 2 Tbsp. water, mustard, and brown sugar over medium heat just until bubbly.

3. Cut steak in 4 portions and top with beets and sauce. Combine cream cheese and seasoning; dollop over all. Makes 4 servings.

EACH SERVING *418 cal, 27 g fat, 83 mg chol, 418 mg sodium, 17 g carb, 4 g fiber, 27 g pro.*

Fall's Best Fruit Butter

Serve this delicious spread of fruit, squash, and nuts on crusty bread alongside roasted meats or cheeses.

`KID FRIENDLY` `LOW FAT`

Harvest Fruit Butter

Use a variety of fruit and squash—interchanging varieties of grapes, apples, and pears—to make this delicious spread. Be sure to follow the ingredient proportions as noted. Depending on the fruit used, there may be color and texture variations; however, flavor will be consistent if you adhere to spice and seasoning amounts.
PREP 25 min. COOK 1¼ hr.

1   lb. red or purple seedless grapes
1   cup of 1-inch pieces peeled, seeded cooking-variety pumpkin and/or butternut squash
1   cup coarsely chopped fresh Mission figs (or ½ cup coarsely chopped dried Mission figs)
½   cup cored chopped pear or apple
½   cup raisins
1   Tbsp. balsamic vinegar
1   tsp. finely shredded orange peel
½   tsp. mustard seeds
½   tsp. sugar
½   tsp. salt
¼   tsp. ground cloves
¼   tsp. ground black pepper
    Chopped toasted hazelnuts

1. In a Dutch oven combine grapes, squash, figs, pear, and raisins. Add remaining ingredients, except nuts, and ½ cup water. Bring to boiling. Reduce heat.
2. Simmer, covered, for 30 minutes, stirring occasionally. Uncover; simmer for 45 minutes (30 minutes if using dried figs) over medium-low heat or until thickened and almost all liquid has evaporated. Cool completely. Transfer to a food processor bowl. Cover and process until nearly smooth. Before serving, sprinkle with hazelnuts. To store, cover and refrigerate up to 1 week or freeze in tightly covered freezer containers up to 3 months. Makes 2½ cups.
EACH 2-TBSP. SERVING *40 cal, 0 g fat, 0 mg chol, 30 mg sodium, 10 g carbo, 1 g fiber, 0 g pro.*

Delicious on a Dollar

This make-ahead brunch dish is flavor-packed with fresh broccoli, gooey cheese, and sweet caramelized onions.

Caramelized Onion Breakfast Casserole

Slowly cooking onions breaks down their natural sugars, which intensifies and concentrates flavor. Make a big batch of caramelized onions and keep them on hand to add depth and a punch of richness to your favorite dishes, sauces, and dips. They'll keep in the refrigerator up to 4 days or in the freezer up to 3 months.

PREP **30 min.** CHILL **2 to 24 hr.**
BAKE **40 min.** STAND **10 min.**
OVEN **325°F**

4	strips bacon
1	sweet onion, halved and thinly sliced
2	cups broccoli florets
5	eggs
1⅓	cups milk
½	tsp. dried basil, crushed
¼	tsp. salt
⅛	tsp. pepper
4	cups crusty sourdough bread, cut into 1-inch cubes
4	oz. Muenster or Swiss cheese, cut into ½-inch cubes

1. In a large skillet cook bacon until crisp; remove bacon, reserving 2 Tbsp. drippings in the skillet. Crumble bacon; set aside. Add onion to skillet. Cover and cook over medium-low heat for 15 minutes, stirring occasionally. Uncover and cook over medium heat until caramelized, about 5 minutes. Meanwhile, in a small saucepan cook broccoli for 3 minutes in enough lightly salted water to cover; drain.
2. In a large bowl combine eggs, milk, basil, salt, and pepper. Stir in bread, broccoli, cooked onion, cheese, and bacon. Transfer to a 2-quart square baking dish. Cover and chill 2 to 24 hours.
3. Preheat oven to 325°F. Bake casserole, covered, for 20 minutes. Uncover and bake 20 to 30 minutes more or until a knife inserted near the center comes out clean. Let stand 10 minutes before serving. Makes 6 servings.

EACH SERVING *302 cal, 18 g fat, 188 mg chol, 542 mg sodium, 19 g carb, 1 g fiber, 17 g pro.*

**ROASTED
BUTTERNUT
SQUASH FILLED
WITH PORT-
SOAKED FRUIT**

FALL IS IN THE AIR Butternut squash is bountiful with the coming of warm days and cool nights and plays nicely in sweet and savory recipes. And give your favorite brew a try in fall favorites.

233

246

251

Delicious Every Day

Fresh and easy ideas for dinner.

PORK AND POBLANO STEW

ASIAN-STYLE FRIED RICE AND BEANS

Pork and Poblano Stew

This stew is low in fat, loaded with vitamin A, and hearty enough to satisfy big appetites. The poblano pepper adds a punch of flavor so you don't miss the fat.
PREP 15 min. COOK 24 min.

1¼ lb. pork tenderloin, cut into ¾- to 1-inch pieces
2 tsp. hot chili powder
2 Tbsp. olive oil
1 fresh poblano chile pepper, seeded and cut into 1-inch pieces (see note, page 69)
1 large red sweet pepper, seeded and cut into 1-inch pieces
1 medium onion, cut into thin wedges
1 14½-oz. can fire-roasted tomatoes with garlic, undrained
1 14½-oz. can reduced-sodium chicken broth
1 3-inch piece stick cinnamon
¼ cup fresh orange juice
2 tsp. finely shredded orange peel

1. Toss pork with chili powder to coat. In a large saucepan heat 1 Tbsp. oil over medium-high heat. Cook pork about 4 minutes or until browned, stirring occasionally. Use a slotted spoon to remove pieces; set aside.
2. Add remaining oil to the saucepan. Add poblano pepper, sweet pepper, and onion; cook over medium-high heat until vegetables are just tender, about 5 minutes.
3. Add tomatoes, broth, and stick cinnamon. Bring to boiling; reduce heat. Simmer, covered, over medium-low heat for 10 minutes. Add pork and orange juice. Simmer, uncovered, for 5 minutes. Stir in orange peel. Remove stick cinnamon before serving. Makes 4 (1½-cup) servings.
PER SERVING 300 cal, 11 g fat, 87 mg chol, 534 mg sodium, 16 g carb, 4 g fiber, 32 g pro.

FLAVOR SECRET:
A HIT OF ORANGE PEEL
Don't skip the orange peel here—it's what makes this stew shine. Use a hand grater to grate in the full 2 teaspoons—don't be skimpy. The combination of fresh orange juice and zest gives the dish a bright kick.

Asian-Style Fried Rice and Beans

PREP 20 min. COOK 14 min.

½ pineapple, peeled, cored, and sliced, or 8-oz. can pineapple slices
1 Tbsp. vegetable oil
2 medium carrots, thinly bias-sliced
4 cloves garlic, minced
2 tsp. grated fresh ginger*
2 cups cooked brown rice (leftover or quick-cooking microwavable rice)
1 15-oz. can garbanzo beans (chickpeas), rinsed and drained
1 cup frozen peas, thawed
3 Tbsp. reduced-sodium soy sauce
⅓ cup snipped fresh cilantro
1 lime, halved

1. Quarter pineapple slices. In a 12-inch nonstick skillet heat 2 tsp. of the oil over medium heat. Add pineapple; cook about 2 minutes per side or until golden brown. Remove from skillet and set aside.
2. Pour the remaining 1 tsp. oil into the hot skillet. Add carrots; cook, stirring frequently, for 5 minutes or until just tender. Add garlic and ginger; cook 30 seconds.
3. Stir in brown rice, garbanzo beans, and peas. Add soy sauce. Cook and stir about 4 minutes or until heated through. Stir in cilantro. Return pineapple to pan.
4. To serve, squeeze lime over all. Top with additional fresh cilantro leaves, if desired. Makes 4 servings.
*Fresh ginger is a freezer gem. Place unpeeled ginger in a freezer bag. When a recipe calls for fresh, peel and grate in its frozen state—no thawing required.
EACH SERVING 350 cal, 6 g fat, 0 mg chol, 711 mg sodium, 65 g carb, 10 g fiber, 11 g pro.

FLAVOR SECRET:
CARAMELIZED PINEAPPLE
It takes less than 5 minutes to caramelize fresh pineapple slices, and the flavor it adds makes all the difference. Get the pan nice and hot before adding the fruit. When the pineapple hits the heat it should sizzle, caramelizing the fruit's natural sugars to sear in bold, savory sweetness. In a pinch, canned pineapple will work— you won't get quite the same browning, but it will still taste delicious.

Harvest Gold

Savory-sweet butternut squash brings fall flavor to the table with delicious ease. These inspiring dishes, from starters to desserts, show how to enjoy this surprisingly versatile veggie all season long.

CITRUSY MASHED
SQUASH WITH
TOASTED PECANS

Citrusy Mashed Squash with Toasted Pecans

PREP 15 min. COOK 21 min.

- 3 lb. butternut squash, peeled, seeded, and cut into chunks
- 2 Tbsp. butter
- ⅓ cup sour cream or ½ cup mascarpone cheese
- ¼ cup maple syrup
- 2 tsp. finely shredded orange peel
- 2 tsp. finely shredded lemon peel
- ¾ tsp. salt
- ¼ tsp. ground black pepper
- 2 Tbsp. snipped fresh sage
- ½ cup pecan halves, toasted and coarsely chopped
  Sliced green onions and/or fresh sage leaves and finely shredded orange and lemon peel

1. In a 5- or 6-quart Dutch oven cook squash in lightly salted boiling water, covered, 16 to 17 minutes or until tender when pierced with a fork. Drain.
2. Meanwhile, melt the butter in a heavy skillet over medium heat, whisking constantly until golden brown, 5 to 6 minutes. Transfer half the squash to a food processor. Add butter, sour cream, maple syrup, orange and lemon peels, salt, and pepper. Cover and process until smooth. Place remaining squash in a bowl; add pureed mixture. Mash slightly. Stir in fresh sage.
3. Top with pecans, green onions and/or sage leaves, and citrus peel. Makes 8 to 10 servings.
EACH SERVING *176 cal, 9 g fat, 12 mg chol, 258 mg sodium, 25 g carb, 4 g fiber, 2 g pro.*

BUTTERNUT MATH

Whole butternut squash can be found in a range of sizes, and some markets offer ready-to-cook chopped fresh squash. Here's a guide to knowing just how much to buy:

1 lb. whole = 2⅓ cups chopped

1½ lb. whole = 3½ cups chopped

2 lb. whole = 4⅔ cups chopped

ROASTED BUTTERNUT SQUASH FILLED WITH PORT-SOAKED FRUIT

Roasted Butternut Squash Filled with Port-Soaked Fruit

To eat this fun starter, top a slice of toasted bread with a slice of white cheddar, then scoop some of the fruit mixture and the roasted squash onto the toast.

PREP 15 min. ROAST 33 min.
COOK 18 min. STAND 10 min.
OVEN 425°F

- 1 1½-lb. butternut squash, halved lengthwise and seeded
- 1 Tbsp. olive oil
- ¾ tsp. salt
- 2 cups port wine or pomegranate juice
- ¼ cup red wine vinegar
- ¼ cup sugar
- 1 cup dried apricots, chopped
- ½ cup dried tart cherries, chopped
- ½ cup salted whole almonds, chopped
  Aged white cheddar cheese or Gruyère cheese, shaved
  Toasted baguette slices

1. Preheat oven to 425°F. Coat a large baking sheet with nonstick cooking spray.
2. Rub squash halves with oil, then sprinkle cut sides with ½ tsp. salt. Place squash, cut sides down, on prepared baking sheet. Roast until easily pierced with the tip of a sharp knife, 33 to 35 minutes. Transfer to a platter, cut sides up.
3. Meanwhile, in a large saucepan combine the port wine, vinegar, sugar, and remaining ¼ tsp. salt. Bring mixture to boiling over medium-high heat and cook, uncovered, 4 minutes. Add the apricots and cherries. Remove from heat; let stand 10 minutes. Remove fruit from saucepan with a slotted spoon; set aside. Return saucepan to the stove over medium-high heat. Bring port mixture to boiling; cook until thick enough to coat the back of a spoon and reduced to about ½ cup, about 14 to 15 minutes. Remove from heat. Stir in the fruit mixture and nuts. Season to taste with salt and ground black pepper.
4. Spoon fruit mixture into squash. Place any remaining mixture in a serving bowl.
5. To serve, place shaved cheese on baguette slices. Spoon on squash and fruit mixture. Makes 6 servings.
EACH SERVING *556 cal, 15 g fat, 20 mg chol, 715 mg sodium, 80 g carb, 7 g fiber, 13 g pro.*

BUTTERNUT SQUASH POSOLE

Butternut Squash Posole

Posole is a Mexican soup made with chili powder and hominy. For this version, we've swapped out half of the usual amount of hominy for tender pieces of squash.

PREP **20 min.** COOK **30 min.**

1   Tbsp. olive oil
1½ lb. skinless, bone-in chicken thighs
3   stalks celery, sliced
2   medium onions, cut into wedges
4   garlic cloves, minced
1   tsp. dried oregano
1   tsp. chili powder
1   tsp. ground cumin
6   cups reduced-sodium chicken broth
1½ lb. butternut squash, peeled, seeded, and cut into chunks
3   cups chopped kale or chard
1   15-oz. can white hominy, rinsed and drained
¼   cup chopped fresh cilantro
1   tsp. salt

¼   tsp. ground black pepper
     Sliced radishes (optional)
     Lime wedges (optional)

1. In a Dutch oven heat oil over medium-high heat. Add chicken; cook until browned, 4 to 5 minutes per side. Transfer to a plate. Drain all but 1 Tbsp. drippings from the Dutch oven.
2. Add the celery, onions, and garlic to the Dutch oven; cook, stirring occasionally, until just tender, 4 to 5 minutes. Stir in the oregano, chili powder, and cumin; cook and stir for 30 seconds.
3. Add the broth, chicken, squash, kale, and hominy to the Dutch oven. Bring to boiling; reduce heat to medium and simmer until chicken is cooked through and squash is tender, 18 to 20 minutes.
4. Remove chicken; cut into cubes. Return chicken to pot. Stir in the cilantro, salt, and pepper. Divide among bowls and top with sliced radishes and lime wedges, if desired. Makes 8 to 10 servings.
EACH SERVING *190 cal, 5 g fat, 48 mg chol, 860 mg sodium, 23 g carb, 4 g fiber, 15 g pro.*

Caramelized Squash Salad with Pistachios and Goat Cheese

PREP **20 min.** MARINATE **1 hr.**
BAKE **26 min.** OVEN **400°F**

1   cup orange juice
3   Tbsp. pure maple syrup
1½ Tbsp. Dijon-style mustard
1   Tbsp. grated fresh ginger
1½ lb. butternut squash, peeled, seeded, halved lengthwise, and cut into ½-inch-wide strips
½   tsp. salt
¼   tsp. ground black pepper
⅓   cup olive oil
6   cups mixed salad greens
1   small head radicchio, cored and thinly sliced
½   cup roasted salted pistachio nuts
3   oz. goat cheese, crumbled (optional)

1. For marinade, in a small bowl stir together orange juice, maple syrup, mustard, and ginger. Set aside ½ cup of the marinade for salad dressing. Place butternut squash pieces in a large resealable plastic bag set in a shallow dish. Pour remaining marinade over squash. Seal bag; marinate, refrigerated, for 1 to 4 hours, turning bag occasionally.
2. Preheat oven to 400°F. Coat a large baking sheet with nonstick cooking spray; set aside. Drain marinade from squash, discarding marinade. Place squash on prepared baking sheet. Roast squash until tender and lightly browned in spots, 26 to 30 minutes. Remove from oven; set aside.
3. For dressing, in small bowl whisk together the reserved marinade, salt, and pepper. Slowly whisk in the oil. Drizzle 2 to 3 Tbsp. of dressing over warm squash; toss to combine. In a large bowl combine the mixed greens, radicchio, and half of the pistachios. Toss with half the dressing. Gently toss roasted squash into salad. Top with remaining pistachios and goat cheese. Pass remaining dressing. Makes 6 to 8 servings.
EACH SERVING *275 cal, 17 g fat, 0 mg chol, 346 mg sodium, 29 g carb, 4 g fiber, 5 g pro.*

CARAMELIZED
SQUASH SALAD
WITH PISTACHIOS
AND GOAT CHEESE

SQUASH AND
SAUSAGE
SHEPHERD'S PIE

A kitchen chameleon, butternut squash takes to hearty and fresh dishes with equally delicious results.

SQUASH PREP
Start by using a large, sturdy knife to cut off the top about 1 inch from the stem end. Insert the knife lengthwise into the center of the squash. Use your other hand to press the knife all the way through the squash. To peel, hold half the squash at an angle on a cutting board. Using a sturdy vegetable peeler, peel down its length. Using a large spoon, scrape the seeds from each half and discard.

KID FRIENDLY

Squash and Sausage Shepherd's Pie

PREP 40 min.   BAKE 15 min.   OVEN 425°F

2½ lb. butternut squash, peeled, seeded, and cut into chunks
5 Tbsp. butter, softened
¼ cup grated Parmesan cheese
1 tsp. salt
½ tsp. ground black pepper
1 lb. bulk sweet Italian sausage or lean ground beef
1 Tbsp. olive oil
1 medium onion, chopped
1 8-oz. package sliced fresh mushrooms
3 cloves garlic, minced
1 cup reduced-sodium beef broth
½ 28-oz. can crushed tomatoes (about 1½ cups)
1 Tbsp. snipped fresh or 1 tsp. dried rosemary
1 tsp. Worcestershire sauce
1 cup frozen peas and carrots
   Shaved Parmesan cheese (optional)
   Sliced green onion (optional)

1. Preheat oven to 425°F. Lightly coat six 10- to 12-oz. individual casseroles with nonstick cooking spray.
2. In a 6-quart Dutch oven cook squash in lightly salted boiling water, covered, for 15 to 17 minutes or until tender when pierced with a fork. Drain; return to Dutch oven. Mash with butter, Parmesan, ½ tsp. salt, and ¼ tsp. pepper; set aside.
3. In a large skillet cook sausage over medium-high heat, breaking up with the back of a wooden spoon until no longer pink. Transfer meat to a colander; drain well. Wipe out skillet with a paper towel.
4. In same skillet heat oil over medium-high heat. Add onion and mushrooms; cook, stirring occasionally, until tender, about 4 to 5 minutes. Add garlic; cook 2 minutes more. Stir in broth, crushed tomatoes, rosemary, and Worcestershire sauce. Bring to boiling; reduce heat to medium and simmer until thickened, about 5 minutes. Stir in meat, peas and carrots, remaining ½ tsp. salt, and ¼ tsp. pepper; cook 2 minutes. Divide mixture among prepared dishes. Spread top with butternut squash. Place on a large baking sheet.
5. Bake, uncovered, for 15 to 20 minutes or until top is lightly browned. Top with shaved Parmesan and green onion, if desired. Makes 6 servings.
EACH SERVING *372 cal, 20 g fat, 51 mg chol, 1,146 mg sodium, 35 g carb, 7 g fiber, 19 g pro.*

BUTTERNUT BREAD PUDDING WITH BOURBON CARAMEL SAUCE

Butternut Bread Pudding with Bourbon Caramel Sauce

PREP **30 min.** BAKE **1 hr.**
COOL **10 min.** OVEN **350°F**

1 Tbsp. butter, softened
1 recipe Bourbon Caramel Sauce
1 cup half-and-half or light cream
3 eggs
1 tsp. vanilla
3 cups ¾-inch cubes peeled butternut squash
¼ cup packed brown sugar
1 tsp. ground cinnamon
2 cups stale or dried whole wheat bread cubes
1 pear, peeled (if desired), cored, and cut into ¾-inch pieces
⅓ cup dried cranberries
1 pear, sliced and/or chopped
Fresh mint and cranberries (optional)

1. Preheat oven to 350°F. Brush a 1½-quart baking dish with softened butter. Prepare Bourbon Caramel Sauce; set aside to cool slightly.

2. In a 4-cup liquid measuring cup combine the half-and-half, eggs, and vanilla; whisk to combine. Whisk in ¾ cup of the Bourbon Caramel Sauce. Set aside. In a large bowl toss squash with brown sugar and cinnamon. Add the whole wheat bread, pear, and cranberries; toss to combine. Place in prepared dish. Slowly and evenly pour egg mixture over top. Let stand for 5 minutes.
3. Bake bread pudding 1 hour. Remove from the oven and let cool 10 minutes. Top with fresh pear and, if desired, mint and cranberries. Reheat remaining sauce. Drizzle some sauce over bread pudding and pass remaining.
Bourbon Caramel Sauce In a heavy medium saucepan combine ¾ cup brown sugar, ½ cup whipping cream, ½ cup butter, and 2 Tbsp. corn syrup. Bring to boiling over medium-high heat, whisking occasionally. Reduce heat to medium. Boil gently for 3 minutes; remove from heat. Stir in 2 Tbsp. bourbon, 1 tsp. vanilla, and ½ tsp. salt. Makes 8 servings.
EACH SERVING *467 cal, 25 g fat, 136 mg chol, 367 mg sodium, 57 g carb, 4 g fiber, 6 g pro.*

Butternut Squash Mac and Cheese

PREP **15 min.** BAKE **14 min.**
COOK **40 min.** OVEN **425°F**

12 oz. dried rigatoni
1½ lb. butternut squash, peeled, seeded, and cut into chunks (3½ cups)
2¾ cups milk
¼ cup all-purpose flour
8 oz. smoked Gruyère cheese, shredded (2 cups)
8 slices bacon
2 small sweet onions, cut into chunks
3 oz. sourdough bread
2 Tbsp. butter, melted
Fresh flat-leaf Italian parsley

1. Preheat oven to 425°F. Lightly butter a 3-quart au gratin or baking dish; set aside. Cook pasta according to package directions. Drain; transfer to a large bowl.
2. Meanwhile, in a large saucepan combine the squash and 2½ cups of the milk over medium-high heat. Bring to boiling; reduce heat to medium, and simmer until the squash is tender when pierced with a fork, 18 to 20 minutes. Stir together remaining ¼ cup milk and flour; stir into squash mixture. Bring to boiling; cook until thickened, 2 to 3 minutes. Stir in 1½ cups of the Gruyère until melted; keep warm.
3. Meanwhile, in a very large skillet cook bacon until crisp; drain on paper towels. Crumble; set aside. Pour off all but 2 Tbsp. bacon drippings. Return skillet to heat.
4. Add onions to skillet; cover and cook over low heat 10 minutes, stirring occasionally. Uncover and increase heat to high. Cook 4 to 6 minutes more, stirring, until onions are golden.
5. Add squash-cheese mixture, onions, and bacon to the bowl with the pasta. Toss well to combine, then transfer to prepared baking dish.
6. Place bread in a food processor; pulse with two or three on/off turns to form large coarse crumbs (you should have about 2 cups). Transfer to a small bowl; mix with melted butter. Sprinkle remaining Gruyère and the bread crumbs over pasta mixture. Bake until top is browned, about 14 to 15 minutes. Cool 5 minutes. Sprinkle with parsley. Makes 6 to 8 servings.
EACH SERVING *686 cal, 29 g fat, 79 mg chol, 668 mg sodium, 77 g carb, 5 g fiber, 30 g pro.*

**BUTTERNUT
SQUASH
MAC AND CHEESE**

**BROWN SUGAR-
BUTTERNUT
SQUASH TART**

Butternut squash is pure fall on a fork. Its mildly sweet pumpkinlike flavor blends with cool-weather standards like smoky bacon and maple.

KID FRIENDLY

Brown Sugar-Butternut Squash Tart

PREP 30 min. CHILL 30 min.
BAKE 32 min. COOL 20 min.
OVEN 450°F/400°F

1   recipe Rich Tart Pastry
⅓   cup butter
⅓   cup packed brown sugar
½   tsp. salt
¾   tsp. ground nutmeg
1½ to 2 lb. butternut squash, peeled, halved, seeded, and cut crosswise into ¼-inch-thick slices
2   Tbsp. coarse sugar
⅓   cup shredded mozzarella or provolone cheese
½   cup whipping cream
1   Tbsp. finely shredded orange peel

1. Preheat oven to 450°F. Prepare Rich Tart Pastry. On a lightly floured surface roll pastry to a 13×10-inch rectangle. Transfer to an 11×8×1-inch tart pan with removable bottom. Ease into bottom and press up the sides of the pan. Trim edges even with edge of pan. Place tart pan on a baking sheet. Line pastry with a double thickness of foil. Bake for 8 minutes. Remove foil. Bake for 4 minutes more or until pastry is set and dry. Set aside to cool slightly. Reduce oven temperature to 400°F.
2. In a 12-inch skillet melt butter over medium heat. Add brown sugar, salt, and ½ tsp. ground nutmeg. Cook and stir until combined and bubbly. Add squash and cook 5 minutes, stirring frequently. Use tongs to remove squash from saucepan, arranging slices in 2 rows lengthwise over pastry. Spoon over any remaining sauce. Sprinkle with 1 Tbsp. coarse sugar.
3. Bake, uncovered, 15 minutes. Sprinkle with cheese. Bake 5 minutes more or until pastry is golden and squash is tender. Cool slightly.

4. For nutmeg whipped cream, in a chilled medium mixing bowl combine whipping cream and remaining 1 Tbsp. sugar and ¼ tsp. nutmeg. Beat with electric mixer on medium speed until soft peaks form.
5. Remove sides of pan; sprinkle with orange peel. Serve warm with whipped cream. Makes 8 servings.
Rich Tart Pastry In a medium bowl stir together 1¼ cups flour and ¼ cup sugar. Using a pastry blender, cut in ½ cup cold butter until pieces are pea size. In a small bowl stir together 2 egg yolks and 1 Tbsp. ice water. Gradually stir egg yolk mixture into flour mixture. Using your fingers, gently knead the pastry just until a ball forms. Cover pastry with plastic wrap and chill for 30 to 60 minutes or until pastry is easy to handle.
EACH SERVING *431 cal, 27 g fat, 120 mg chol, 360 mg sodium, 44 g carb, 2 g fiber, 5 g pro.*

MEET DAVID

Recipe whiz and *Better Homes and Gardens®* regular David Bonom created these savory and sweet squash recipes. "Butternut squash is one of my favorite fall ingredients," he says. "You can store it in the cupboard for up to a month, then cut into it and prepare it in a number of ways. The flavor of butternut squash really shines in savory cooking, bringing complexity to a dish and balance to intensely flavored ingredients," he says. "Then, just as easily, you can douse it in a buttery brown sugar sauce and bring out all of its sweet goodness."

**BROWN ALE-
BRAISED CHICKEN**

Home Cooking

COOKING WITH BEER Beer lovers, take note: Your top brew makes a delicious ingredient in favorite fall foods, from a hearty stew to a stout-soaked steak. Here are four new recipes that showcase its ability to shine in the kitchen.

Brown Ale-Braised Chicken

PREP 25 min. STAND 10 min.
COOK 15 min. BAKE 40 min. OVEN 350°F

1   Tbsp. packed brown sugar
½   Tbsp. chili powder
½   tsp. salt
¼   tsp. ground black pepper
¼   tsp. crushed red pepper
8   skin-on chicken thighs
1   Tbsp. vegetable oil
1   medium onion, sliced
2   stalks celery, chopped
8   small whole carrots with tops, peeled and tops trimmed to 1 inch
2   Tbsp. all-purpose flour
1   12-oz. bottle brown ale
½   cup reduced-sodium chicken broth
4   cloves garlic, peeled
     Coarsely chopped celery leaves
     Fresh thyme

1. Preheat oven to 350°F. In a small bowl combine brown sugar, chili powder, salt, ground black pepper, and crushed red pepper; rub into chicken thighs. Let stand 10 minutes.
2. In an extra-large ovenproof skillet heat oil over medium-high heat. Add chicken; cook until well browned on both sides and skin is crispy. Remove chicken from skillet. Drain fat, reserving 1 Tbsp.
3. In the same skillet cook and stir the onion, celery, and carrots in the reserved fat about 5 minutes or until tender. Stir in flour; cook and stir 1 minute. Stir in beer and broth. Bring to a simmer. Return chicken to skillet. Add garlic. Cover and bake 40 minutes. Sprinkle with celery leaves and thyme. Makes 4 servings.
EACH SERVING *552 cal, 34 g fat, 183 mg chol, 571 mg sodium, 23 g carb, 4 g fiber, 33 g pro.*

Beer's rich flavor intensifies during cooking, giving dishes a hearty, perfect-for-fall taste. Like wine, beer can be used as a braising liquid or as a marinade. It also makes a great addition to a batter or a glaze—all recipe ideas we've included here. Match a beer to the flavors in the recipe—heavier beers tend to go well with heartier dishes—or just cook with what you like. Start with our suggestions, then experiment with your favorite brews.

BROWN ALE
This hearty beer is a natural for cool-weather soups and braises. It has a nutty flavor that can border on bitter, along with a sweetness that can range from caramel toffee to rich molasses. Try Newcastle Brown Ale, Samuel Smith's Nut Brown Ale, and Abita Turbodog.

BRAISE Low, slow braising in beer results in tender, juicy meat. Using brown ale as the simmering liquid benefits the dish beyond just flavor: Its richness lends a velvety texture to the sauce.

MARINATE Soaking a meaty porterhouse in a dark, hearty stout quickly punches up the flavor, infusing the meat with a bold coffeelike taste.

STOUT

Use stout in marinades, as a basting liquid, or in a slow-cooking stew. Stouts can range from velvety and sweet to sharp and almost bitter. The bold flavor is a great match for beef or lamb, and the hints of chocolate and coffee make a nice addition to chili and barbecue sauce. Try Guinness Extra Stout, Murphy's Irish Stout, and Old No. 38 Stout.

Stout-Soaked Porterhouse with Beer Butter

One porterhouse usually serves 2 or 3 people. If serving more than that, add another porterhouse and use the same amount of marinade as you would for one steak.

PREP **35 min.** MARINATE **4 hr.**
BROIL **12 min.** STAND **5 min.**

1	porterhouse steak, 1 inch thick (about 1¼ lb.)
1	12-oz. bottle stout beer
1	Tbsp. Dijon-style mustard
1	Tbsp. Worcestershire sauce
2	tsp. dried tarragon, crushed
½	tsp. salt
½	tsp. ground black pepper
1	shallot, finely chopped
2	tsp. olive oil
½	cup butter, softened

1. Place steak in a resealable plastic bag set in a shallow dish. Set aside 2 Tbsp. beer. In a small bowl combine remaining beer, mustard, Worcestershire, 1 tsp. of the tarragon, the salt, and pepper. Pour beer mixture over steak in bag. Marinate in the refrigerator for 4 to 6 hours, turning occasionally.

2. Meanwhile, in a small skillet over medium heat cook shallot in hot oil 5 minutes or until tender. Stir in reserved 2 Tbsp. beer. Remove from heat. Cool 10 minutes. In a small bowl combine softened butter, shallot mixture, and remaining 1 tsp. tarragon. Transfer to waxed paper; shape into a log. Wrap and freeze.

3. Preheat broiler. Drain steak; reserve marinade. Season steak with additional salt and pepper. Place steak on the unheated rack of a broiler pan. Broil 3 to 4 inches from heat to desired doneness, turning once, 12 to 15 minutes for medium-rare (145°F) or 15 to 20 minutes for medium (160°F). Transfer to platter. Tent with foil and let stand 5 minutes.

4. Place reserved marinade in a small saucepan. Bring to boiling. Reduce heat to medium and simmer, uncovered, 15 minutes. (Do not overcook; marinade can become bitter.)

5. To serve, slice steak into portions. Drizzle with some of the marinade reduction and top each with a slice of frozen butter. Makes 2 to 3 servings.

EACH SERVING *502 cal, 25 g fat, 134 mg chol, 1,339 mg sodium, 12 g carb, 0 g fiber, 41 g pro.*

STOUT-SOAKED PORTERHOUSE WITH BEER BUTTER

BEER-CHEESE
HUSH PUPPIES

BATTER Foamy, bubbly beer lightens batter and results in lacy, super-crisp fried deliciousness. Using a light beer, such as lager, lets the corn and cheese flavors in these hush puppies shine.

KID FRIENDLY | FAST

Beer-Cheese Hush Puppies

PREP 25 min. COOK 3 min. per batch

1   cup yellow cornmeal
½   cup all-purpose flour
1½ tsp. baking powder
1   tsp. sugar
½   tsp. salt
2   oz. pepper Jack cheese or cheddar cheese, shredded (½ cup)
⅓   cup finely chopped onion
⅓   cup finely chopped red sweet pepper
1   egg, lightly beaten
⅔   cup light lager
     Vegetable oil for deep-fat frying
     Snipped fresh flat-leaf Italian parsley (optional)
     Green or red jalapeño jelly

1. In a medium bowl mix cornmeal, flour, baking powder, sugar, and salt. Add cheese, onion, and red sweet pepper; toss to combine. Make a well in the center of flour mixture. In another bowl mix egg and beer. Add all at once to flour mixture. Stir just until moistened.

2. In a 3-quart saucepan heat 2 inches of oil to 375°F. For each hush puppy, drop 1 rounded Tbsp. batter into hot oil. Fry three or four at a time for 3 minutes or until golden brown, turning once. Drain on paper towels. Sprinkle with parsley, if desired.

3. Meanwhile, in a small saucepan heat pepper jelly just until melted. Serve hush puppies warm with pepper jelly. Makes 20 to 24 hush puppies.

EACH HUSH PUPPY *128 cal, 7 g fat, 12 mg chol, 124 mg sodium, 15 g carb, 1 g fiber, 2 g pro.*

LIGHT LAGER

A high level of carbonation makes this beer a natural for fried food because it gives batters a flavorful, airy crunch. It also makes a good neutral-tasting liquid for chili or for poaching sausages. It will impart that familiar beer flavor without overpowering other ingredients. Try Budweiser, Corona Extra, and Rolling Rock Extra Pale.

GLAZE After a few minutes of cooking, beer becomes a light glistening glaze for smoky seared sausage, tender-crisp apples, and green beans.

Beer-Glazed Sausage and Apples

START TO FINISH 35 min.

1   12-oz. bottle Belgian-style wheat beer
½   tsp. crushed red pepper
1   14- to 16-oz. pkg. smoked sausage, such as kielbasa, cut in 3-inch pieces
½   lb. fresh green beans
2   Tbsp. butter
2   medium cooking apples, cored and thinly sliced
2   Tbsp. packed brown sugar
1   Tbsp. cider vinegar
1   tsp. finely shredded orange peel
8   small sage leaves

1. In a large saucepan combine ½ of the beer and the crushed red pepper; bring to boiling. Add sausage and green beans. Return to a simmer; cook, covered, 5 to 8 minutes or until beans are tender. Drain. Set aside.

2. Meanwhile, in a large skillet melt 1 Tbsp. butter; add apples. Cook, turning occasionally, until apples are just tender. Transfer to a platter.

3. Add sausage to skillet. Cook, turning occasionally, until browned on all sides. Add to platter; cover. Drain fat from skillet.

4. Carefully add remaining beer to skillet (mixture may foam); stir to scrape up browned bits. Add remaining 1 Tbsp. butter, brown sugar, cider vinegar, and orange peel. Bring to boiling; reduce heat and boil gently, uncovered, 5 to 6 minutes or until slightly thickened. Return sausage and green beans to skillet to coat in glaze. Heat through. Fold in apples. Return to serving platter. Sprinkle with sage. Makes 4 servings.

EACH SERVING 409 cal, 24 g fat, 85 mg chol, 1,250 mg sodium, 31 g carb, 4 g fiber, 15 g pro.

BELGIAN-STYLE WHEAT
With enough sweet flavor notes to be a good base for a glaze, citrusy wheat beer provides a nice balance for smoky meats such as sausage. It's also delicious paired with seared chicken, pork, or seafood. Also known as Belgian white or Belgian witbier, this brew has a fruity flavor with hints of orange and coriander. Try Blue Moon Belgian White, Hoegaarden Original White Ale, and Shock Top Belgian White.

Delicious on a Dollar

Tempted by takeout? Make it at home with wallet-friendly sizzling and spicy lime-marinated fajitas.

Fall Vegetable Fajitas

Thinly slicing tougher cuts of meat, such as beef chuck eye steak, flank steak, and skirt steak, ensures tenderness. To slice with ease, pop the steak in the freezer for about 20 minutes before slicing—it should be firm but not frozen. Hold a chef's knife at a 45-degree angle to the meat and thinly slice across the grain.

PREP 20 min. MARINATE 2 hr. GRILL 9 min.

3   Tbsp. chili-lime hot sauce
2   tsp. vegetable oil
1   tsp. dried marjoram, crushed
8   oz. boneless beef chuck eye steak, cut into very thin slices
1   medium zucchini, halved lengthwise and sliced
1   green sweet pepper, cut into strips
½   large red onion, sliced
6   8-inch flour tortillas
2   Tbsp. snipped fresh cilantro
⅛   tsp. black pepper
     Sour cream, salsa, and cilantro sprigs (optional)

1. In a large shallow dish combine hot sauce, oil, and marjoram. Add beef, zucchini, sweet pepper, and red onion; toss to coat. Cover and refrigerate for 2 hours, tossing once. Drain.
2. Preheat charcoal or gas grill over medium-high heat. Add meat and vegetables to grill basket. Grill, covered, for 8 to 10 minutes, stirring once, until meat is browned. Remove from grill. Place tortillas on grill grates and cook 1 minute, turning once.
3. Divide meat and vegetables among tortillas. Sprinkle with cilantro and black pepper. Top with sour cream, salsa, and cilantro sprigs, if desired. Serve immediately. Makes 6 servings.
PER SERVING 254 cal, 11 g fat, 25 mg chol, 598 mg sodium, 27 g carb, 1 g fiber, 12 g pro.

FALL VEGETABLE FAJITAS

CARAMEL APPLE-
CHERRY PIE

THANKSGIVING Nothing says autumn like pie! Author Gesine Bullock-Prado shares her sweet—and beautiful—holiday recipes. Add a succulent turkey and all the trimmings for a truly memorable gathering.

261

272

279

MARMELADE-
GLAZED ROAST
TURKEY

A Maine-Made Thanksgiving

Jonathan King and Jim Stott, creators of the specialty food company Stonewall Kitchen, play favorites with the iconic ingredients of their home state.

KID FRIENDLY | **LOW FAT**

Marmalade-Glazed Roast Turkey

"Thanksgiving is only once a year, so we go all out and buy a really nice organic fresh turkey," Jonathan says. If using a frozen turkey, be sure to thaw it completely over 3 to 4 days in the refrigerator.

PREP 35 min. ROAST 4 to 5 hr.
OVEN 325°F

1   15- to 20-lb. fresh turkey (preferably organic)
1½ Tbsp. vegetable oil
    Salt and freshly ground black pepper
1   recipe Herbed Bread and Cherry-Cranberry Stuffing, page 262
1   slice bread
½   tsp. smoked paprika
1   recipe Garlic Roasted Root Vegetables, right
1   recipe Homemade Giblet Gravy, page 262
¼   cup citrus or desired flavor marmalade
½   tsp. orange peel

1. Remove turkey from refrigerator 30 minutes before working with it so it comes to room temperature. Preheat oven to 325°F. Arrange oven rack so turkey will fit on middle shelf without touching top shelf.
2. Rinse turkey and remove giblets. Reserve neck, heart, and gizzard for Homemade Giblet Gravy. Discard liver. Pat turkey dry with paper towels.
3. Lightly grease bottom of a large roasting pan with vegetable oil. Season all over and in the cavity with salt and pepper. Loosely stuff both the body and neck cavities of the turkey with the stuffing, being careful not to overstuff the turkey. Use the whole slice of bread as a "door" to keep stuffing inside body cavity as it roasts. Carefully place turkey in roasting pan, breast side up.
4. Sprinkle top of turkey with paprika. Using a piece of 100-percent-cotton kitchen string, tie drumsticks together.
5. Loosely cover with foil. Roast 4 to 5 hours, about 15 to 20 minutes per pound. (Fresh turkey tends to cook faster than thawed frozen turkeys.) Meanwhile, prepare Garlic Roasted Root Vegetables and turkey stock for Homemade Giblet Gravy.
6. Spoon juices from bottom of roasting pan over turkey every hour or so, removing foil for the last hour of roasting to give turkey a golden-brown glaze. During the last 30 minutes of roasting, add Garlic Roasted Root Vegetables to roasting pan, brush turkey with marmalade, and sprinkle with orange peel.
7. To test for doneness: The turkey should be golden brown; when a drumstick is wiggled, it should feel slightly loose; and juices should run clear. Internal temperature should be 170°F in the breast, 180°F in the thigh, and 165°F in the stuffing. Gently remove turkey from roasting pan and place on a serving platter; cover loosely with foil. Let rest 20 minutes before carving. Remove the stuffing from turkey and place in a serving bowl; discard slice of bread. Arrange Garlic Roasted Root Vegetables around turkey and garnish with sage sprigs. Carve and serve with the hot gravy on the side. Makes 10 to 12 servings plus leftovers.
EACH SERVING *216 cal, 10 g fat, 99 mg chol, 86 mg sodium, 1 g carb, 0 g fiber, 28 g pro.*

KID FRIENDLY | **LOW FAT**

Garlic Roasted Root Vegetables

PREP 30 min. COOK 6 min.

1   lb. baby carrots with tops, trimmed and peeled
1   lb. parsnips, peeled
1   Tbsp. vegetable oil
3   cloves garlic, thinly sliced
8   oz. cipollini onions, peeled

1. Split large carrots in half lengthwise. Quarter parsnips lengthwise. In a Dutch oven bring salted water to boiling. Add carrots and parsnips and simmer 5 minutes; drain.
2. In a very large skillet heat oil over medium heat. Add garlic and cook 30 seconds or until fragrant and beginning to brown. Add carrots, parsnips, and cipollini onions to skillet. Cook and stir for 5 minutes or until coated in oil and beginning to soften. Sprinkle with salt and ground black pepper. (Vegetables will continue to cook when roasting with the turkey.) Makes 10 servings.
EACH SERVING *67 cal, 2 g fat, 0 mg chol, 148 mg sodium, 13 g carb, 3 g fiber, 1 g pro.*

"We want to give our guests something we know they'll enjoy. After all, it's our family, our friends—and our Thanksgiving," Jim says.

MULLED CIDER AND PINEAPPLE COCKTAIL

NEW ENGLAND CRANBERRY ORANGE COMPOTE

LOW FAT
Mulled Cider and Pineapple Cocktail
PREP 15 min. CHILL 2 hr.

½ gallon apple cider
8 cinnamon sticks
8 star anise
Pineapple juice
Rum
Pineapple spears

In a large saucepan bring cider, cinnamon, and star anise to a simmer. Reduce heat and simmer 5 minutes. Cool and transfer to a pitcher. Chill 2 to 4 hours. To serve, in a cocktail shaker combine ½ cup spiced cider, ¼ cup pineapple juice, ¼ cup rum, and ice. Shake to combine and strain into 2 glasses. Add a pineapple spear to each. Reserve remaining cider for additional cocktails. Makes 2 cocktails.
EACH COCKTAIL *126 cal, 0 g fat, 0 mg chol, 7 mg sodium, 15 g carb, 0 g fiber, 0 g pro.*

KID FRIENDLY | LOW FAT
New England Cranberry Orange Compote
"I always make an extra batch and spoon it into jars to give guests," Jonathan says.
PREP 25 min. COOK 20 min.

1¼ cups sugar
⅓ cup maple syrup
1 lb. fresh cranberries
¼ cup fresh orange juice
¼ cup orange rind, cut into thin strips
1 Tbsp. grated orange zest
2 Tbsp. coarsely chopped candied ginger
1 cup walnuts, pecans, or your favorite nut, coarsely chopped

1. Place sugar and 1¼ cups water in large saucepan; bring to boiling. Reduce heat to low and cook 10 to 15 minutes or until sugar syrup begins to thicken slightly and turn pale amber.

2. Add maple syrup and cranberries. Cook, stirring occasionally, until cranberries begin to pop. Add orange juice, rind, and zest. Cook another 5 to 10 minutes or until sauce thickens slightly.
3. Remove from heat. Add ginger and nuts, stirring well. Cool completely. Place in a clean glass jar and cover; refrigerate up to 1 week or freeze 6 months. Makes 4 cups.
EACH (2-TBSP.) SERVING *77 cal, 2 g fat, 0 mg chol, 2 mg sodium, 14 g carb, 1 g fiber, 1 g pro.*

KID FRIENDLY
Chutney Cheese Balls
PREP 30 min. CHILL 2 hr.

16 oz. cream cheese, softened
½ cup desired-flavor chutney
¼ cup green onion, diced
1 clove garlic, crushed
4 oz. Colby cheese, shredded (1 cup)
4 oz. Monterey Jack cheese, shredded (1 cup)
½ cup chopped pecans
½ cup snipped dried apricots
½ cup chopped pistachio nuts
2 Tbsp. snipped fresh flat-leaf Italian parsley

1. In large bowl combine cream cheese, chutney, green onion, and garlic. Season to taste with salt and pepper. Beat with electric mixer on medium until combined. Fold in Colby and Monterey Jack cheeses. Divide mixture in half and chill at least 2 hours or until firm enough to handle; shape into balls.
2. In shallow dish combine pecans and apricots. In another shallow dish combine pistachios and parsley. Roll one ball in pecan and apricot mixture to completely coat. Roll remaining ball in pistachio and parsley mixture to completely coat. Cover lightly; chill until ready to serve. Makes 16 servings.
EACH SERVING *228 cal, 18 g fat, 44 mg chol, 264 mg sodium, 10 g carb, 1 g fiber, 6 g pro.*

CHUTNEY
CHEESE BALLS

ROASTED
ACORN
SQUASH
AND BEET
SALAD

HOMEMADE
GIBLET
GRAVY

CHEESE AND
CHIVE
POPOVERS

MARMALADE-
GLAZED ROAST
TURKEY

PARMESAN
POTATO GRATIN

HERBED BREAD AND CHERRY-CRANBERRY STUFFING

NEW ENGLAND CRANBERRY ORANGE COMPOTE

GREEN BEANS AND PANCETTA WITH BROWNED BUTTER

GREEN BEANS AND
PANCETTA WITH
BROWNED BUTTER

Green Beans and Pancetta with Browned Butter

PREP 20 min. COOK 14 min.

2 lb. thin green beans or haricots verts, trimmed
4 oz. pancetta
2 shallots, thinly sliced
6 Tbsp. butter
6 oz. peeled and roasted chestnuts, sliced

1. In 4-quart saucepan cook green beans, covered, in boiling salted water 4 to 7 minutes or until crisp-tender. Drain; set aside.
2. In an extra-large skillet cook pancetta over medium heat until crisp. Drain pancetta on paper towels, reserving drippings in skillet.
3. Reduce heat to medium-low. Add shallots to reserved drippings. Cook for 4 minutes or until golden brown and beginning to crisp, stirring frequently. Using tongs, transfer shallots to a paper towel-lined plate. Season to taste with salt.
4. Add butter to drippings in skillet. Melt butter over medium heat. Reduce heat to medium-low. Continue to cook, without stirring, for 4 minutes or until butter becomes light brown and fragrant. Reduce heat to low. Add chestnuts, green beans, and pancetta. Cook 2 to 4 minutes to heat through, stirring occasionally. Season to taste with salt and freshly ground black pepper. Serve immediately topped with shallots. Makes 8 to 10 servings.
EACH SERVING *213 cal, 13 g fat, 28 mg chol, 310 mg sodium, 20 g carb, 4 g fiber, 6 g pro.*

Parmesan Potato Gratin

PREP 45 min. BAKE 1 hr. 45 min.
OVEN 325°F/400°F

1 Tbsp. olive oil
1 lb. chunk Parmesan cheese
4 slices bacon, crisp-cooked and crumbled
2 green onions, thinly sliced
2 Tbsp. snipped fresh chives
4 lb. potatoes, peeled and finely sliced
1 Tbsp. snipped fresh thyme
1 Tbsp. snipped fresh rosemary
¼ cup unsalted butter, cut in small cubes
¾ cup whole milk
¾ cup heavy cream

CHEESE AND CHIVE POPOVERS

3 Tbsp. all-purpose flour
   Snipped fresh rosemary and/or minced thyme

1. Preheat oven to 325°F. Brush the bottom of a 3-quart rectangular or oval baking dish with olive oil; set aside. Using a wide vegetable peeler, shave Parmesan into thin strips (about 4 cups); set aside.
2. In a small bowl combine bacon, green onions, and chives. In prepared baking dish place half the potatoes. Sprinkle with ½ tsp. each salt and freshly ground black pepper, half the bacon mixture, and half the herbs. Top with half the Parmesan. Dot with half the butter. Repeat layers. In a small bowl whisk together milk, heavy cream, and flour; pour over potatoes.
3. Bake, covered, for 1½ hours. Increase temperature to 400°F. Bake, uncovered, for 15 to 20 minutes more or until potatoes are tender and top is golden brown. Sprinkle with snipped fresh rosemary. Makes 24 (½-cup) servings.
EACH SERVING *192 cal, 11 g fat, 30 mg chol, 392 mg sodium, 15 g carb, 1 g fiber, 9 g pro.*

Cheese and Chive Popovers

PREP 25 min. BAKE 35 min. OVEN 400°F

2 cups whole or 2 percent milk
4 large eggs

¼ cup snipped fresh herbs such as rosemary, thyme, sage, and chives
⅛ tsp. salt
   Freshly ground black pepper
2 cups all-purpose flour
1½ cups shredded Gruyère or Parmesan cheese

1. Place rack in middle of oven; preheat to 400°F.
2. Place 1 large or 2 small popover pans in the preheated oven (you'll need 8 or 9 cups total).
3. Meanwhile, in a small saucepan heat milk over low heat for 3 to 4 minutes or until warm to the touch. In a large bowl whisk together eggs, herbs, salt, and a generous grinding of pepper. Add the warm milk while whisking to keep the milk from cooking the eggs. Sift flour into the milk mixture; whisk well.
4. Remove the pan(s) from oven and spray with nonstick cooking spray, making sure the entire cups are well coated. Fill each cup three-fourths full and sprinkle 3 heaping Tbsp. of cheese on top of each.
5. Bake 35 minutes or until popovers have risen and are golden brown. Serve immediately. Makes 8 or 9 popovers.
EACH POPOVER *276 cal, 12 g fat, 122 mg chol, 170 mg sodium, 27 g carb, 1 g fiber, 15 g pro.*

Homemade Giblet Gravy

PREP 25 min. COOK 2 hr.

1   turkey neck, heart, and gizzard
2   onions, peeled and quartered
2   ribs celery, chopped
2   carrots, peeled and chopped
½   cup coarsely chopped fresh parsley
6   peppercorns
1   bay leaf
2½ Tbsp. flour

1. For the turkey stock, in a large saucepan combine the reserved neck, heart, and gizzard. Add the onions, celery, carrots, parsley, peppercorns, and bay leaf. Cover with about 6 cups water. Bring to a boil over high heat; reduce heat and let simmer, partially covered, on very low heat for 1 to 2 hours. Remove from heat. Strain through a sieve; discard solids. Set aside.
2. To finish gravy, once you've removed turkey from the roasting pan, place pan over two burners over moderate heat. Use a spatula to loosen any browned bits clinging to the bottom of pan. Sprinkle on the flour and, using a whisk, mix flour with the juices in pan. Let cook 1 minute, stirring, until paste has come together and is beginning to turn a pale golden color. Pour 3 cups of the turkey stock into the pan and whisk to create a smooth gravy. Let simmer 5 to 10 minutes, stirring frequently, until slightly thickened and flavorful. Thin the gravy by adding additional stock as needed. Season to taste with salt and freshly ground black pepper. Keep gravy warm over low heat, stirring occasionally, until ready to serve. Makes 10 servings.
EACH SERVING *74 cal, 7 g fat, 7 mg chol, 245 mg sodium, 2 g carb, 0 g fiber, 1 g pro.*

KID FRIENDLY   LOW FAT
Herbed Bread and Cherry-Cranberry Stuffing

"For a stuffing that just bursts with flavor, we use a mix of dried cranberries, dried cherries, dried tomatoes, and smoked oysters depending on what we have on hand," Jonathan says. "Any combination of them will work."
PREP 25 min. COOK 15 min.

2   Tbsp. unsalted butter
1   Tbsp. olive oil
3   medium onions, chopped
6   cloves garlic, thinly sliced
2   Tbsp. chopped fresh thyme leaves or 2 tsp. crumbled dried thyme
5   stalks celery, chopped
½   cup very thinly sliced basil leaves
1½   cups chopped fresh parsley leaves
10   cups cubed bread
1   cup dried cranberries, dried cherries, dried tomatoes, and/or smoked oysters (any combination)
1   cup pecan halves, coarsely chopped
1   to 1½ cups milk

1. In a large skillet heat 1 Tbsp. of the butter and the olive oil over medium-low heat. When butter has melted and begins to sizzle, add the onions and garlic. Cook, stirring, for about 8 minutes or until the onions are soft. Season with half the thyme and some salt and pepper. Add the celery, half of the basil, and half of the parsley. Cook 5 minutes, stirring frequently, or until the celery is just beginning to soften.
2. Meanwhile, place the bread in a large bowl and mix in the remaining thyme, basil, and parsley; the dried fruit mixture; and the pecans. Pour the celery mixture from the skillet on top of the bread and gently toss to mix all of the ingredients. Place the skillet back over low heat. Add 1 cup milk and the remaining 1 Tbsp. butter and simmer for 2 to 4 minutes, using a spatula to scrape up any bits on the bottom of the skillet. Pour 1 cup of the hot milk mixture over the bread and toss; the stuffing should be somewhat moist. If the stuffing seems dry, add the remaining ½ cup milk. Season to taste. Use to stuff Marmalade-Glazed Roast Turkey, page 255. Makes 8 to 10 (½-cup) servings plus leftovers.
EACH SERVING *107 cal, 5 g fat, 3 mg chol, 127 mg sodium, 14 g carb, 2 g fiber, 2 g pro.*

Roasted Acorn Squash and Beet Salad

"This is a perfect make-ahead salad," Jonathan says. "The beets, squash, and dressing can all be prepped ahead and refrigerated overnight. Then add it all to the salad greens and serve the salad at room temperature."
PREP 30 min. BAKE 1 hr. 10 min.
OVEN 400°F

1   lb. small yellow, red, and/or Chioggia beets
1   acorn squash (1¼ lb.), peeled, seeded, and cut into ½-inch slices
1   Tbsp. olive oil
⅓   cup maple syrup
1   tsp. Dijon mustard
¼   cup fresh lemon juice
¼   cup maple syrup
⅓   cup olive oil
3   cups mixed greens
⅓   cup fresh pomegranate seeds

1. Preheat oven to 400°F. Tightly wrap beets, separated by color, in aluminum foil bundles. Place on middle oven shelf. Roast 45 minutes to 1 hour or until tender when tested with a sharp knife. Remove from oven; cool slightly. Peel beets and set aside.
2. Place squash slices on a rimmed baking sheet. Toss with salt, pepper, and 1 Tbsp. olive oil. Place on middle shelf in oven; roast 15 minutes. Drizzle ⅓ cup maple syrup over squash and roast another 10 minutes or until tender; cool.
3. To make dressing, in a small bowl whisk the mustard, lemon juice, and ¼ cup maple syrup together. Add the ⅓ cup olive oil and whisk until smooth. Season to taste.
4. To assemble, place salad greens in middle of a large plate. Arrange beets and squash on lettuce. Pour half of dressing over salad. Sprinkle with pomegranate seeds. Pass remaining dressing. Makes 6 to 8 servings.
EACH SERVING *281 cal, 15 g fat, 0 mg chol, 379 mg sodium, 38 g carb, 4 g fiber, 2 g pro.*

ROASTED
ACORN
SQUASH
AND BEET
SALAD

MOLASSES
SPICE CAKE
WITH FRESH
BLUEBERRY
JAM COMPOTE
AND PUMPKIN
ICE CREAM

Molasses Spice Cake

"This is such a nice spice cake to serve all through the holidays—it's so versatile," Jonathan says. "We'll serve it with Fresh Blueberry Jam Compote for Thanksgiving, but it is equally good with just a sprinkling of powdered sugar."

PREP **25 min.** BAKE **18 min.**
COOL **10 min.** OVEN **350°F**

2½ cups all-purpose flour
1 tsp. baking soda
¾ tsp. ground cloves
½ cup butter, softened
¾ cup packed brown sugar
2 eggs
¾ cup mild-flavor molasses
⅔ cup milk
1 recipe Fresh Blueberry Jam Compote
   Finely shredded lemon peel

1. Preheat oven to 350°F. Grease and lightly flour three 8×2-inch round pans; set aside. In a small bowl stir together flour, baking soda, and cloves; set aside.
2. In a large bowl beat butter with an electric mixer on medium speed for 30 seconds. Add brown sugar; beat until well mixed. Beat in eggs until fluffy. Beat in molasses on low speed.
3. Alternately add flour mixture and milk, beating on low speed after every addition just until combined. Divide batter evenly into prepared pans, spreading to level.
4. Bake 18 to 20 minutes or until a toothpick inserted near center comes out clean. Cool in pans on wire racks for 10 minutes. Remove from pans; cool completely on rack.
5. To assemble the cake, place one layer on a serving plate. Spoon about ¾ cup Fresh Blueberry Jam Compote over this layer, allowing it to flow down the side. Repeat with remaining layers and jam. Sprinkle with lemon peel. Makes 8 to 10 servings.
EACH SERVING *553 cal, 14 g fat, 79 mg chol, 309 mg sodium, 100 g carb, 3 g fiber, 7 g pro.*

Fresh Blueberry Jam Compote

"Make this jam up to two days ahead and refrigerate it," Jonathan says. "Its bright, sweet berry flavor goes really well with the richly flavored Molasses Spice Cake."

PREP **15 min.** COOK **7 min.**

⅓ cup sugar
1 Tbsp. cornstarch
3 cups fresh or frozen blueberries
⅓ cup orange juice
¼ cup mild-flavor molasses
3 Tbsp. blueberry brandy or orange juice

1. In a large saucepan combine sugar and cornstarch. Stir in 2 cups of the blueberries, the orange juice, molasses, and brandy. Bring to boiling; reduce heat. Cook and stir over medium heat until thickened and bubbly. Stir in remaining blueberries and cook 2 minutes more. Cool slightly.
2. To store, cover and chill for up to 2 weeks. Makes 2½ cups.
PER TBSP. *23 cal, 0 g fat, 0 mg chol, 1 mg sodium, 5 g carb, 0 g fiber, 0 g pro.*

Pumpkin Ice Cream

"Serve a scoop or two of this alongside a slice of the Molasses Spice Cake," Jonathan says. "As the ice cream melts, it will turn into a creamy sauce for the cake to soak up."

PREP **10 min.** COOK **8 min.** CHILL **3 hr.**
FREEZE **According to manufacturer's instructions**

3 cups half-and-half
¾ cup packed brown sugar
5 egg yolks
1 tsp. pumpkin pie spice
¼ tsp. salt
1 Tbsp. cognac or brandy (optional)
1 tsp. vanilla
1 cup canned pumpkin

1. In a medium saucepan combine the half-and-half and brown sugar. Cook over medium heat, stirring to dissolve sugar, about 4 minutes until bubbles form around the edges of the pan.

2. In a small bowl whisk together the egg yolks, pumpkin pie spice, and salt. Gradually whisk about ½ cup of the hot half-and-half mixture into the egg mixture and continue to whisk until smooth. Pour the egg mixture into the half-and-half mixture in the pan. Cook and stir over medium heat until the mixture coats the back of a large metal spoon, about 4 minutes. Do not boil. Strain mixture through a fine-mesh sieve into a large bowl. Stir in the cognac, if desired, and vanilla. Whisk the pumpkin into the mixture until thoroughly combined. Cover surface with plastic wrap to prevent a skin from forming and refrigerate until well chilled, at least 3 hours or overnight.
3. Pour the pumpkin custard into a 1½- or 2-quart ice cream maker; freeze according to the manufacturer's directions. Pack the ice cream into a freezer-safe container. Cover and freeze until firm, at least 3 hours or up to 3 days, before serving. Makes 10 (½-cup) servings.
EACH SERVING *195 cal, 11 g fat, 119 mg chol, 98 mg sodium, 22 g carb, 1 g fiber, 4 g pro.*

Home Cooking

TIME FOR PIE Bake along with pie maker and cookbook author Gesine Bullock-Prado as she shares mouthwatering recipes and tips for the sweetest (and most beautiful!) holiday desserts.

No other dessert says autumn quite like pie. "It's the time of year when you're waiting and waiting for all of those delicious harvest flavors, and then all at once, boom, the season is here," says Gesine Bullock-Prado, author of *Pie It Forward*. Cranberries, apples, plums, clementines, and, of course, pumpkins—all are the base for big fall flavor. "If you're seeing it at the grocery store, you should be baking with it," she says. Here Gesine shares four must-try flavor combinations, techniques for decorative touches, and tips for ensuring pie success. So grab your rolling pin because after the biggest of Thanksgiving meals, there's always room for dessert.

"A great pie is worth every drop of effort."

Gesine's tricks for a really spectacular pie:

1. "Make sure your work surface is cool enough that when you roll out the dough it doesn't start melting," Gesine says. Work away from the hot cooking areas in the kitchen. Flour the surface, rolling pin, and top of the dough. "I roll from the middle and make ⅛ turns to make it as round as I can," she says.

2. With particularly juicy fruit, Gesine sprinkles "crust dust" (equal parts sugar and cornstarch) over the bottom crust to absorb some of the juice and ensure a cooked pastry.

3. An elegant pastry web created with a lattice roller is a showstopper. "If you don't have a lattice roller, a traditional lattice or even a double crust with a few decorative cutouts on top to vent are great options," she says.

4. Work quickly with the latticed dough. "It's already a delicate dough and will get even more fragile the warmer it gets," Gesine says. Gently roll crust onto a floured rolling pin to transfer it to the top of the filled pie, and use your fingers to carefully spread the lattice apart. "Don't worry about being perfect," Gesine says. "There's beauty in those bumps and imperfections."

5. Give the crust edge a flourish. "My philosophy is that pie should be beautiful and reflect the occasion," she says. For this autumn pie, Gesine uses a small leaf piecrust cutter that cuts out and embosses leftover dough for the edge.

6. A bit of egg wash around the crust keeps decorative cutouts in place.

7. Gesine's finishing touches are an egg wash for perfect browning and a sprinkle of coarse sugar. "It gives a little sparkle and sweet crunch," she says.

"I love how unexpected cherries are for fall, and they give sweet balance to something tart like cranberries."

Caramel Apple-Cherry Pie

PREP 2 hr. CHILL 40 min.
BAKE 1 hr. 15 min. OVEN 375°F/350°F

1   Recipe Gesine's Piecrust, page 275
Cranberry Compote
1   12-oz. bag fresh cranberries
1   cup granulated sugar
¼   cup orange juice
2   tsp. finely shredded orange peel
20 fresh sweet cherries, pitted, or
    1 cup frozen unsweetened pitted
    dark sweet cherries
Caramel Apple Filling
8   tart baking apples, such as Granny
    Smith, peeled, cored, and sliced
    ¼ inch thick (2 to 2¼ lb.)
2   Tbsp. lemon juice
1   tsp. finely shredded lemon peel
1   cup packed dark brown sugar
¼   cup all-purpose flour
1   tsp. ground cinnamon
2   Tbsp. unsalted butter
¼   cup whipping cream
1   tsp. vanilla bean paste or pure
    vanilla extract
1   egg
2   to 3 Tbsp. coarse sugar

1. Prepare Gesine's Piecrust. Divide pastry into 3 balls. Combine 2 to form 1 large ball. Wrap both balls and refrigerate 20 minutes.
2. For Cranberry Compote, in a small saucepan combine cranberries, granulated sugar, orange juice, orange peel, and a pinch of salt. Cook over medium heat until the cranberries begin to burst and mixture begins to thicken, stirring occasionally. Carefully stir in cherries. Remove from heat; cool.
3. For Caramel Apple Filling, in a large bowl gently toss together apples, lemon juice, and lemon peel. In a small bowl stir together brown sugar, flour, cinnamon, and ½ tsp. salt. Sprinkle over apples; stir gently to coat.
4. In a large pot melt butter over medium heat. Add apple mixture. Cook about 5 minutes, stirring frequently. Add whipping cream and vanilla. Continue cooking, stirring often, until juices thicken and apples are tender, about 5 minutes. Remove from heat; cool completely.
5. Preheat oven to 375°F. On a lightly floured surface use your hands to slightly flatten the large pastry ball. Roll pastry from center to edges into a circle 13 inches in diameter. Transfer to a 9-inch deep-dish pie plate with a flat-edge rim. Trim pastry 1 inch beyond pie plate edge. Turn edges under, pressing down on rim. Prick bottom and sides of pastry with a fork. Wrap and refrigerate 20 minutes.
6. Line dough with parchment; fill to top with dried beans or pie weights. Bake 20 minutes. Remove parchment and weights; bake 2 to 3 minutes more or until lightly golden brown. Cool on a wire rack. Reduce oven to 350ºF.

7. Roll out the remaining ball to ⅛ inch thick. Using 1½- to 2-inch leaf or acorn cookie cutters, stamp out shapes; transfer to a parchment-lined sheet pan.
8. Using a slotted spoon, spoon one-third of the cranberry mixture into the bottom of the prebaked crust. Layer half the apple mixture on top of the cranberries. Spoon another third of the cranberry mixture on top of the apples in random dollops. Spoon over remaining apples. Spoon remaining cranberry mixture on top in random dollops, leaving pockets of apple visible on top (placing the cranberry mixture in little pockets keeps the apples from being dyed red). Leave the flat edge of the crust free from filling.
9. Whisk together egg and 2 Tbsp. water; gently brush on edge of crust. Place some of the cutouts on the edge, pressing gently to adhere. Place remaining cutouts on top of filling; brush with egg wash. Sprinkle with coarse sugar.
10. Place a foil-lined baking sheet on rack below pie in oven to catch any dripping. Bake 40 minutes. Cover edges with foil; bake 10 to 15 minutes more or until crust is deep golden brown and filling is bubbly. Cool on wire rack at least 3 hours before serving. Makes 10 servings.
EACH SERVING *567 cal, 24 g fat, 82 mg chol, 385 mg sodium, 88 g carb, 5 g fiber, 5 g pro.*

CARAMEL APPLE-
CHERRY PIE

"Clementines are everywhere come Thanksgiving, and after a heavy meal it's so nice to have that sweet, citrusy spark. Their mellow flavor pairs beautifully with anything creamy."

Clementine Chess Pie

PREP **1 hr.** CHILL **1 hr. 5 min.**
BAKE **55 min.** OVEN **350°F**

1   recipe Shortbread Crust
1½ cups sugar
½   cup unsalted butter, softened
2   tsp. all-purpose flour
2   tsp. fine cornmeal
5   eggs
2   drops orange food coloring (optional)
¾   cup crème fraîche
3   Tbsp. clementine or orange juice
1   Tbsp. lemon juice
1   tsp. finely grated clementine or orange peel
2   tsp. finely grated lemon peel
1   tsp. vanilla extract
1   recipe Quick Candied Clementines

1. Preheat oven to 350°F. Prepare Shortbread Crust. Crumble two-thirds of the shortbread dough over the surface of a 9-inch deep-dish pie plate. Gently press dough evenly onto bottom and sides; trim excess. Prick bottom and sides of pastry with a fork. Chill 45 minutes. Line pan with parchment; fill to the top with dried beans or pie weights. Bake 15 minutes. Carefully remove parchment and weights; loosely cover with foil. Bake 5 to 8 minutes

more or until dough begins to brown. Cool on a wire rack.
2. For filling, in a large mixing bowl beat together sugar, butter, and a pinch of salt until light and fluffy. Add flour and cornmeal; mix until just incorporated. Add eggs, one at a time, until incorporated, scraping down sides of bowl between additions. Add orange food coloring, if desired.
3. In a small bowl whisk together crème fraîche, clementine and lemon juices and peels, and vanilla; beat into butter and sugar mixture. Scrape down sides; mix until incorporated. (It may look curdled—this is OK.) Pour into prepared crust. Bake 35 to 40 minutes or until pie is just set but still has a very slight wiggle in center. Cool on a wire rack.
4. Prepare gold cookie medallions (see "Golden Dress-Up," right) and Quick Candied Clementines. Serve on pie. Makes 10 servings.

Shortbread Crust In the bowl of a food processor fitted with the blade attachment combine 1 cup all-purpose flour, 6 Tbsp. unsalted butter (cold and cut into small pieces), ½ cup cornstarch, ¼ cup sugar, and ½ tsp. salt. Pulse until mixture resembles coarse cornmeal. In a small bowl whisk together 1 egg yolk, 2 Tbsp. cold water, and 1 tsp. vanilla extract until well combined. While pulsing, slowly pour egg mixture into flour mixture. Pulse until just moistened; turn onto plastic wrap. Gently knead until any dry patches are incorporated. Wrap and refrigerate at least 20 minutes.

Quick Candied Clementines Cut 2 clementines into paper-thin slices; brush generously with melted orange marmalade; let dry completely.

EACH SERVING *469 cal, 26 g fat, 178 mg chol, 184 mg sodium, 55 g carb, 1 g fiber, 5 g pro.*

GOLDEN DRESS-UP
Gesine uses an embossed cookie stamp and a round cutter to make medallions out of extra Shortbread Crust dough. "Edible gold spray adds sparkle—like autumn light hitting golden leaves," she says. Roll dough to ⅛ inch thick; stamp and cut out cookies. Bake at 350°F for 5 to 10 minutes. Cool completely; spray with Wilton Gold Color Mist ($4.29; wilton.com).

"Pumpkin is so iconic. Each Thanksgiving is a chance to try something new. Play with your spices, try a marshmallowy meringue, mix up the crust, but don't skip the pumpkin pie—it's like leaving out the turkey."

KID FRIENDLY

Caramel Cream Pumpkin Pie

This pie has two layers—one smooth, custardy caramel and one fluffy, light caramel-pumpkin. It takes time, but just one bite is worth every minute.

PREP **1 hr. 45 min.** BAKE **30 min.** CHILL **6 hr. 50 min** OVEN **375ºF**

1   recipe Gesine's Piecrust, page 275
1   cup granulated sugar
1   tsp. lemon juice
2   cups half-and-half
8   egg yolks (reserve whites for Meringue Topping)
⅓   cup packed dark brown sugar
¼   cup cornstarch
1   tsp. vanilla bean paste or pure vanilla extract
4   tsp. unflavored gelatin
1   cup pumpkin puree or canned pumpkin (room temperature)
½   tsp. ground cinnamon
¼   tsp. each ground nutmeg, cloves, and ginger
6   drops orange food coloring (optional)
½   cup whipping cream
1   recipe Meringue Topping

1. Prepare Gesine's Piecrust. Divide pastry into 3 balls. Combine 2 to form 1 large ball; wrap and refrigerate 30 minutes. Reserve remaining ball for another use.
2. For filling, in a large saucepan combine granulated sugar, ⅓ cup water, and lemon juice. Stir over low heat until sugar has dissolved. Brush sides of pan with a moist pastry brush to remove clinging sugar. Increase heat to medium-high; cook until a medium amber color (slightly lighter than a penny), about 10 minutes. Remove from heat; pour in half-and-half (mixture will bubble vigorously but calm down quickly). Return to low heat; stir until caramel dissolves into cream. Keep warm.
3. In a large bowl whisk together egg yolks, brown sugar, cornstarch, vanilla, and ½ tsp. salt until well combined. While whisking, slowly pour warm caramel mixture into bowl; continue whisking until well combined. Transfer to a large saucepan; whisk over medium heat until thickened, about 8 minutes. Transfer to a large bowl; cover surface of cream completely to avoid forming a skin. Refrigerate at least 2 hours.
4. Preheat oven to 375ºF. On a lightly floured surface use your hands to slightly flatten the large pastry ball. Roll pastry from center to edges in a circle 13 inches in diameter. Transfer to a 9-inch deep-dish pie plate. Trim to ½ inch over edge; crimp edge lightly to the lip of the plate. Prick bottom and sides of pastry with a fork. Wrap and refrigerate 20 minutes.
5. Line dough with parchment; fill with dried beans or pie weights to the top. Bake 15 minutes. Remove parchment and weights; bake 15 minutes more or until lightly golden. Cool on wire rack. Once cool, spread half the caramel mixture in an even layer onto prepared crust.
6. In a large microwave-safe bowl soften gelatin in ⅔ cup water; let stand several minutes. Heat in microwave on 50 percent power 1½ to 2 minutes or until gelatin is dissolved, swirling every 30 seconds. Stir in pumpkin puree, spices, orange food coloring, if desired, and remaining half of the caramel cream.
7. In a small bowl beat whipping cream until stiff peaks form; gently fold into pumpkin mixture. Spread over caramel in prepared crust. Refrigerate at least 4 hours. Top with Meringue Topping. Makes 10 servings.

Meringue Topping In a large glass bowl combine 8 egg whites, 1⅔ cups sugar, and a pinch salt. Place bowl over a large saucepan half-filled with simmering water. Beat with a handheld electric mixer until egg whites are warm to the touch. Continue beating and remove when egg whites exceed 160ºF when tested with a candy thermometer, about 15 minutes. If necessary, continue beating until stiff, shiny peaks form.

EACH SERVING *586 cal, 26 g fat, 216 mg chol, 374 mg sodium, 80 g carb, 1 g fiber, 10 g pro.*

FLUFFY PEAKS
"You've already used the egg yolks in the filling, so use the whites to make beautifully fluffy meringue," Gesine says. "I use a pastry bag fitted with a large star tip to pipe it on, but you could also spoon it on in swirls. It's the perfect thing for kids to do—and it brings a little cloud of happiness to your table." For extra drama, brown lightly with a kitchen torch.

**CARAMEL CREAM
PUMPKIN PIE**

"Last-of-the-season plums are baking gems. They're so juicy and have the most gorgeous jewel-like color—perfect for a harvest pie as they soak up even the most subtle of spices. I love them with something like candied ginger that adds a sweet, chewy zing—just what you need to wake up after all that turkey."

KID FRIENDLY

Spiced Plum Pie

The riper your plums, the juicier your pie. "I love a pie that's so juicy you could almost eat it with a spoon," Gesine says. "But if you prefer a little less juice, choose plums that are firm to the touch."
PREP 45 min. BAKE 1 hr. 30 min.
OVEN 350°F

1   recipe Gesine's Piecrust, right
10 large dark plums, pitted and cut into quarters (3 to 3½ lb.)
¾   cup packed brown sugar
¼   cup cornstarch
2   Tbsp. chopped candied ginger
2   tsp. finely shredded orange peel
1   tsp. ground cinnamon
½   tsp. salt
¼   tsp. each ground nutmeg and cloves
1   Tbsp. vanilla bean paste or pure vanilla extract
1   Tbsp. sugar
1   Tbsp. cornstarch
1   egg
¼   cup coarse sugar

1. Preheat oven to 350°F. Prepare Gesine's Piecrust. Divide pastry in half; form halves into balls. Wrap and refrigerate 30 minutes.
2. For plum filling, in a 5- to 6-quart Dutch oven combine plums with ½ cup water. Bring to boiling; reduce heat. Simmer, covered, for 3 minutes. Remove from heat; drain well. Return plums to Dutch oven. In a small bowl stir together brown sugar, cornstarch, candied ginger, orange peel, cinnamon, salt, nutmeg, and cloves; add to plums in the Dutch oven. Add vanilla. Toss gently to combine.
3. For bottom crust, on a lightly floured surface use your hands to slightly flatten one pastry ball. Roll pastry from center to edges into a circle 12 inches in diameter, about ⅛ inch thick. Transfer to a 9-inch deep-dish pie plate without stretching. Trim pastry to ½ inch beyond edge of pie plate. In a small bowl stir together sugar and 1 Tbsp. cornstarch; sprinkle over dough. Cover with plastic wrap and refrigerate.
4. For top crust, roll remaining ball into a 12-inch-diameter circle or large rectangle. Use a lattice roller (see "Lattice Web," right) to roll through dough. Remove bottom crust from refrigerator; spoon in filling. Cover with lattice crust; trim edges. Crimp or decorate edge as desired. Whisk together egg and 1 Tbsp. water; brush on top crust. Sprinkle with coarse sugar.
5. Place a foil-lined baking sheet on the rack below the pie in the oven. Bake pie 1½ to 1¾ hours until filling is thick and bubbly and crust is golden brown. (If after 1 hour crust is already golden, gently cover with aluminum foil for remaining baking time.) Cool on a wire rack. Makes 10 servings.

Gesine's Piecrust In the bowl of a food processor fitted with the blade attachment pulse together 2 cups cold all-purpose flour, 1 cup unsalted butter (cut into small pieces and chilled in the freezer about 10 minutes), 1 Tbsp. sugar, and 1 tsp. salt until mixture resembles coarse cornmeal. In a small bowl whisk together ½ cup ice-cold water (or ¼ cup each vodka* and water) and 1 tsp. lemon juice. Slowly add to the flour mixture, pulsing until dough just comes together. Squeeze a small piece of dough between your thumb and index finger to make sure it holds its shape. Follow pie recipe for dividing and refrigerating dough.
*Alcohol forms less gluten (the protein in flour that can create tough dough) than water, so using half flavorless vodka will yield tender, easy-to-roll dough and an extra-flaky crust.
EACH SERVING *421 cal, 20 g fat, 67 mg chol, 364 mg sodium, 59 g carb, 3 g fiber, 4 g pro.*

LATTICE WEB

A lattice roller makes the top of this pie impressive enough for any bakeshop window. "It's such a fun contraption," Gesine says. "Flour the roller and be sure to push with enough pressure so it cuts through the dough."

Sides for Sharing

Skip the fuss and still have all the fixings with these quick recipes for veggies, potatoes, salads, and stuffing.

BROCCOLINI WITH PEAS AND SEARED LEMONS

Goat Cheese Mashed Sweet Potatoes

START TO FINISH 30 min.

3 lb. sweet potatoes, peeled and cubed
   Salt
½ cup half-and-half
¼ cup butter
2 ounces goat cheese
1 tsp. fresh sage
½ cup roasted and salted pistachios,
   coarsely chopped
   Fresh sage

1. Place potatoes in a large saucepan. Add enough water to cover. Bring to a boil and add salt. Reduce heat to medium-high and simmer, covered, until potatoes are tender when pierced with a knife, about 10 minutes. Drain and return to the saucepan. Heat half-and-half and butter in a glass measuring cup in the microwave for 1 minute.
2. Toast pistachios with butter and salt in a skillet. Sprinkle pistachios, additional goat cheese, and fresh sage over potatoes. Makes 12 (½-cup) servings.
EACH SERVING 209 cal, 11 g fat, 22 mg chol, 22 mg chol, 277 mg sodium, 25 g carb, 4 g fiber, 5 g pro.

GOAT CHEESE MASHED SWEET POTATOES

LOW FAT

Broccolini with Peas and Seared Lemons

PREP 25 min. COOK 6 min.

2 lbs. Broccolini, trimmed
8 oz. Swiss chard, trimmed and cut into 2- to 3-inch lengths
1 cup frozen peas
2 Tbsp. butter
1 lemon, thinly sliced
¼ cup chicken broth
¼ tsp. crushed red pepper
¼ cup chopped fresh chives
½ tsp. coarse salt

1. Bring a 6- to 8-quart pot of salted water to a boil. Add broccolini, cook for 2 minutes, and then add Swiss chard and peas. Simmer, covered, for 4 minutes or until bright green. Drain. Meanwhile, melt butter in a large skillet. Add lemon slices and cook over medium to medium-high heat until lemons are soft and browned and butter is browned, 3 minutes each side (Do not move lemons around too much so that they will get a nice sear.) Return the drained Broccolini,

Swiss chard, and peas to the pot. Add broth and crushed red pepper; toss gently. Transfer the Broccolini mixture to a serving platter and top with the lemons. Top with chives and coarse salt before serving. Makes 12 (½-cup) servings.
EACH SERVING 48 cal, 2 g fat, 5 mg chol, 186 mg sodium, 6 g carb, 2 g fiber, 2 g pro.

LOW FAT

Orange-Farro Salad

PREP 20 min. COOK 30 min.

2 oranges
1 small shallot, minced
1 Tbsp. red wine vinegar
3 Tbsp. olive oil
   Salt and ground black pepper
2 cups cooked farro or brown rice
⅓ cup pitted green olives
2 cups baby arugula

1. Peel oranges; slice 1½ oranges and juice the remaining half orange into a large bowl. Add shallot, red wine vinegar, and olive oil to bowl. Season with salt and pepper.
2. To bowl add farro, olives, and arugula. Fold in orange slices. Makes 12 (½-cup) servings.

EACH SERVING 110 cal, 4 g fat, 0 mg chol, 369 mg sodium, 15 g carb, 2 g fiber, 3 g pro.

Blue Cheese-Garlic Potatoes

PREP 20 min. COOK 12 min.

3 lb. russet or Yukon gold potatoes, peeled and cubed
1½ tsp. salt
¼ cup olive oil
2 garlic cloves, thinly sliced
4 oz. crumbled blue cheese
   Crushed red pepper flakes

1. In a Dutch oven combine potatoes, water to cover, and about half of the salt. Bring to boiling. Reduce heat and simmer, covered, until potatoes are tender, reserving ½ cup cooking water. Drain potatoes and return to pot.
2. In a skillet heat olive oil with garlic and cook for 1 minute until garlic starts to brown. Mash into potatoes along with cooking water, crumbled blue cheese, and crushed red pepper to taste. Makes 12 to 14 (½-cup) servings.
EACH SERVING 156 cal, 9 g fat, 8 mg chol, 453 mg sodium, 15 g carb, 1 g fiber, 4 g pro.

HARVEST SLAW

Parmesan Roasted Cauliflower

PREP 15 min. ROAST 25 min.
COOK 12 min. OVEN 425°F

6   cups cauliflower florets
1   Tbsp. olive oil
     Salt
     Ground black pepper
½   cup freshly shredded Parmesan cheese
¼   cup butter
2   garlic cloves, chopped
⅔   cup slivered almonds, chopped
⅔   cup panko

1. Preheat oven to 425°F. Place cauliflower in a 15×10×1-inch baking pan and toss with olive oil, salt, and pepper. Roast for 20 minutes. Toss and sprinkle with the Parmesan cheese. Roast 5 minutes more. Meanwhile, in a medium skillet melt butter. Add garlic; cook 20 seconds. Stir in almonds and bread crumbs and stir to coat with butter. Cook over medium-low to medium heat until golden. Transfer cauliflower to a serving dish and top with the almond mixture. Makes 8 to 10 (¾-cup) servings.
EACH SERVING *175 cal, 14 g fat, 19 mg chol, 319 mg sodium, 9 g carb, 3 g fiber, 6 g pro.*

Seared Brussels Sprouts

PREP 25 min. COOK 10 min.

2   Tbsp. all-purpose flour
2   shallots, thinly sliced and separated into rings
     Canola oil
     Salt and ground black pepper
2   Tbsp. olive oil
1½   lb. fresh Brussels sprouts, trimmed and halved (about 6 cups)
¼   cup white wine

1. In a small bowl place flour. Toss shallot rings in flour and let stand 10 to 15 minutes to become sticky. In a 12-inch skillet heat 1 inch of canola oil over medium-high heat. Using a slotted spoon, add half the shallots. Fry 3 to 4 minutes until crisp and dark golden brown. Remove from oil; drain. Fry remaining shallots. Sprinkle with salt; set aside. Pour frying oil from skillet and wipe clean.
2. Add 1 Tbsp. of the olive oil to the skillet and return to medium heat. Arrange half

Honey Balsamic Beet Salad

PREP 20 min. ROAST 40 min.
OVEN 400°F

2   lb. baby beets, trimmed and scrubbed
½   cup balsamic vinegar
1   Tbsp. olive oil
1   Tbsp. honey
⅛   tsp. salt
⅛   tsp. ground black pepper
2   cups watercress or arugula
1½   cups cooked quinoa
     Chopped fresh tarragon

1. In a 3-quart rectangular baking dish place beets. In a small bowl whisk together the balsamic vinegar, olive oil, and honey. Pour over beets. Sprinkle with salt and pepper. Cover; roast 40 minutes or until beets are tender.
2. On a platter combine watercress, quinoa, and beets. Drizzle with the roasting liquid. Top with chopped tarragon. Makes 8 to 10 (½-cup) servings.
EACH SERVING *113 cal, 3 g fat, 0 mg chol, 106 mg sodium, 20 g carb, 3 g fiber, 3 g pro.*

Harvest Slaw

START TO FINISH 30 min.

3   Tbsp. olive oil
2   garlic cloves, coarsely chopped
2   tsp. caraway seeds, lightly crushed
¼   cup cider vinegar
1   Tbsp. honey
     Salt and ground black pepper
4   cups finely shredded red cabbage
2   red apples, cored and thinly sliced
½   cup dried cranberries
½   cup pecan halves, toasted
2   Tbsp. cilantro or parsley leaves

1. In a large skillet heat olive oil over medium heat. Add garlic and caraway seeds; cook and stir 1 minute. Whisk in vinegar and honey; bring to a simmer. Season with salt and pepper.
2. In a bowl toss together the cabbage, apples, cranberries, and pecans. Add dressing and toss to combine. Top with cilantro. Makes 12 (¾-cup) servings.
EACH SERVING *108 cal, 7 g fat, 0 mg chol, 56 mg sodium, 13 g carb, 2 g fiber, 1 g pro.*

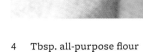

the sprouts, cut sides down, in the hot skillet. Cook, uncovered, 3 to 4 minutes or until the sprouts are well browned. Remove sprouts from pan. Repeat with remaining olive oil and sprouts. Return reserved sprouts to the skillet. Add wine and scrape any browned bits from the bottom. Cover and cook 4 to 6 minutes or until tender. Season with salt and pepper. Transfer to a serving dish and top with crispy shallots. Makes 8 (¾-cup) servings.
EACH SERVING *144 cal, 10 g fat, 0 mg chol, 59 mg sodium, 10 g carb, 3 g fiber, 3 g pro.*

KID FRIENDLY

Corn Bread Stuffing with Sausage

PREP 25 min. BAKE 45 min.
OVEN 325°F

8	corn bread muffins, broken into large pieces (4 cups)
8	oz. bulk pork sausage
1	cup onion wedges
4	cups fresh spinach
1	tsp. fennel seeds, crushed
½	tsp. salt
¼	tsp. ground black pepper
1	to 1⅓ cups chicken or turkey broth

1. Preheat oven to 325°F. Spread corn bread in a 15×10×1-inch baking pan. Bake, uncovered, for 10 minutes stirring once. Cool on a wire rack.
2. In a large skillet cook sausage until browned. Drain fat, reserving 1 Tbsp. of drippings. Set sausage aside. In the same skillet cook onion in reserved drippings for 3 to 5 minutes or until starting to brown. Stir in spinach, fennel, salt, and pepper. In a large bowl combine corn bread pieces, sausage, and spinach mixture. Drizzle with broth, tossing gently to combine. Spoon into a 2-quart round baking dish.
3. Bake, uncovered, 45 minutes or until top is browned and heated through. Makes 11 (½-cup) servings.
EACH SERVING *166 cal, 9 g fat, 26 mg chol, 499 mg sodium, 16 g carb, 1 g fiber, 5 g pro.*

FAST

Creamed Kale

START TO FINISH 30 min.

1¾	lb. fresh kale (about 2 bunches)
¼	cup butter
1	medium onion, chopped (½ cup)
4	Tbsp. all-purpose flour
1½	cups milk
1½	oz. Gruyère cheese or finely shredded Parmesan cheese (⅓ cup)
¼	tsp. crushed red pepper
⅛	tsp. ground nutmeg

1. Trim and discard stems from kale. Thoroughly wash and drain. Cut kale into ½-inch-wide ribbons; set aside.
2. For sauce, in a medium skillet melt butter over medium heat. Add onion and cook about 5 minutes or until tender. Stir in flour. Add milk all at once; cook and stir until thickened and bubbly. Cook and stir for 1 minute more. Stir in ⅓ cup cheese, nutmeg, and crushed red pepper. Keep warm.
3. Meanwhile, bring an 8-quart Dutch oven or kettle of lightly salted water to boiling. Gradually add kale to boiling water; cook for 5 minutes or until tender. Drain well. Return to Dutch oven or kettle. Stir sauce into cooked kale. Heat through. Makes 7 (½-cup) servings.
EACH SERVING *207 cal, 12 g fat, 33 mg chol, 251 mg sodium, 18 g carb, 3 g fiber, 9 g pro.*

FAST

Harvest Succotash

START TO FINISH 25 min.

2	slices bacon, chopped
1	clove garlic, sliced
4	cups finely chopped mustard greens
1	12-oz. package frozen corn kernels, thawed (2½ cups)
1	10-oz. package frozen lima beans (2 cups)
¾	cup half-and-half or light cream
2	Tbsp. snipped fresh sage
½	tsp. salt
¼	tsp. ground black pepper

1. In a 12-inch large skillet cook bacon over medium heat until crisp. Remove bacon from skillet and drain on paper towels. Add garlic to skillet. Cook for 30 seconds. Stir in the mustard greens, corn, and beans; cook and stir 3 minutes or until mustard greens soften. Stir in half-and-half, sage, salt, and pepper. Bring to boiling. Transfer to a serving dish. Sprinkle with reserved bacon. Makes 8 (½-cup) servings.
EACH SERVING *170 cal, 7 g fat, 15 mg chol, 262 mg sodium, 21 g carb, 4 g fiber, 7 g pro.*

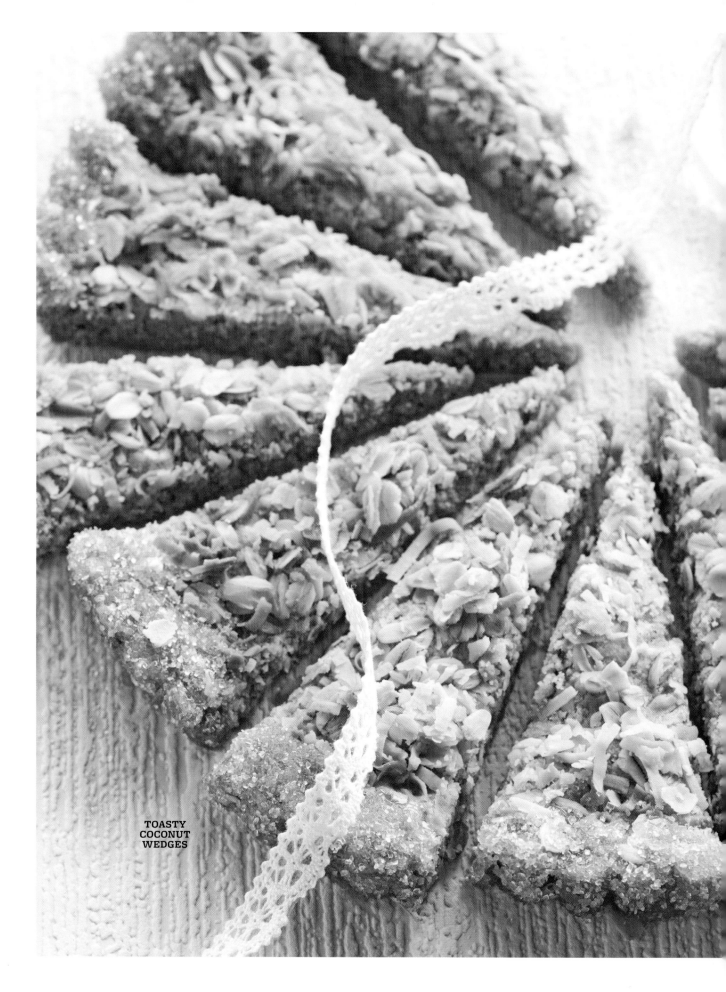

TOASTY
COCONUT
WEDGES

HOLIDAY TIME IS HERE Create cookies for your dessert plate that are as beautiful as they are delicious. And let chef Melissa Perello guide you through hosting the holiday meal—stress-free style.

285

293

296

ROSEMARY-SCENTED
EVERGREENS

...and Nature Sings

Gather round our woodland-inspired cookie collection. From zingy gingerbread "twigs" and sugar-and-spice-dusted "bark" to glitter-capped "evergreens," these edible (and easy-to-make) wonders sparkle on any holiday dessert plate.

Rosemary-Scented Evergreens

The bold, piney quality of fresh rosemary is tamed and seems only gently herbal, which most people find both intriguing and enticing. The cookies also have a noticeable crisp-tender texture.

PREP 40 min. CHILL 1 hr.
BAKE 8 min. per batch
COOL 3 min. OVEN 350°F

¾ cup plus 2 Tbsp. powdered sugar
3½ Tbsp. finely chopped fresh rosemary
2   tsp. finely shredded lemon peel
⅛ tsp. salt
1   cup unsalted butter, slightly softened and cut into chunks
¼ cup granulated sugar
1   Tbsp. orange juice
2   tsp. vanilla
3⅓ cups unbleached all-purpose flour
2   cups powdered sugar
    Gold decorating sugar

1. Position a rack in middle of oven. Preheat to 350°F. Line a baking sheet with parchment. Set out 6 additional large pieces of parchment.
2. In a food processor combine powdered sugar, rosemary, lemon peel, and salt. Cover and process for 2 to 4 minutes or until rosemary is pulverized into very fine bits but not pureed. Reserve 6 Tbsp. of the rosemary-sugar mixture; set aside.
3. In a large bowl add remaining rosemary-sugar mixture, butter, granulated sugar, orange juice, and vanilla. Beat with an electric mixer on medium speed about 2 minutes or until well blended and lightened in color, scraping sides of bowl occasionally. Beat in half the flour on low speed. Beat or stir in remaining flour until smoothly incorporated.
4. Divide dough into thirds. Roll each portion to a scant ¼-inch thickness between 2 pieces of parchment. Check undersides; smooth out wrinkles. Stack dough portions with parchment on the baking sheet. Refrigerate for 1 hour until firm. (To speed chilling, freeze for 20 to 30 minutes.)
5. Working with one dough portion (keep others chilled), peel off one piece of parchment; pat dough back into place. Invert dough; peel off and discard second piece of parchment. Using a 3-inch Christmas tree cutter, cut out dough (for larger cookies, see "Cut and Create," right). Using a spatula, place cookies about 2 inches apart on baking sheets. If dough becomes too soft to work with, return to the refrigerator or freezer until firm.
6. Bake one sheet at a time for 8 to 11 minutes or until lightly browned on the edges (watch carefully as they brown rapidly near the end of baking). Transfer to a wire rack; let cool until firm, about 3 minutes. Using a wide spatula, gently transfer cookies to wire rack. Cool completely before icing.
7. For icing, stir reserved rosemary-sugar mixture through a very fine sieve into a small, deep bowl. Add additional powdered sugar and 2 to 3 Tbsp. water. Stir until well blended and smooth. If necessary, stir in more water or more powdered sugar to yield piping consistency.
8. Place cookies, slightly separated, on a wire rack set over waxed paper. Using a piping bag fitted with a fine writing tip,* pipe around cookie edge. Sprinkle with gold sugar. Let stand until icing sets, at least 30 minutes. Thin remaining icing with water; fill in the piped borders. Let stand at least 30 minutes more (preferably longer before packing airtight). Makes 44 3-inch cookies or 4 11-inch cookies.
*If you don't have a piping bag, use a heavy resealable plastic bag with the tip of one corner snipped off.

EACH 3-INCH COOKIE *107 cal, 4 g fat, 11 mg chol, 8 mg sodium, 16 g carb, 0 g fiber, 1 g pro.*

CUT AND CREATE
To make a showstopping large cookie, trace around a tree cutter on a sheet of paper. Use a copy machine to increase size to about 11 inches long; use scissors to cut out shape. Press fresh rosemary sprigs into cookie, if desired. Use dough scraps to form star for top of cookie. Bake 15 minutes for large tree and 8 to 10 minutes for stars or until faintly browned on the edges. Pipe and decorate. Glaze star and attach with icing; sprinkle with gold sugar.

Fruit and Nut Biscotti Logs

These quietly handsome, not-too-sweet biscotti are crunchy-crisp but have a slight chew from golden raisins.

PREP 30 min. **BAKE** 43 min.
STAND 10 min. **OVEN** 325°F

¾ cup sugar
5 Tbsp. unsalted butter, melted and cooled
2½ tsp. vanilla
1 tsp. baking powder
¾ tsp. almond extract
½ tsp. salt
2 large eggs
2 large egg whites
1 cup golden raisins and/or snipped dried apricots
1½ cups lightly salted dry-roasted pistachio nuts, chopped
2½ cups unbleached all-purpose flour

1. Preheat oven to 325°F. Lightly coat two 8×4×2-inch (or similar) loaf pans with nonstick spray. Line a large baking sheet with parchment; set aside.
2. In a large bowl stir together sugar, butter, vanilla, baking powder, almond extract, and salt. Beat or vigorously stir in eggs and egg whites until evenly incorporated. Fold in raisins, then nuts until thoroughly incorporated. Gradually stir in flour until very well blended (if desired, work in last of it with your hands). If dough seems very soft or sticky, let stand to firm up for 5 minutes.
3. Divide dough in half; place each half in a loaf pan. Using greased hands, press dough to the edges until smooth on top and evenly thick all over. (Alternatively, line a large baking sheet with parchment. Using greased hands, shape and smooth each half into an 8×4-inch, evenly thick loaf, spacing them as far apart as possible on the sheet.)

4. Bake for 24 to 28 minutes or until edges are tinged with brown and a toothpick tested in the center comes out clean. Set aside; cool completely. Refrigerate until lightly chilled for easier cutting. Transfer to a cutting board. Using a large, serrated knife, cut each log into about ¼-inch-thick slices. Using a spatula, transfer slices to prepared baking sheet, laying flat and slightly separated.
5. Return to oven. Bake slices until toasted and lightly tinged with brown, 12 to 15 minutes. Cool slightly. Gently turn over. Bake 7 to 10 minutes longer until just barely tinged, watching closely to avoid overbrowning. Turn off oven. Let stand in oven to crisp 10 minutes longer. Remove from oven; cool completely. Makes 36 cookies.
EACH COOKIE 113 cal, 4 g fat, 15 mg chol, 77 mg sodium, 16 g carb, 1 g fiber, 3 g pro.

FRUIT AND NUT BISCOTTI LOGS

Chocolaty Cookie Stones

Both fresh and dried sweetened cranberries add zip to these colorful, flavorful, super-convenient cookies. Due to the use of some oil instead of all butter, they don't freeze hard and can be sliced immediately upon removal from the freezer.

PREP **45 min.** STAND **10 min.**
FREEZE **1 hr.** BAKE **11 min. per batch**
COOL **3 min.** OVEN **350°F**

⅔ cup sugar
1 Tbsp. finely shredded orange peel
1¼ cups dried sweetened cranberries
½ cup fresh (or partly thawed, frozen) cranberries
½ cup semisweet chocolate pieces
½ cup unsalted butter, slightly softened
⅓ cup corn oil, canola oil, or other flavorless vegetable oil
2 tsp. vanilla extract
¼ tsp. salt
2½ cups unbleached all-purpose white flour
¼ tsp. baking soda
2 Tbsp. orange juice concentrate

1. In a food processor combine half the sugar and the orange peel. Cover and process until sugar is colored and very fragrant, about 30 seconds. Add dried and fresh cranberries and ½ cup chocolate pieces. Pulse until chopped moderately fine but not pureed. (Chocolate bits should be ⅛ inch or smaller or dough will be hard to slice.)

2. In a large bowl beat butter, oil, remaining sugar, vanilla, and salt with an electric mixer on low speed until evenly blended. Beat in half the flour and the baking soda until evenly incorporated. Vigorously stir in orange-sugar mixture and orange juice concentrate until thoroughly incorporated. Stir in remaining flour until evenly incorporated. If dough is slightly dry or crumbly, gradually knead in 1 to 2 tsp. more orange juice concentrate until cohesive. Let stand about 10 minutes or until soft but not sticky.

3. Divide dough in half; place each on a 12-inch square of plastic wrap. With lightly oiled hands, use plastic to shape each into an evenly thick 11½-inch-long log. Roll each log in plastic wrap; twist ends to close (see "Well Rounded," right). Freeze at least 1 hour before slicing.

4. Position a rack in middle of oven; preheat to 350°F. Line baking sheets with parchment; set aside.

5. Working with one dough portion (keep the other frozen) slice crosswise into ¼-inch slices. Place slices about 1½ inches apart on baking sheets. If dough becomes too soft to work with, return to freezer until firm. Repeat with second portion.

6. Bake one baking sheet at a time for 7 minutes. Rotate from front to back; bake 4 to 6 minutes more or until cookies are faintly tinged and rimmed with brown at the edges (watch carefully—they brown rapidly near the end of baking). Transfer to a wire rack; let cool until cookies firm up, about 3 minutes. Using a wide spatula, transfer cookies to wire rack. Cool completely. Dip in melted chocolate, if desired. Makes 60 cookies.

EACH COOKIE *84 cal, 4 g fat, 14 mg chol, 29 mg sodium, 12 g carb, 6 g fiber, 1 g pro.*

CHOCOLATY COOKIE STONES

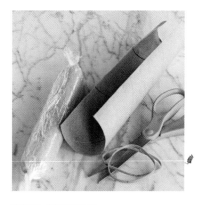

WELL ROUNDED
To keep slice-and-bake dough logs round, slip them into discarded paper towel tubes that have been cut lengthwise. Use tape or rubber bands to secure. Label logs with recipe name and baking instructions. Chill or freeze per recipe instructions.

SPICY
GINGERBREAD
TWIGS

This gingerbread is as grabbable and munchable as breadsticks. Coarse sugar "glitter" only enhances their crunchy snap, and ground red pepper adds a nippy bite if you choose. They're oh-so-hard to resist! Tie them up in little bundles for gift giving.

KID FRIENDLY | **LOW FAT**
Spicy Gingerbread Twigs

These cookies look like pretzel sticks and have crackerlike crunch but serve up the sweet taste and aroma of gingerbread cookies.

PREP 35 min. BAKE 23 min. per batch
OVEN 350°F/200°F

2   cups unbleached all-purpose flour
⅓   cup packed dark brown sugar
1   Tbsp. ground cinnamon
2   tsp. ground ginger
½   tsp. salt
½   tsp. ground cloves
½   tsp. ground allspice
¼   tsp. ground cayenne pepper (optional)
⅓   cup unsalted butter, melted and cooled
⅓   cup mild or medium molasses (not blackstrap)
¼   cup brewed coffee, cooled
⅓   cup coarse clear or green sugar, coarse sugar, or other plain coarse sparkling sugar
     White or clear edible decorating glitter (optional)

1. Position a rack in middle of oven; preheat to 350°F. Set aside two large baking sheets and four 15-inch-long pieces of parchment.
2. In a large bowl stir together flour, brown sugar, cinnamon, ginger, salt, cloves, allspice, and cayenne pepper, if using, until well blended. Thoroughly mash out sugar lumps with the back of a spoon.
3. In a small bowl whisk together butter, molasses, and coffee until very well blended. Immediately vigorously stir into flour mixture until evenly incorporated. Knead dough with your hands for 30 seconds to make it smoother and more malleable. If dough is too dry or crumbly to roll out, work in a few drops of water until

it holds together; if too wet, thoroughly knead in 1 to 2 Tbsp. more flour.
4. Divide dough in half. Roll each portion between two pieces of parchment into a 6×12-inch rectangle. If necessary, cut and patch to make sides even. (Don't worry about making it perfect.) Peel off top piece of parchment. Evenly sprinkle each portion of dough with about 3 Tbsp. coarse sugar. If desired, sprinkle each with about 1 Tbsp. edible glitter. Lay parchment over dough; pat and press all over to imbed sugar. Remove top piece of parchment.
5. Using a pizza cutter or a large knife, cut each piece of dough into a grid of ¼ to ⅓×6-inch sticks (see "Clean Cut," right). Leave the uneven edges. Slide cookie grids and parchment onto baking sheets.
6. Working with one grid at a time, bake for 13 to 16 minutes or until just firm when pressed in the center top and uneven edges are browned. Immediately slide cookie grid and parchment onto a cutting board. Cut away and discard the uneven, overbake edges. Quickly (before grid cools and becomes brittle) retrace the cuts between sticks. (If necessary, return grid to the oven; warm until soft enough to work with.)
7. Reduce oven to 200°F. When cool enough to handle, use your hands to gently separate sticks. Place sticks on a parchment-lined baking sheet, placing underdone ones around the perimeter. If desired, sprinkle with edible glitter. Bake for 10 minutes. Slide sticks and parchment onto a wire rack; cool completely. Makes 80 gingerbread sticks.
EACH GINGERBREAD STICK *29 cal, 1 g fat, 2 mg chol, 16 mg sodium, 5 g carb, 0 g fiber, 0 g pro.*

CLEAN CUT
To easily cut the gingerbread into sticks, use a ruler and a pizza cutter to slice through gingerbread dough. Don't worry if they aren't all exactly the same.

KEEP 'EM FRESH
Here are a few must-dos for storing cookies:

• When the recipe says "cool completely," it really means completely. Still-warm cookies can become soggy in a storage container.

• Layer cookies between waxed paper and use storage containers with tight-fitting lids.

• Avoid storing crisp cookies and soft cookies in the same container—one can change the consistency of the other.

BROWNED
BUTTER-PECAN
SANDIES

SUGAR AND SPICE
BARK COOKIES

KID FRIENDLY
Sugar and Spice Bark Cookies

Simple, buttery sugar cookies take on a woodsy persona—no special tools required.
PREP 30 min. STAND 30 min.
CHILL 1 hr. 20 min.
BAKE 12 min. per batch OVEN 350°F

1 cup unsalted butter, cut into chunks
1 egg
½ cup plus 1 Tbsp. granulated sugar
1 Tbsp. molasses
2½ tsp. vanilla
½ tsp. salt
2¼ cups unbleached all-purpose flour
½ tsp. grated fresh nutmeg
½ tsp. ground cinnamon
  Edible gold spray (optional)
  Coarse white decorating sugar

1. Position a rack in middle of oven; preheat to 350°F. Let butter and egg stand at room temperature for 30 minutes.
2. In a large bowl vigorously beat butter and sugar with an electric mixer until well blended and smooth. Add egg, molasses, vanilla, and salt; beat for 1 minute or until well blended, scraping sides of bowl occasionally. Beat in flour, cinnamon, and nutmeg on low speed just until evenly incorporated. Divide dough in half; wrap and chill 1 hour or until easy to handle.
3. Roll one portion of dough between two pieces of parchment to a 9×9-inch square; chill 20 minutes. Gently peel off top parchment (if it sticks, chill for 5 minutes first). Score with a fork. Using a pizza cutter, cut into sixteen 3×1½-inch rectangles. Do not separate. Transfer

dough and parchment to a baking sheet. Repeat with remaining dough.
4. Bake one baking sheet at a time for 12 to 14 minutes or until lightly browned at the edges. Transfer to a wire rack. Immediately spray with gold spray, if using. Sprinkle with coarse sugar and additional nutmeg and cinnamon. Let stand until cookies firm up slightly, about 4 minutes. Recut rectangles with pizza cutter. Using a wide spatula, transfer cookies to wire rack. Cool completely. Makes 36 cookies.
EACH COOKIE 92 cal, 5 g fat, 19 mg chol, 35 mg sodium, 10 g carb, 0 g fiber, 1 g pro.

KID FRIENDLY
Browned Butter-Pecan Sandies

Browning the pecans in brown butter not only toasts the nuts, it permeates the butter with sweet, earthy flavor.
PREP 45 min. COOK 8 min.
COOL 15 min. BAKE 10 min. per batch
OVEN 350°F

1 cup unsalted butter, cut into chunks
1 cup chopped pecans
¾ cup powdered sugar
¼ cup packed brown sugar
3 to 4 Tbsp. half-and-half or light cream
2 tsp. vanilla
½ tsp. salt
2 cups unbleached all-purpose flour
  Coarse sugar (optional)
36 pecan halves

1. Position a rack in upper third of oven; preheat to 350°F. Grease baking sheets or line with parchment; set aside.

2. In a medium heavy saucepan bring butter to boiling over medium heat (it will be foamy). Adjust heat so it bubbles gently. Cook, stirring the bottom frequently, until fragrant and golden, about 8 to 10 minutes. Watch carefully to avoid burning. Stir in chopped pecans (it's normal for mixture to foam up). Return to a gentle boil. Cook, watching carefully, for 1 to 2 minutes (if pecans begin to darken, immediately remove pan from heat). Transfer to a large bowl. Cool about 15 minutes.
3. Stir powdered sugar, brown sugar, half-and-half, vanilla, and salt into cooled butter-pecan mixture until smoothly incorporated. Stir in flour until fully incorporated. If mixture is crumbly, work in more cream until it holds together but is not wet. If mixture is wet, let stand 5 to 10 minutes more.
4. Divide dough into thirds. Divide each third into 12 equal balls. Roll each ball in coarse sugar, if desired. Place balls about 2½ inches apart on prepared baking sheets; press a pecan half firmly into each. If edges of the rounds crack, just push back together.
5. Bake one baking sheet at a time for 10 to 13 minutes or until cookies are just light golden all over and slighter darker at the edges.
6. To ensure even browning, rotate baking sheet from front to back about halfway through. Transfer to a wire rack. Let cool 5 minutes to firm up (they are too tender to move while hot). Using a wide spatula, transfer cookies to wire rack. Cool completely. Makes 36 cookies.
Store at room temperature up to 10 days. Freeze up to 2 months.
EACH COOKIE 117 cal, 8 g fat, 14 mg chol, 34 mg sodium, 10 g carb, 1 g fiber, 1 g pro.

Fruit and Cheese Cocktail Cookies

Unusual semisavory sandwich cookies are irresistibly tasty and lend a gourmet touch to any occasion. A slightly tangy fruity filling is the perfect pairing for tender cheese-flavored cookies.

PREP 35 min. FREEZE 45 min.
BAKE 11 min. per batch OVEN 350°F

Savory Fruit
1   cup trimmed and coarsely chopped dried Calimyrna figs
1   cup chopped fresh (or frozen, thawed) cranberries
¼   cup clover honey or other mild honey

Cheese Cocktail Cookies
½   cup unsalted butter, slightly softened and cut into chunks
4   oz. blue cheese, slightly softened and cut into chunks
2   oz. sharp cheddar cheese, cut into small pieces
1   large egg
1   Tbsp. sugar
½   tsp. baking powder
1½   cups unbleached all-purpose white flour
     Red, pink, or white coarse-crystal sea salt, or poppy or sesame seeds (optional)

FRUIT AND
CHEESE
COCKTAIL
COOKIES

1. For Savory Fruit, in a food processor combine figs and cranberries. Process until finely chopped but not pureed. Transfer to a medium heavy nonreactive saucepan. Stir in honey and 3 Tbsp. water. Cook and stir over medium heat until mixture just comes to a boil. Cook and stir 1 minute more. Cool completely; set aside.*
2. For Cheese Cocktail Cookies, in a food processor combine butter, blue cheese, cheddar, egg, sugar, and baking powder. Cover and process until very well blended, about 1½ minutes, scraping sides of bowl occasionally. Add 1 cup of the flour. Cover and pulse until partially incorporated.
3. Turn mixture onto waxed paper. Fully knead in remaining flour. If dough is very soft, knead in up to 3 Tbsp. more flour; if still soft, let stand to firm up for 5 minutes.
4. Divide dough in half. On waxed paper, using greased hands, stretch and shape each half into an evenly thick 9-inch log. Roll each log in plastic wrap; twist ends to close (see "Well Rounded," page 285). Freeze at least 45 minutes or until just firm enough to cut neatly.*

5. Position a rack in middle of oven; preheat to 350°F. Line large baking sheets with parchment; set aside.
6. Using a very sharp knife, cut each log crosswise into slices slightly less than ¼ inch thick. Turn log a quarter turn after each slice to keep round. Place slices about 1½ inches apart on baking sheets. If desired, sprinkle with a few grains of coarse salt or seeds, patting down lightly.
7. Bake one baking sheet at a time for 11 to 15 minutes or until cookies are lightly browned at edges. Transfer to a wire rack; let cool 2 minutes. Using a wide spatula, transfer cookies to wire rack. Cool completely.
8. Stir Savory Fruit. If mixture seems dry or crumbly, add a few teaspoons of warm water until spreadable. Spread about 2 tsp. on each cookie. Top with another cookie, pressing down until fruit is just spread out to edges. Serve immediately. Makes 30 sandwich cookies.

***Tip** To make ahead Cheese Cocktail Cookies, pack unbaked cookies in freezer bags; freeze up to 3 months. Let frozen logs soften at room temperature about 15 minutes before slicing. To make ahead Savory Fruit, cover and refrigerate in a nonreactive container up to 1 week. Bring to room temperature before serving. Store unfilled cookies in the refrigerator up to 2 days. Freeze up to 1 month; thaw before using.
EACH COOKIE *97 cal, 11 g fat, 19 mg chol, 76 mg sodium, 11 g carb, 1 g fiber, 2 g pro.*

Lime and Ginger Chewies

The secret to the full-bodied flavor of these crinkle-topped, crisp-chewy sugar cookies is lime zest and both ground and fresh ginger.

PREP 45 min. BAKE 6 min. per batch
STAND 5 min. OVEN 350°F

1⅓ cups granulated sugar
2 Tbsp. finely shredded lime peel
1 Tbsp. peeled minced fresh ginger
¾ cup plus 2 Tbsp. unsalted butter, cut into chunks and just slightly softened
1 egg yolk
1½ Tbsp. fresh lime juice
1½ Tbsp. light-color corn syrup
2 to 3 tsp. ground ginger, to taste
½ tsp. lemon or vanilla extract
½ tsp. baking soda
¼ tsp. salt
2¼ cups unbleached all-purpose flour
Powdered sugar
Finely shredded lime peel
Coarse green sugar (optional)

1. Position a rack in middle of oven; preheat to 350°F. Lightly grease baking sheets; set aside.
2. In a food processor combine sugar, lime peel, and fresh ginger. Cover and process for 2 to 3 minutes, scraping sides of bowl occasionally, until ginger is completely pulverized and mixture is thoroughly blended and smooth. Reserve ½ cup; transfer to a saucer to use as garnish.
3. In a large bowl combine remaining lime-sugar mixture, butter, egg yolk, lime juice, corn syrup, ground ginger, lemon extract, baking soda, and salt. Beat with an electric mixer on low, then medium speed until very well blended and lightened in color, about 1½ minutes. Beat in half the flour on low speed just until evenly incorporated, scraping sides of bowl occasionally. Beat or stir in remaining flour until evenly incorporated. If dough seems too wet, stir in up to 3 Tbsp. more flour; if too dry, stir in up to 1 tsp. water.
4. Shape dough into a flat disk; cut into quarters. Divide each quarter into 11 or 12 equal portions. Shape portions into balls; roll in reserved lime-sugar mixture. Gently reshape as needed. Space about 2½ inches apart on prepared baking sheets; flatten to ⅛- to ¼-inch thickness with the bottom of a glass.
5. Bake one sheet at a time, for 6 to 8 minutes, or until cookies are lightly tinged with brown at the edges and not quite firm when pressed in the center top. (For chewier cookies underbake slightly; for crisper ones, over-bake slightly.) Let stand on baking sheet 5 minutes. Using a spatula, transfer cookies to wire rack. Dust with powdered sugar; sprinkle with lime peel. If desired, sprinkle with coarse green sugar. Cool completely. Makes 44 to 48 cookies.

EACH COOKIE *84 cal, 4 g fat, 14 mg chol, 29 mg sodium, 12 g carb, 6 g fiber, 1 g pro.*

LIME AND GINGER CHEWIES

Toasty Coconut Wedges

These golden brown shortbreads have a pronounced buttery, nutty-sweet taste from an abundance of well-toasted oats and coconut and, of course, a good amount of butter.

PREP 30 min. BAKE 50 min.
COOL 5 min. OVEN 300°F

2	to 3 Tbsp. coarse green sugar
1½	cups flaked or shredded sweetened coconut
1	cup old-fashioned rolled oats
1	cup unsalted butter, softened slightly and cut into chunks
½	cup granulated sugar
¼	cup packed light brown sugar
½	tsp. salt
⅛	tsp. almond extract
1½	cups unbleached all-purpose flour
¼	cup flaked or shredded coconut
2	Tbsp. old-fashioned rolled oats

1. Position a rack in middle of oven; preheat to 300°F. Grease a 10-inch fluted tart pan, 10-inch springform pan or line a large baking sheet with parchment. Sprinkle edges with 1 Tbsp. of the coarse green sugar; set aside.

2. On a large baking sheet spread 1½ cups coconut in an even layer. Bake, stirring every 3 minutes, until evenly toasted, about 6 to 8 minutes. Stir in 1 cup oats. Continue baking, stirring every 3 minutes, until coconut is well toasted and the color of graham crackers, about 6 to 8 minutes more. Cool slightly.

3. In a food processor add toasted coconut-oat mixture. Cover and process until ground almost to flour consistency but not clumped or oily looking, scraping sides of bowl occasionally.

4. In a large bowl beat butter, granulated and brown sugars, salt, and almond extract with an electric mixer on medium speed until very well blended and lightened in color, about 2 minutes. On low speed, beat in ground coconut-oat mixture. Add half the flour; beat until evenly incorporated, scraping sides of bowl occasionally. Beat or stir in remaining flour until evenly incorporated. If dough is crumbly, work in up to 3 tsp. water until it holds together.

5. Press dough evenly into bottom of prepared pan. Lay a piece of waxed paper over dough, smoothing and pressing down with your fingertips. Remove waxed paper. Using a table knife, carefully score dough into quarters; score each quarter into 4 or 5 wedges.

TOASTY COCONUT WEDGES

6. For coconut topping, sprinkle generously with remaining coconut; sprinkle lightly with remaining oats. Sprinkle edge with remaining coarse green sugar; press down to embed sugar.

7. Bake for 30 minutes. If coconut topping becomes too brown, cover loosely with foil. Continue baking, covered, for 20 minutes or until shortbread is fragrant, nicely browned all over, and feels almost firm when pressed in the center.

8. Transfer to a wire rack; let cool for 5 to 10 minutes so shortbread can firm up slightly. To ensure wedges will separate, retrace cuts. Let stand until cooled or barely warm. If using a springform pan, carefully remove sides. Separate wedges. Using a spatula, transfer wedges to wire rack. Cool completely. Makes 16 to 20 cookies.

EACH COOKIE WEDGE *260 cal, 16 g fat, 31 mg chol, 102 mg sodium, 29 g carb, 1 g fiber, 2 g pro.*

FREEFORM SHORTBREAD
If you don't have a fluted tart pan or a springform pan, you can still make this shortbread. Press dough into a 10-inch circle. To create decorative edges, press with a fork all around or use the dowel-like part of a wooden spoon handle and press into sides. Place on a parchment-lined baking sheet, then score wedges.

Home Cooking

OPEN TABLE It's your turn to host the holiday feast? Don't stress. We asked chef Melissa Perello to share her favorite menu with step-by-step instructions on how to get it to the table beautifully.

Holiday Rib Roast with Grain Mustard Sauce

PREP 30 min. ROAST 2 hr.
STAND 15 min. OVEN 350°F

1   recipe Garlic-Herb Rub
1   6- to 7-lb. beef rib roast (3 bones)
1   Tbsp. vegetable oil
½   cup unsalted butter, melted
4   medium shallots, sliced
6   cloves garlic, halved
1   Tbsp. olive oil
½   cup dry white wine
2   cups low-sodium beef broth
1   Tbsp. fresh grated horseradish or 1 tsp. prepared horseradish
1½   Tbsp. coarse-grain mustard*
2   Tbsp. cold unsalted butter

1. Position oven rack just below center. Preheat oven to 350°F. Prepare Garlic-Herb Rub; set aside. Season roast with salt.

2. In a large skillet brown roast on all sides in hot vegetable oil. Place meat, fat side up, on a rack in a shallow roasting pan. Spread Garlic-Herb Rub evenly over roast; spoon over butter. Roast, uncovered, 2 to 2¼ hours for medium rare (135°F) or 2¼ to 2½ hours for medium (150°F), spooning butter from the pan over occasionally.

3. Meanwhile, in a large skillet cook shallots and garlic in hot olive oil 5 to 8 minutes or until shallots are golden brown. Remove from heat. Carefully add wine. Return to heat. Simmer, uncovered, 5 minutes or until reduced by half. Stir in beef broth. Simmer, uncovered, 8 minutes more or until reduced to 1½ cups.

4. Transfer roast to a cutting board. Cover with foil; let stand 15 minutes before slicing. Temperature of meat after standing should be 145°F for medium rare and 160°F for medium. Sprinkle with fresh thyme, if desired.

5. While roast stands, prepare grain mustard sauce. Drain fat from roasting pan. Add ½ cup water and the 1½ cups beef broth mixture. Cook and stir, scraping up browned bits from bottom of pan. Simmer; strain sauce through a fine sieve into a small saucepan. Return to simmering. Add mustard and horseradish. Whisk in butter, 1 Tbsp. at a time. Season with salt and ground black pepper. Serve sauce with sliced meat. Makes 10 to 12 servings.

Garlic-Herb Rub In a food processor combine 2 Tbsp. chopped fresh thyme, 1½ Tbsp. cracked black peppercorns, and 7 cloves garlic. Cover and process until combined. Add 3 Tbsp. olive oil; pulse to a coarse paste.

***Make your own** In a small jar pour 4 Tbsp. water over 2 Tbsp. mustard seeds. Let stand at room temperature overnight. Crush slightly.

EACH SERVING *488 cal, 37 g fat, 119 mg chol, 373 mg sodium, 3 g carb, 0 g fiber, 31 g pro.*

TWIST ON TRADITION
"Most people use red wine in a sauce with beef, but I prefer white here," Melissa says. "It gives the sauce a different depth. Grainy mustard gives it this amazing texture, and horseradish adds zing at the end. The butter takes the sauce to the next level—an over-the-top richness that most people expect at a holiday dinner."

"I love a rib roast because it's got a great tenderness to it, and when slow-cooked, all the juices and fats caramelize and give you this amazing crispy, salty crust."

Butter Bean Ragout

Melissa likes to soak beans a night or two before. Marrow or gigandes beans are both good substitutes for butter beans because they provide similar texture.
PREP 30 min. COOK 1 hr.
SOAK 8 hr. or overnight

1   lb. dried butter beans (about 2½ cups)
8   cloves garlic, peeled
4   sprigs fresh thyme
½   tsp. whole black peppercorns
1   Tbsp. vegetable oil
2   large onions, peeled and split in half
12 cups reduced-sodium chicken broth
½   cup cold unsalted butter, cubed
½   cup finely shredded Parmesan cheese
¼   cup chopped fresh flat-leaf Italian parsley
2   tsp. finely shredded lemon peel
⅛   tsp. crushed red pepper
½   cup Seasoned Breadcrumbs

1. In a large bowl add beans and enough water to cover by 3 inches. Soak at room temperature at least 8 hours or overnight. Drain.

2. In a 6- to 8-quart Dutch oven cover beans with fresh water; bring to boiling. Drain. Rinse beans once.

3. Wrap garlic, thyme, and peppercorns in cheesecloth. Tie with 100%-cotton kitchen string; set aside. In the Dutch oven heat oil over medium heat. Cook onions, cut sides down, 5 minutes or until golden. Add chicken broth, cheesecloth packet, and rinsed beans. Bring to boiling; reduce heat. Simmer until beans are fully tender but still hold shape, stirring occasionally, about 1 hour. Add broth as needed to cover beans. Drain, reserving 1½ cups cooking liquid. Discard cheesecloth packet and onions.

4. In a Dutch oven cook drained beans and ½ cup reserved cooking liquid over medium heat. Add butter one cube at a time. Add ½ to 1 cup more cooking liquid until desired consistency. Cook and stir until butter is incorporated. Season with salt and ground black pepper.

5. In a small bowl combine Parmesan, parsley, lemon peel, and crushed red pepper; sprinkle on beans. Top with Seasoned Breadcrumbs. Makes 8 servings.

Seasoned Breadcrumbs Preheat oven to 425°F. In a medium bowl toss 2 cups 1-inch cubes of artisan bread with 1 Tbsp. olive oil to coat. Spread on a 15×10×1-inch baking pan. Bake, uncovered, 8 to 10 minutes or until golden brown. In a food processor combine toasted bread cubes, 1 tsp. finely shredded lemon peel, 1 tsp. snipped fresh thyme, and 1 clove minced garlic. Cover; process until coarse crumbs form. Makes 1 cup.
EACH SERVING 367 cal, 16 g fat, 34 mg chol, 1,087 mg sodium, 38 g carb, 14 g fiber, 20 g pro.

SOMETHING UNEXPECTED

Melissa likes to deliver a surprise flavor in almost every dish she prepares. Here, the Parmesan cheese and lemon provide the aha moment. "This ragout is hearty and filling," she says. "It's my version of comfort food—and as a side dish, it's a bit healthier than your average mashed potatoes."

Brown Butter and Sausage Quick Bread

For the best browned butter, slice the stick of butter so it melts evenly. Stir it constantly—the butter will froth a bit. Remove from heat immediately to keep from burning.

PREP 30 min. COOK 15 min.
BAKE 25 min. OVEN 425°F

½ cup unsalted butter
1 sprig fresh sage
8 oz. Italian or fennel sausage
1 Tbsp. vegetable oil
1½ cups all-purpose flour
1 Tbsp. sugar
1 Tbsp. baking powder
½ tsp. salt
1 tsp. ground black pepper
6 eggs, room temperature
2 tsp. finely shredded lemon peel
3 oz. Pecorino cheese, coarsely shredded
⅓ cup golden raisins, roughly chopped
Fresh sage leaves (optional)

1. In a small saucepan melt butter over low heat. Add sage. Cook and stir, allowing the butter to brown to a nutty color. Remove sage. Cool to room temperature.

2. Remove sausage from casing, if necessary. In a large skillet heat vegetable oil over medium heat. Lightly sear the sausage, stirring and breaking it into small chunks as it cooks. Cook through (but don't allow it to sear too heavily). Transfer to a plate. Cool to room temperature or chill in the refrigerator.

3. Preheat oven to 350°F. Butter an 8-inch cast-iron skillet or 9-inch cake pan; set aside. In a medium bowl sift together flour, sugar, baking powder, and salt. Stir in pepper.

4. In a large bowl whisk eggs and lemon peel about 2 minutes or until frothy. Stir in flour mixture. Add brown butter. Fold in sausage, Pecorino, and raisins.

5. Pour batter into prepared skillet. Bake about 30 minutes (if using a cast-iron skillet) or about 25 minutes (if using a cake pan) or until a wooden toothpick inserted into the center comes out clean. Remove from pan; cool on a wire rack. Top with fresh sage leaves, if desired. Serve warm. Makes 16 servings.

EACH SERVING 204 cal, 13 g fat, 100 mg chol, 334 mg sodium, 13 g carb, 1 g fiber, 7 g pro.

"This is the most satisfying cake. It's always sweet, always moist, always good. There's something about it that takes you back to your childhood."

Fruit and Date Lumberjack Cake

PREP 30 min. COOK 10 min.
BAKE 45 min. COOL 2 hrs. OVEN 350°F

1   cup pitted dates
1   tsp. baking soda
1¼   cups all-purpose flour
¾   tsp. baking powder
¼   tsp. salt
½   cup butter, softened
1¼   cups granulated sugar
1   egg
1   tsp. vanilla
1   pear or apple, peeled and chopped
½   cup flaked coconut
        Powdered sugar
1   recipe Glazed Pears and Kumquats

1. Preheat oven to 350°F. Grease a 9-inch springform baking pan; line bottom with parchment paper. In a small saucepan bring dates and 1 cup water to boiling; remove from heat. Stir in baking soda (mixture will foam); set aside. Cool to room temperature.
2. In a small bowl stir together flour, baking powder, and salt. Set aside.
3. In a large bowl beat butter, sugar, egg, and vanilla with an electric mixer on medium speed until combined. Slowly beat into date mixture until combined. Add flour mixture gradually, beating just until combined. Fold in pears or apples and coconut.

4. Spread mixture evenly into prepared pan. Bake 45 to 50 minutes or until a wooden toothpick inserted near center comes out clean. If necessary, rotate pan; bake about 5 minutes more (center of cake may dip). Cool on a wire rack. Carefully remove sides of pan; remove parchment paper. Sprinkle with powdered sugar. With a slotted spoon, top with Glazed Pears and Kumquats. Makes 10 servings.
Glazed Pears and Kumquats In a small skillet combine ½ cup water and ½ cup sugar. Cook and stir over medium-high heat until mixture comes to boiling and sugar is dissolved. Add pear wedges (from 1 pear) and a few sliced kumquats. Cook and gently stir 10 minutes or until tender. Remove from heat; cool to room temperature.
EACH SERVING *374 cal, 11 g fat, 43 mg chol, 312 mg sodium, 69 g carb, 4 g fiber, 3 g pro.*

SWEET FINISH
"Traditional lumberjack cake comes with a gooey topping of butter, brown sugar, and coconut. In my version, I put all the gooey elements inside. It's impossible to stop with one piece," Melissa says. Packed with dates and pear, it's rich, moist, and perfect for the season. Her version is a big crowd-pleaser at her restaurant, Frances, in San Francisco. "We can't take it off the menu—people love it so much."

Prize Tested Recipes®

Every year thousands of *Better Homes and Gardens*® readers enter the monthly Prize Tested Recipe® contest and one winner is selected in each category. This year's creative collection is sure to please!

KID FRIENDLY

$500 PRIZE: CREATIVE TWISTS ON HUMMUS

Baked Asiago Hummus

Angela Ness Rosemount, MN

PREP 15 min. COOK 20 min.
BAKE 8 min. OVEN 450°F

1   Tbsp. butter
1   onion, thinly sliced
½   tsp. sugar
1   15-oz. can garbanzo beans, rinsed
    and drained
1   Tbsp. olive oil
1   Tbsp. sesame oil
1   clove garlic
½   tsp. snipped fresh rosemary
6   Tbsp. shredded Asiago cheese
    Fresh rosemary sprig (optional)
    Toasted baguette slices, carrot
    sticks, and celery sticks

1. Preheat oven to 450°F. In a large skillet melt butter over medium heat. Add onion and sugar; reduce heat to medium-low. Cook and stir for 20 to 25 minutes or until onion is very tender and caramelized. Coarsely chop; set aside.
2. In food processor combine beans, olive oil, sesame oil, garlic, rosemary, 2 Tbsp. water, ½ tsp. salt, and ¼ tsp. ground black pepper. Process until smooth. Stir in 2 Tbsp. of the cheese. Transfer to a 12- to 16-ounce individual casserole.
3. Top with caramelized onion and remaining cheese. Bake 8 to 10 minutes or until cheese is browned and hummus is heated through. Garnish with rosemary. Serve with baguette slices and carrot and celery sticks. Makes 6 servings.
EACH SERVING *183 cal, 10 g fat, 13 mg chol, 427 mg sodium, 18 g carb, 3 g fiber, 6 g pro.*

BAKED ASIAGO HUMMUS

VEGETABLE-LOADED PASTA BAKE

KID FRIENDLY

$500 PRIZE: HEALTHY CASSEROLES

Vegetable-Loaded Pasta Bake

Audra Macejka Santa Fe, NM

PREP 40 min. BAKE 40 min.
OVEN 350°F

8   oz. dried whole wheat penne pasta
     (2¾ cups)
2½   cups cauliflower florets (½ medium
     head)
1   medium onion, chopped
2   cloves garlic, minced
1   Tbsp. olive oil
2   medium carrots, sliced
1   stalk celery, chopped
12   oz. kale, stems removed, leaves torn
     (12 cups)
½   cup frozen peas
½   cup frozen whole kernel corn
1   recipe Cheese Sauce
2   Tbsp. finely shredded Parmesan
     cheese

1. Preheat oven to 350°F. In large Dutch oven cook pasta according to package directions; add cauliflower the last 4 minutes of cooking. Drain; rinse.
2. In same pan cook onion and garlic in hot oil over medium heat 2 minutes. Add carrots and celery; cook just until tender. Add kale; cook just until wilted. Stir in pasta mixture, peas, and corn. Stir in Cheese Sauce. Transfer to 2½-quart casserole. Cover; bake 35 minutes. Uncover; sprinkle with Parmesan. Bake 5 minutes more. Makes 6 servings.
Cheese Sauce In a small saucepan melt 2 Tbsp. butter; stir in 2 Tbsp. all-purpose flour, ¼ tsp. salt, and ¼ tsp. ground black pepper. Add 1 cup fat-free milk all at once; cook and stir until thickened and bubbly. Reduce heat; add 4 oz. shredded extra-sharp cheddar cheese (1 cup). Cook and stir until melted.
EACH SERVING *365 cal, 14 g fat, 32 mg chol, 355 mg sodium, 47 g carb, 4 g fiber, 15 g pro.*

CAJUN CHICKEN CURRY

FAST | LOW FAT

$500 PRIZE: EASY CHICKEN CURRIES

Cajun Chicken Curry

Pat Banta Kreml Winter Haven, FL

PREP 15 min. COOK 21 min.

½ tsp. fennel seeds, crushed
1 Tbsp. olive oil
1 lb. skinless, boneless chicken breast halves, cut in 1-inch pieces
¼ cup butter
1 large green sweet pepper, cut in strips
1 large red onion, cut in thin wedges
1 stalk celery, sliced (½ cup)
6 cloves garlic, minced (2 Tbsp.)
2 to 3 tsp. curry powder
1 tsp. garam masala
¼ cup all-purpose flour
1 14.5-oz. can chicken broth
½ cup tangerine or orange marmalade
1 tsp. bottled hot pepper sauce
4 cups hot cooked basmati or jasmine rice

1. In a 4-quart Dutch oven cook fennel seeds in hot oil over medium heat 1 minute. Stir in chicken. Cook and stir for 5 minutes or until chicken is browned. Remove chicken with a slotted spoon.
2. In same pan heat butter and cook pepper, onion, celery, garlic, curry powder, garam masala, and ½ tsp. salt over medium heat for 5 to 10 minutes or until tender. Stir in flour. Gradually add broth, stirring until combined. Stir in chicken, marmalade, and hot pepper sauce. Bring to boiling; reduce heat. Simmer, covered, 10 minutes or until chicken is no longer pink; stir occasionally. Serve over rice. Makes 4 servings.
EACH SERVING *641 cal, 17 g fat, 97 mg chol, 925 mg sodium, 88 g carb, 2 g fiber, 33 g pro.*

INSIDE-OUT S'MORES BROWNIES

KID FRIENDLY

$500 PRIZE: BROWNIES AND BLONDIES

Inside-Out S'mores Brownies

Angela Johnson Edmond, OK

PREP 15 min. COOK 5 min.
BAKE 25 min. OVEN 350°F

½ cup butter
2 oz. unsweetened chocolate, chopped
1 cup sugar
2 eggs
1 tsp. vanilla
¾ cup all-purpose flour
9 honey graham cracker squares
1 cup tiny marshmallows

1. Preheat oven to 350°F. Line a 11×7×1½-inch baking pan with parchment paper or lightly grease the pan. Set aside.
2. In a medium saucepan melt butter and chocolate over low heat. Remove from heat. Stir in sugar, eggs, and vanilla until combined. Stir in flour.
3. Spread half the batter in the prepared pan. Top with graham crackers (divide as needed to evenly top the batter). Sprinkle marshmallows on the graham crackers, but do not let them touch the sides of the pan. Carefully spread the remaining batter on the marshmallows and graham crackers, covering them completely.
4. Bake for 25 minutes or until set. Cool completely on a wire rack. Cut into bars. Makes 15 brownies.
EACH SERVING *189 cal, 9 g fat, 44 mg chol, 84 mg sodium, 26 g carb, 1 g fiber, 2 g pro.*

CHILE-ORANGE
SHORT RIBS

$500 PRIZE: SLOW-COOKER BEEF

Chile-Orange Short Ribs

Susan Asanovic Wilton, CT

PREP 10 min.
COOK 11 hr. (low) or 5½ hr. (high)

4	to 5 lb. beef short ribs
3	medium leeks, trimmed and cut into 2-inch lengths
6	cloves garlic, sliced
1	1-inch piece fresh ginger, peeled and sliced
1	star anise, broken
1	dried chile de arbol pepper
½	cup dry sherry or beef broth
4	2-inch strips orange peel
½	cup orange juice
¼	cup reduced-sodium soy sauce
2	Tbsp. packed brown sugar
3	Tbsp. chopped fresh cilantro

1. Place ribs on a broiler pan; sprinkle with 1½ tsp. kosher salt and ½ tsp. black pepper. Broil 4 to 5 inches from heat for 10 minutes or until browned.
2. Place leeks in a 5- to 6-quart slow cooker. Place ribs on top of leeks. Add garlic, ginger, star anise, and chile pepper. Combine sherry, orange peel, orange juice, soy sauce, and sugar. Pour over ribs in cooker. Cover; cook on low-heat setting for 11 to 12 hours or on high-heat setting for 5½ to 6 hours.
3. Using a slotted spoon or sieve, transfer ribs to a platter; cover and keep warm. Strain cooking liquid; discard solids. Skim fat from cooking liquid. Sprinkle ribs with cilantro. Serve cooking liquid with ribs for dipping. Serve ribs with peeled and sectioned oranges or tangerines if desired. Makes 6 servings.
EACH SERVING *834 cal, 66 g fat, 152 mg chol, 986 mg sodium, 20 g carb, 2 g fiber, 34 g pro.*

SPICED NUTS AND ZUCCHINI CORN BREAD

$500 PRIZE: CREATIVE CORN BREADS

Spiced Nuts and Zucchini Corn Bread

Anita Lindsay St. Petersburg, FL

PREP 25 min. BAKE 50 min.
OVEN 300°F

1	cup all-purpose flour
1	cup yellow cornmeal
½	cup spiced mixed nuts (salt and pepper mixed nuts), finely chopped
⅓	cup sugar
4	tsp. baking powder
¼	tsp. salt
4	eggs
½	cup butter, melted
½	cup unsweetened applesauce
1	14.75-oz. can cream-style corn
1	cup coarsely shredded zucchini
1	cup shredded sharp cheddar cheese (4 oz.)
½	cup finely chopped onion

1. Preheat oven to 300°F. Grease a 13×9×2-inch baking pan; set aside. In a large bowl stir together flour, cornmeal, nuts, sugar, baking powder, and salt; set aside.
2. In a bowl whisk together the eggs, butter, and applesauce. Stir in the corn, zucchini, cheese, and onion. Add butter mixture all at once to cornmeal mixture. Stir just until moistened. Pour batter into prepared pan.
3. Bake for 50 to 60 minutes or until edges are golden brown. Cool slightly; serve warm. Makes 18 servings.
EACH SERVING *201 cal, 11 g fat, 67 mg chol, 326 mg sodium, 21 g carb, 1 g fiber, 5 g pro.*

**PAN-SEARED SHRIMP
SALAD WITH MANGO-
LIME DRESSING**

$500 PRIZE: MAIN-DISH SALADS
Pan-Seared Shrimp Salad with Mango-Lime Dressing

Jan Cole Lawrenceburg, TN

PREP 20 min. MARINATE 30 min.
COOK 3 min.

24 medium fresh or frozen shrimp
⅓ cup olive oil
3 Tbsp. lemon juice
1 Tbsp. Old Bay seasoning
1 Tbsp. bottled cocktail sauce
¼ tsp. garlic powder
1 medium mango, halved, seeded, peeled, and cut up
2 Tbsp. honey
2 Tbsp. water
1 Tbsp. lime juice
1 Tbsp. red wine vinegar
½ tsp. poppy seeds
1 8-oz. pkg. spring lettuce mix

1 cup pecan halves and/or chopped pecans, toasted
⅓ cup thinly sliced red onion

1. Thaw shrimp, if frozen. Peel and devein shrimp. Place a large resealable plastic bag in a shallow dish; add olive oil, lemon juice, Old Bay seasoning, cocktail sauce, and garlic powder. Add shrimp. Seal and turn bag to coat shrimp. Marinate in the refrigerator for 30 minutes to 1 hour.
2. For dressing, in a blender or food processor combine mango, honey, the water, lime juice, vinegar, and poppy seeds. Cover and blend or process until smooth. Divide greens among four serving plates. Top with pecans and onion rings.
3. Heat a large skillet over medium heat. Add shrimp and marinade to skillet. Cook and stir for 3 to 4 minutes or until shrimp are opaque. Spoon shrimp over greens. Drizzle with dressing. Makes 4 servings.
EACH SERVING *518 cal, 39 g fat, 115 mg chol, 660 mg sodium, 27 g carb, 5 g fiber, 19 g pro.*

KID FRIENDLY   LOW FAT

$500 PRIZE: MEAT LOAF MAKEOVERS
Southwestern Turkey Meat Loaf

Kaycee Mason Siloam Springs, AR

PREP 30 min. COOL 20 min. BAKE 1 hr. 15 min. STAND 10 min. OVEN 350°F

¼ cup chopped onion
1 Tbsp. vegetable oil
1 cup uncooked long grain rice
1 Tbsp. minced fresh garlic
1 14.5-oz. can beef broth
1 15-oz. can black beans, rinsed and drained
2 lb. uncooked ground turkey
1 cup frozen whole kernel corn, thawed
½ cup bottled picante sauce
¼ to ½ cup crushed tortilla chips
1 tsp. taco seasoning
   Shredded cheese, chopped tomato, cilantro, sliced jalapeño, and/or lime wedges (optional)

1. In saucepan cook onion in hot oil over medium heat 5 minutes or until tender. Stir in rice and garlic. Cook and stir 5 minutes, until rice is brown. Add broth. Bring to boiling; reduce heat. Simmer, covered, 10 to 15 minutes or until rice is tender. Stir in beans; cool slightly.
2. Preheat oven to 350°F. Line a 15×10×1-inch baking pan with parchment. In bowl combine turkey, corn, picante sauce, chips, and seasoning. Stir in rice mixture. In baking pan lightly pat turkey mixture into 10×5-inch loaf. Bake 1¼ to 1½ hours, until an instant-read thermometer inserted near center of loaf registers 165°F. Let stand 10 minutes. Sprinkle with cheese, tomato, cilantro, and/or jalapeño and serve with lime if desired. Makes 8 servings.
EACH SERVING *343 cal, 11 g fat, 78 mg chol, 722 mg sodium, 33 g carb, 3 g fiber, 29 g pro.*

Coffee-Dunked Doughnut Bread Pudding

Mildred Smith Jefferson, GA

PREP **25 min.** BAKE **40 min.**
OVEN **350°F**

12 day-old unfrosted plain and/or chocolate doughnuts, torn in 1-inch pieces
2 cups milk
1 14-oz. can sweetened condensed milk
1¼ cups strong brewed coffee, cooled
6 egg yolks
1½ tsp. ground cinnamon
½ tsp. granulated sugar
Butterscotch Sauce (optional)
Multicolor sprinkles (optional)

1. Preheat oven to 350°F. Place doughnut pieces in a 3-quart baking dish; set aside. In large bowl whisk together milk, sweetened condensed milk, coffee, egg yolks, and 1 tsp. of the cinnamon. Pour evenly over doughnuts. Combine granulated sugar and remaining cinnamon; sprinkle over pudding.

2. Bake, uncovered, for 40 to 45 minutes or until a knife inserted near center comes out clean. Cool slightly. If desired, serve with Butterscotch Sauce and top with sprinkles. Makes 16 servings.
EACH SERVING *260 cal, 12 g fat, 91 mg chol, 185 mg sodium, 33 g carb, 1 g fiber, 6 g pro.*
Butterscotch Sauce In a small saucepan melt ½ cup butter over low heat. Stir in ½ cup dark brown sugar and ¼ cup whipping cream. Cook and stir until sugar is dissolved. Remove from heat. Stir in ½ tsp. vanilla. Spoon over pudding.

KID FRIENDLY

$500 PRIZE: POTATO SIDE DISHES

Mashed Potato Veggie Strata

Linda Cobb San Diego, CA

PREP 30 min. COOK 20 min.
BAKE 30 min. STAND 20 min.
OVEN 350°F

2¼ lb. russet potatoes, peeled and cut up
½ cup bottled roasted red sweet peppers
1 8-oz. carton sour cream
1 Tbsp. purchased basil pesto
¼ tsp. salt
2 medium zucchini, halved lengthwise, sliced
1 medium yellow summer squash, halved lengthwise and sliced
1 medium red sweet pepper, chopped
1 medium yellow sweet pepper, chopped
1 medium green sweet pepper, chopped
1 medium onion, chopped (½ cup)
1 Tbsp. olive oil
½ tsp. salt
8 oz. cheddar cheese, shredded (2 cups)

1. Preheat oven to 350°F. Lightly coat a 3-quart rectangular baking dish with nonstick cooking spray; set aside. In large saucepan cook potatoes in enough lightly salted water to cover for 20 to 25 minutes, until tender. Drain potatoes. Return to saucepan, mash, then spread evenly in baking dish.

2. In blender or small food processor blend or process roasted sweet peppers until smooth. Transfer to medium bowl. Whisk in sour cream, pesto, and ¼ tsp. salt until smooth. Spread sweet pepper mixture on mashed potatoes.

3. In 12-inch skillet cook zucchini, summer squash, sweet peppers, and onion in hot oil over medium-high heat until crisp-tender. Season with ½ tsp. salt. Spoon vegetables on roasted pepper layer. Sprinkle with cheese. Bake, uncovered, about 30 minutes, until heated through. Let stand 20 minutes before serving. Makes 10 servings.
EACH SERVING 269 cal, 14 g fat, 36 mg chol, 598 mg sodium, 27 g carb, 4 g fiber, 9 g pro.

PINEAPPLE-BLACK BEAN GUACAMOLE

$500 PRIZE: CROWD-PLEASING DRINKS

Sparkling Basil Lemonade

Wendy O'Connor Spokane, WA

PREP 15 min. COOK 20 min.
CHILL 2 hr.

4 cups water
3 cups sugar
2 cups fresh basil leaves (about 1½ oz.)
2 1-liter bottles club soda, chilled
2 cups lemon juice
   Ice cubes
1 fresh jalapeño chile pepper, sliced (see note, page 69)
   Fresh basil leaves

1. For basil syrup, in large saucepan combine the water, sugar, and 2 cups basil leaves. Bring to boiling over medium-high heat. Reduce heat. Simmer, uncovered, for 20 minutes. Strain and discard leaves. Cover and chill syrup for 2 to 24 hours.
2. For lemonade, in very large punch bowl combine chilled syrup, club soda, and lemon juice. Serve over ice and garnish with jalapeño slices and fresh basil leaves. Makes 16 servings.
EACH SERVING 155 cal, 0 g fat, 0 mg chol, 29 mg sodium, 40 g carb, 0 g fiber, 0 g pro.

SPARKLING BASIL LEMONADE

$500 PRIZE: ULTIMATE GUACAMOLE

Pineapple-Black Bean Guacamole

Beth McDonald Churchville, NY

PREP 15 min. CHILL 2 hr.

2 medium avocados, halved, seeded, and peeled
¼ cup bottled green salsa (salsa verde)
1 Tbsp. sour cream
½ cup finely chopped fresh pineapple or canned crushed pineapple, drained
½ cup canned black beans, rinsed and drained
1 fresh jalapeño chile pepper, seeded and minced (see note, page 69)
2 Tbsp. finely chopped red onion
2 Tbsp. chopped fresh cilantro
1 Tbsp. minced garlic
1 Tbsp. lime juice
¼ tsp. salt
¼ tsp. ground cumin
¼ cup shredded Monterey Jack cheese
   Fresh cilantro (optional)
   Tortilla chips (optional)

In large bowl mash avocados. Stir in salsa and sour cream until combined. Stir in pineapple, beans, jalapeño, onion, cilantro, garlic, lime juice, salt, and cumin. Cover and chill for 2 hours or until ready to serve. Sprinkle with Monterey Jack cheese. If desired, sprinkle guacamole with fresh cilantro and serve with tortilla chips. Makes 18 servings.
EACH SERVING 42 cal, 3 g fat, 2 mg chol, 88 mg sodium, 4 g carb, 1 g fiber, 1 g pro.

HAWAIIAN BURGER

LOW FAT

$500 PRIZE: FROM THE VEGETABLE GARDEN

Garden Salsa Jam

Jean Groen Apache Junction, AZ

PREP 30 min. STAND 10 min.

1¾ cups peeled, seeded, and chopped tomatoes
¾   cup nopalitos* (canned marinated tender cactus), rinsed, drained, and chopped
½   cup chopped onion
½   cup finely chopped fresh cilantro
½   cup tomato sauce
⅓   cup chopped pickled jalapeños
1   tsp. finely shredded lime peel
2   Tbsp. fresh lime juice
¼   tsp. bottled hot pepper sauce
4½ cups sugar
1   tsp. salt
¾   cup water
1   1.75-oz. pkg. regular powdered fruit pectin

1. In a very large bowl stir together tomatoes, nopalitos, onion, cilantro, tomato sauce, jalapeños, lime peel and juice, hot pepper sauce, sugar, and salt. Let stand 10 minutes, stirring occasionally.
2. In a small saucepan stir together the water and pectin. Bring to full rolling boil, stirring occasionally. Boil 1 minute. Pour over vegetables. Stir for 5 minutes.
3. Spoon jam into half-pint freezer containers, leaving ¼ inch headspace. Seal, label, and freeze up to 3 months. Thaw before using. Serve with crackers and cheese. Makes 7 half-pint containers (fifty-six 2-Tbsp. servings).
*Find marinated cactus in the Mexican food section of grocery or specialty stores.
EACH SERVING 66 cal, 0 g fat, 0 mg chol, 64 mg sodium, 17 g carb, 0 g fiber, 0 g pro.

$500 PRIZE: BURGER LOVE
Hawaiian Burger

Theresa M. Busby Mount Pleasant, MI

PREP 20 min. GRILL 14 min.

2½ lb. lean ground beef
1   cup crumbled blue cheese (4 oz.)
1   cup finely chopped onion
1   8-oz. can crushed pineapple, drained
½   cup diced ham
1   2.8-oz. package cooked bacon pieces
2   tsp. ground black pepper
1   tsp. garlic powder
8   slices sharp cheddar cheese
8   hamburger buns or plain bagel thins
    Leaf lettuce (optional)
2   medium tomatoes, sliced (optional)
1   medium sweet onion, sliced (optional)

1. In a very large bowl combine beef, blue cheese, onion, pineapple, ham, bacon pieces, pepper, and garlic powder; mix well. Shape meat mixture into eight 1-inch-thick patties.
2. For a charcoal grill, place patties on the grill rack directly over medium coals. Grill, covered, for 12 to 14 minutes or until done (160°F to 165°F), turning once halfway through grilling. Top patties with cheddar cheese. Continue to grill, covered, for 2 minutes more or until cheese is melted. (For a gas grill, preheat grill. Reduce heat to medium. Place patties on grill rack over heat. Cover; grill as directed.) Serve patties on buns. If desired, top with lettuce, tomatoes, and onion. Makes 8 burgers.
EACH SERVING 596 cal, 32 g fat, 137 mg chol, 951 mg sodium, 27 g carb, 2 g fiber, 46 g pro.

GARDEN SALSA JAM

BERRY COBBLER
CAKE

KID FRIENDLY

$500 PRIZE: BERRY DESSERTS

Berry Cobbler Cake

Barbara Piccinino Redding, CA

PREP 20 min. BAKE 45 min.
COOL 45 min. OVEN 350°F

1½ cups all-purpose flour
2 tsp. baking powder
3 cups fresh blackberries
1 cup fresh blueberries
¼ cup butter, softened
1 cup sugar
1 cup milk

2 Tbsp. butter, cut in small pieces
1 recipe Fluffy Cream Cheese Frosting

1. Preheat oven to 350°F. Lightly coat two 8×1½-inch or 9×1½-inch round cake pans with nonstick cooking spray; set aside.
2. In a small bowl combine flour, baking powder, and ¼ tsp. salt. In medium saucepan combine berries and ⅔ cup water. Cook over very low heat to warm and release juices. In large mixing bowl beat ¼ cup butter on medium to high for 30 seconds. Beat in sugar. Alternately add flour and milk; beat on low just until combined. Spread in prepared pans.

3. Remove berries from heat. Use slotted spoon to spoon berries on batter. Pour on remaining juice; dot with butter. Bake 45 minutes or until lightly browned. Cool in pans on racks 45 minutes. Serve with frosting. Makes 12 servings.
Fluffy Cream Cheese Frosting In mixing bowl beat 12 oz. softened cream cheese until smooth. Beat in one 7-oz. jar marshmallow creme until combined. Beat in 1 Tbsp. lemon juice.
EACH SERVING *354 cal, 16 g fat, 48 mg chol, 282 mg sodium, 50 g carb, 3 g fiber, 5 g pro.*

BOURBON-SAUCED PORK CHOPS

$500 PRIZE: PORK ON THE GRILL
Bourbon-Sauced Pork Chops

Chris Gegorek Boone, NC

PREP 15 min. COOK 10 min.
GRILL 14 min.

⅓ cup bourbon or apple juice
3 Tbsp. reduced-sodium soy sauce
3 Tbsp. packed brown sugar
2 Tbsp. cider vinegar
2 cloves garlic, thinly sliced
½ tsp. grated fresh ginger
¼ tsp. ground black pepper
1 Tbsp. cold water
½ tsp. cornstarch
4 1¼-inch-thick bone-in pork chops
  Hot cooked Broccolini or mashed
  potatoes (optional)

1. For sauce, in a small saucepan combine bourbon, soy sauce, brown sugar, vinegar, garlic, ginger, and pepper. Bring to boiling; reduce heat. Simmer, uncovered, about 10 minutes or until reduced to ½ cup. Combine the water and cornstarch. Stir into bourbon mixture. Cook and stir until slightly thickened and bubbly; cook and stir 2 minutes more.
2. For a gas or charcoal grill, grill chops on the rack of a covered grill directly over medium heat for 14 to 16 minutes or until 145°F when tested with an instant-read thermometer or slightly pink in the center, turning once halfway through grilling. Brush occasionally with the sauce during the last 5 minutes of grilling time. If desired, serve chops with Broccolini or mashed potatoes drizzled with any unused sauce. Makes 4 servings.
EACH SERVING 558 cal, 23 g fat, 193 mg chol, 575 mg sodium, 12 g carb, 0 g fiber, 60 g pro.

**DOUBLE CHERRY
CRUNCH PIE**

KID FRIENDLY

$500 PRIZE: BOWLFUL OF CHERRIES
Double Cherry Crunch Pie

Vivian F. Jury East Canton, OH

PREP 35 min. BAKE 20 min.
OVEN 375°F

12 oz. frozen tart cherries, thawed
6 oz. frozen sweet cherries, thawed
¾ cup sugar
3 Tbsp. quick-cooking tapioca
2 3×1-inch strips lemon peel
1 9-inch baked pastry shell
1 cup flaked coconut
½ cup coarsely chopped almonds
½ cup white baking chocolate pieces
¼ cup quick-cooking rolled oats
¼ cup whole wheat flour
2 Tbsp. packed brown sugar
¼ cup butter, melted

1. Preheat oven to 375°F. Drain cherries, reserving juices; if necessary, add water to equal 1 cup. In a medium saucepan combine sugar and tapioca. Stir in reserved juices and lemon peel. Cook and stir over medium heat until thickened and bubbly. Remove and discard lemon peel. Add drained cherries (you should have about 2 cups). Cook and stir 5 minutes more. Pour filling into baked pastry.
2. For topping, in a bowl combine coconut, nuts, baking pieces, oats, flour, and brown sugar. Add butter; stir to combine. Sprinkle topping over filling. Bake 20 to 25 minutes or until topping is golden brown. Cool on rack. Makes 8 servings.
EACH SERVING 545 cal, 28 g fat, 31 mg chol, 271 mg sodium, 68 g carb, 4 g fiber, 6 g pro.

KIDS LOVE 'EM
HEALTH CUPS

KID FRIENDLY | **LOW FAT**

$500 PRIZE: HEALTHY SNACKS

Kids Love 'em Health Cups

Diane Emick-Smith Olean, NY

PREP 15 min. BAKE 12 min.
COOL 10 min. OVEN 325°F

1   cup quick-cooking rolled oats
⅓   cup all-purpose flour
2   tablespoons flaxseed meal
2   tablespoons packed brown sugar
½   teaspoon baking soda
½   cup dried cranberries, coarsely chopped
½   cup slivered almonds, coarsely chopped
2   tablespoons flaked coconut
1   tablespoon unsalted dry-roasted sunflower kernels
3   tablespoons honey or agave nectar
2   tablespoons canola oil
1   tablespoon butter, melted

½   teaspoon vanilla
    Vanilla yogurt, unsalted dry-roasted sunflower kernels, and/or honey (optional)

1. Preheat oven to 325°F. Lightly coat twenty-four 1¾-inch muffin cups with nonstick cooking spray; set aside. Combine oats, flour, flaxseed meal, sugar, and baking soda; stir in cranberries, almonds, coconut, and sunflower kernels. In bowl combine honey, oil, butter, and vanilla; add to oat mixture. Mix well.
2. Press tightly into muffin cups. Bake 12 minutes. Gently press with back of spoon; cool on rack in cups for 10 minutes. Remove from cups and cool.
3. If desired, top with vanilla yogurt, additional sunflower kernels, and a drizzle of honey just before serving. Makes 24 servings.
EACH SERVING 73 cal, 3 g fat, 1 mg chol, 32 mg sodium, 10 g carb, 1 g fiber, 5 g pro.

$500 PRIZE: WALNUT DISHES

Holiday Kale Salad

Nancy Thompson Seattle, WA

PREP 25 min. ROAST 20 min.
OVEN 375°F

2   cups fresh cranberries
4   to 5 cloves garlic, unpeeled
⅓   cup olive oil
¼   cup lemon juice
1   Tbsp. Dijon-style mustard
2   tsp. finely shredded lemon peel
4   cups chopped kale
2   cups cooked wild rice, cooled
1   small bulb fennel, cored and shaved or cut into very thin wedges
1   cup chopped walnuts, toasted
½   cup thinly sliced red sweet pepper
½   cup thinly sliced red onion

1. Preheat oven to 375°F. Line a 15×10×1-inch baking pan with foil or parchment. Place cranberries and garlic cloves on pan. Drizzle with 1 Tbsp. of the olive oil; sprinkle with ¼ tsp. each salt and ground black pepper. Roast, uncovered, for 20 to 25 minutes or until garlic is softened and cranberries are browned at the edges and wrinkled. Cool slightly. Remove garlic peels; finely chop garlic cloves.
2. For dressing, in a screw-top jar combine garlic, remaining olive oil, lemon juice, mustard, and lemon peel. Cover and shake well. Season to taste with salt and ground black pepper.
3. In a large bowl combine cranberries, kale, wild rice, fennel, walnuts, sweet pepper, and onion. Pour dressing over salad; toss to coat. Makes 12 servings.
EACH SERVING 187 cal, 14 g fat, 0 mg chol, 112 mg sodium, 14 g carb, 3 g fiber, 4 g pro.

SALTED ALMOND
PRALINE TART

**$500 PRIZE: CROWD-PLEASING
ALMOND DISHES**

Salted Almond
Praline Tart

Gloria Pleasants Williamsburg, VA

PREP 35 min. BAKE 35 min.
CHILL 2 hr. OVEN 325°F

1   recipe Almond Crust
12   oz. cream cheese, softened
4½   oz. white baking chocolate, chopped
⅓   cup sugar
½   cup light sour cream
¼   tsp. almond extract
1   egg and 1 egg yolk
     Whipped cream
1   recipe Salted Almond Praline
     Fresh raspberries

1. Prepare crust. In saucepan combine 8 oz. cream cheese and chocolate. Stir over low heat until melted. In bowl beat remaining cream cheese on medium to high for 30 seconds. Beat in sugar until smooth. Beat in melted mixture until combined. Beat in sour cream and extract until combined. Beat in egg and yolk until combined. Pour into crust.
2. Bake in 325°F oven 35 minutes or until center is nearly set when gently shaken. Cool on rack 30 minutes. Loosen crust from side of pan, but do not remove. Chill at least 2 hours. Remove tart from pan. Top with whipped cream, Salted Almond Praline, and berries. Makes 12 servings.
Almond Crust Preheat oven to 325°F. In food processor combine 2½ cups broken cinnamon graham crackers, 1 cup toasted sliced almonds, and ⅓ cup sugar. Cover; process until finely ground. Add ⅓ cup softened butter. Pulse to combine. Press into bottom and sides of 10-inch fluted tart pan with removable bottom. Chill 15 minutes. Place on foil-lined baking sheet. Bake 20 minutes or until lightly browned; cool.
Salted Almond Praline Preheat oven to 325°F. Line baking pan with foil and spray with nonstick cooking spray. In a medium bowl combine 1 cup sliced almonds, ½ cup sugar, 2 Tbsp. melted butter, 1 Tbsp. water, 1 tsp. ground cinnamon, and ½ tsp. sea salt. Spread evenly in pan. Bake 20 minutes or until golden brown. Cool completely on rack. Break into pieces.
EACH SERVING *562 cal, 30 g fat, 91 mg chol, 237 mg sodium, 69 g carb, 22 g fiber, 10g pro.*

**MELON AND
HERB
BREAD SALAD**

$500 PRIZE: HOLIDAY BRUNCH SALADS

Melon and Herb Bread Salad

Kelly Ortigara Chicago, IL

PREP 30 min. BAKE 10 min.
OVEN 375°F

2	6-inch pita bread rounds, torn into bite-size pieces
1	Tbsp. olive oil
½	tsp. dried thyme, crushed
¼	tsp. sesame seeds
5	oz. mixed baby greens (4 to 5 cups)
½	cup fresh mint leaves
¼	cup fresh parsley, coarsely chopped
2	cups cubed seedless watermelon and/or cantaloupe
1¾	cups sliced cucumber (1 medium)
½	cup sliced red onion
½	cup crumbled feta cheese
2	Tbsp. pomegranate seeds
1	recipe Lemon Vinaigrette

1. Preheat oven to 375°F. Arrange pita pieces on a 15×10×1-inch baking pan. In a bowl whisk together olive oil, thyme, sesame seeds, ¼ tsp. salt, and ¼ tsp. ground black pepper. Drizzle mixture over pita pieces; toss to coat. Spread in an even layer. Bake 10 to 12 minutes or until golden and crisp, stirring once.
2. On a large platter arrange greens, mint, parsley, melon, cucumber, and red onion. Sprinkle with cheese and pomegranate seeds. Top with pita chips. Pour over Lemon Vinaigrette; toss to coat. Makes 6 to 8 servings.
Lemon Vinaigrette In a screw-top jar combine ¼ cup olive oil, 2 Tbsp. pomegranate juice, 2 Tbsp. red wine vinegar, 4 tsp. lemon juice, 1½ tsp. finely shredded lemon peel, and ½ tsp. honey. Cover; shake well.
EACH SERVING *228 cal, 14 g fat, 11 mg chol, 352 mg sodium, 21 g carb, 2 g fiber, 5 g pro.*

PEACH MANGO PIE

KID FRIENDLY

$500 PRIZE: SUMMER PIES

Peach Mango Pie

Jane Ozment Purcell, OK

PREP 30 min. BAKE 50 min.
OVEN 375°F

1	recipe Pastry
1	cup sugar
2	Tbsp. all-purpose flour
¼	tsp. each ground ginger and ground cinnamon
⅛	tsp. ground nutmeg
3	cups thinly sliced, peeled fresh peaches or frozen unsweetened peach slices, thawed
3	cups sliced, seeded, and peeled fresh mangoes
2	tsp. fresh lime juice
1	egg white
	Vanilla ice cream (optional)

1. Preheat oven to 375°F. Prepare Pastry. For filling, combine sugar, flour, spices, and ¼ tsp. salt. Add fruit; toss. Transfer to pastry-lined pie plate. Drizzle with lime juice. Trim pastry. Roll remaining pastry into a 12-inch circle. Cut slits in pastry; place on filling. Trim to ½ inch beyond edge; fold under bottom pastry. Crimp edge. Combine egg white and 1 Tbsp. water. Brush over pie. Sprinkle with 1 tsp. coarse sugar. Cover edge with foil. Place pie on middle oven rack with a foil-lined baking sheet on rack below. Bake 25 minutes. Remove foil from pie; bake 25 minutes more or until filling is bubbly. Cool. Serve with vanilla ice cream if desired. Makes 8 servings.
Pastry In bowl combine 2½ cups flour and 1 tsp. salt. Cut in ¾ cup shortening until pieces are pea size. Using ½ to ⅔ cup milk, sprinkle 1 Tbsp. milk over mixture; toss with fork. Repeat, 1 Tbsp. at a time, until moistened. Gather into a ball; knead gently. Divide in half. On a lightly floured surface roll 1 ball into a 12-inch circle. Transfer to a 9-inch pie plate. Cover; set aside.
EACH SERVING *489 cal, 20 g fat, 1 mg chol, 380 mg sodium, 73 g carb, 3 g fiber, 6 g pro.*

BERRY-ORANGE
COFFEE CAKES

$500 PRIZE: COOKING WITH CRANBERRIES

Berry-Orange Coffee Cakes

Mary Beth Mandola Houston, TX

PREP 25 min. BAKE 20 min.
OVEN 350°F

2	cups all-purpose flour
1½	tsp. ground cinnamon
½	tsp. baking soda
½	tsp. baking powder
⅓	cup butter, softened
½	cup each packed brown and granulated sugars
1	cup whole-milk ricotta cheese
1	egg
1	Tbsp. finely shredded orange peel
1	Tbsp. orange juice
½	tsp. vanilla
1½	cups fresh cranberries, coarsely chopped
2	Tbsp. finely chopped crystallized ginger
1	recipe Orange Glaze
½	cup walnuts, toasted and chopped
	Orange peel (optional)

1. Preheat oven to 350°F. Grease fifteen 2½-inch muffin cups. In a bowl combine flour, cinnamon, baking soda, baking powder, and ¼ tsp. salt. In a large bowl beat butter and sugars with an electric mixer until fluffy. Beat in ricotta, egg, orange peel, orange juice, and vanilla. Stir in flour mixture just until combined. Fold in cranberries and ginger.
2. Fill muffin cups ⅔ full. Bake 20 to 25 minutes or until a toothpick inserted near center comes out clean. Cool in pan 5 minutes. Remove; cool slightly. Spoon on glaze. Sprinkle with nuts and additional orange peel if desired. Makes 15 cakes.
Orange Glaze Combine 1 cup powdered sugar, 1 Tbsp. orange juice, and ½ tsp. vanilla. Stir in 2 Tbsp. melted butter and ½ tsp. shredded orange peel.
EACH SERVING *268 cal, 11 g fat, 36 mg chol, 169 mg sodium, 39 g carb, 1 g fiber, 5 g pro.*

SPICY MARINATED PORK AND EGGS

$500 PRIZE: SLOW COOKER BRUNCH

Spicy Marinated Pork and Eggs

Nora Romero Albuquerque, NM

PREP 30 min. MARINATE overnight
COOK 6 hr. (low) or 3 hr. (high)
+ 15 min.

1	lb. boneless pork shoulder
1	cup bottled thick and chunky salsa
1	Tbsp. vegetable oil
1	large white onion, coarsely chopped
2	lb. potatoes, peeled and cut into 1-inch pieces
2	fresh green chile peppers, seeded and chopped (1 cup) (see note, page 69)
2	cloves garlic, minced
6	eggs
1	cup shredded cheddar cheese (4 oz.)
	Fresh cilantro
	Sliced fresh jalapeño chile peppers (see note, page 69)

1. Trim fat from pork. Cut meat into 1-inch pieces. Place meat in a resealable plastic bag set in a shallow dish. Top with salsa. Seal bag; turn to coat. Refrigerate overnight.
2. Lightly grease an oval 3½- to 4-quart slow cooker* with the oil. Place onion in cooker. Add pork and marinade mixture, potatoes, green chile peppers, and garlic. Cover; cook on low-heat setting for 6 to 7 hours or on high-heat setting for 3 to 3½ hours.
3. Using the bottom of a ladle or serving spoon, make 6 indentations in the top of the mixture. Crack an egg into each indentation. If using low-heat setting, turn cooker to high-heat setting. Cover; cook 15 minutes more or until egg whites are set and yolks are thickened. Top with cheese, cilantro, and, if desired, jalapeño slices. Makes 6 servings.
EACH SERVING *405 cal, 16 g fat, 251 mg chol, 494 mg sodium, 33 g carb, 3 g fiber, 32 g pro.*
***Note** If you don't have an oval slow cooker, you can still make the recipe. Just be aware that the eggs might run together on top.

CHICKEN
POT PIE SOUP

$500 PRIZE: HEARTY SOUPS

Chicken Pot Pie Soup

Beth Seuferer West Des Moines, IA

PREP 35 min. BAKE 10 min.
OVEN 450°F

½ cup each chopped carrot and celery
⅓ cup chopped onion
2 cloves garlic, minced
1 Tbsp. butter
½ tsp. seasoned salt
½ tsp. dry mustard
½ tsp. chili powder
½ tsp. ground black pepper
¼ tsp. curry powder
4 cups chicken broth
2 cups chopped cooked chicken breast
2 cups dried medium egg noodles
1 cup half-and-half or light cream
1 Tbsp. all-purpose flour
1 cup chopped fresh broccoli
⅓ cup frozen peas
1 recipe Quick Biscuits

1. In a saucepan cook carrot, celery, onion, and garlic in hot butter about 5 minutes or until tender. Stir in seasoned salt, mustard, chili powder, pepper, curry powder, broth, chicken, and noodles. Bring to boiling; reduce heat. Simmer, covered, 10 minutes or until noodles are tender. Meanwhile, prepare Quick Biscuits.
2. In a small bowl whisk together half-and-half and flour; add to saucepan. Add broccoli and peas. Simmer, uncovered, 5 minutes or until slightly thickened. To serve, spoon soup into bowls. Top with Quick Biscuits. Makes 6 servings.
Quick Biscuits Preheat oven to 450°F. In a bowl combine 2 cups all-purpose flour, 4 tsp. baking powder, 4 tsp. sugar, and ½ tsp. cream of tartar. Cut in ½ cup butter to make coarse crumbs. Make a well in center; add ⅔ cup milk. Using a fork, stir just until moistened. On a lightly floured surface gently knead dough until it holds together. Pat into an 8-inch square. Cut into 12 rectangles; place 1 inch apart on an ungreased baking sheet. Bake 10 to 12 minutes or until golden.
EACH SERVING *544 cal, 26 g fat, 117 mg chol, 1,272 mg sodium, 54 g carb, 3 g fiber, 25 g pro.*

GRAND PRIZE WINNER

Banana-Nut Pound Cake

Brenda Camp Orbell Pittsboro, NC

Not only delicious straight out of the oven with a big scoop of melty ice cream, this cake freezes like a dream. With this moist, dense cake, pecans give the cake bottom a delightfully unexpected crunch. "I was snowed in one day, had some ripe bananas on hand, and wanted to bake something other than a banana bread," Brenda says. "The first time I made the recipe, I took it to work for a going-away party—there was hardly a crumb left. It's a moist cake that's not heavy."
PREP 25 min. BAKE 1 hr. 20 min.
COOL 10 min. OVEN 325°F

3 cups all-purpose flour
½ tsp. baking powder
½ cup butter, softened
3 cups granulated sugar
4 eggs
2 medium bananas, mashed (about 1 cup)
¼ cup bourbon or low-fat milk
1 Tbsp. vanilla
1 cup chopped pecans, toasted
   Powdered sugar

1. Preheat oven to 325°F. Grease and flour a 10-inch fluted tube pan; set aside. Combine flour, baking powder, and ½ tsp. salt; set aside.
2. In large bowl beat cream cheese and butter with an electric mixer on medium speed until combined. Gradually add sugar, beating about 7 minutes or until light. Add eggs, one at a time, beating 1 minute after each; scrape bowl frequently. In a bowl combine bananas, bourbon, and vanilla. Alternately add flour mixture and banana mixture to butter mixture; beat on low to medium speed after each addition just until combined. Stir in pecans. Spread evenly in pan.
3. Bake for 80 minutes or until a toothpick inserted near center comes out clean. Cool cake in the pan on a wire rack for 10 minutes. Remove from pan; cool on rack. Sprinkle with powdered sugar. Serve with berries or ice cream if desired. Makes 12 servings.
EACH SERVING *573 cal, 23 g fat, 103 mg chol, 271 mg sodium, 84 g carb, 2 g fiber, 8 g pro.*

Recipe Index

Nutrition information.

With each recipe, we give important nutrition information you can easily apply to your own needs. You'll find the calorie count of each serving and the amount, in grams, of fat, saturated fat, cholesterol, sodium, carbohydrates, fiber, and protein to help you keep tabs on what you eat. To stay in line with the nutrition breakdown of each recipe, follow the suggested number of servings.

How we analyze.

The Better Homes and Gardens® Test Kitchen computer analyzes each recipe for the nutritional value of a single serving.

• The analysis does not include optional ingredients.

• We use the first serving size listed when a range is given. For example: If we say a recipe "Makes 4 to 6 servings," the nutrition information is based on 4 servings.

• When ingredient choices (such as butter or margarine) appear in a recipe, we use the first one mentioned for analysis. The ingredient order does not mean we prefer one ingredient over another.

• When milk and eggs are recipe ingredients, the analysis is calculated using 2 percent (reduced-fat) milk and large eggs.

What you need.

The dietary guidelines below suggest nutrient levels that moderately active adults should strive to eat each day. There is no real harm in going over or under these guidelines in any single day, but it is a good idea to aim for a balanced diet over time.

Calories: About 2,000

Total fat: Less than 65 grams

Saturated fat: Less than 20 grams

Cholesterol: Less than 300 milligrams

Carbohydrates: About 300 grams

Sodium: Less than 2,400 milligrams

Dietary fiber: 20 to 30 grams

Low Fat icon.

Certain recipes throughout the book have an icon above the recipe title that indicates the recipe is low fat. For a recipe to earn this icon, it must meet certain nutritional requirements. For a main dish one serving should have 12 grams of fat per serving or less, one serving of a side dish should have 5 grams of fat or less, an appetizer serving should have 2 grams of fat or less, and cookies and desserts should have 2 grams of fat or less per serving. Occasionally the fat level will slightly exceed one of the recommended numbers, but typically they remain below the listed amounts.

Metric Information

The charts on this page provide a guide for converting measurements from the U.S. customary system, which is used throughout this book, to the metric system.

Product Differences

Most of the ingredients called for in the recipes in this book are available in most countries. However, some are known by different names. Here are some common American ingredients and their possible counterparts:

- Sugar (white) is granulated, fine granulated, or castor sugar.
- Powdered sugar is icing sugar.
- All-purpose flour is enriched, bleached or unbleached white household flour. When self-rising flour is used in place of all-purpose flour in a recipe that calls for leavening, omit the leavening agent (baking soda or baking powder) and salt.
- Light-color corn syrup is golden syrup.
- Cornstarch is cornflour.
- Baking soda is bicarbonate of soda.
- Vanilla or vanilla extract is vanilla essence.
- Green, red, or yellow sweet peppers are capsicums or bell peppers.
- Golden raisins are sultanas.

Volume and Weight

The United States traditionally uses cup measures for liquid and solid ingredients. The chart below shows the approximate imperial and metric equivalents. If you are accustomed to weighing solid ingredients, the following approximate equivalents will be helpful.

- 1 cup butter, castor sugar, or rice = 8 ounces = ½ pound = 250 grams
- 1 cup flour = 4 ounces = ¼ pound = 125 grams
- 1 cup icing sugar = 5 ounces = 150 grams

Canadian and U.S. volume for a cup measure is 8 fluid ounces (237 ml), but the standard metric equivalent is 250 ml.

1 British imperial cup is 10 fluid ounces.

In Australia, 1 tablespoon equals 20 ml, and there are 4 teaspoons in the Australian tablespoon.

Spoon measures are used for smaller amounts of ingredients. Although the size of the tablespoon varies slightly in different countries, for practical purposes and for recipes in this book, a straight substitution is all that's necessary. Measurements made using cups or spoons always should be level unless stated otherwise.

Common Weight Range Replacements

Imperial / U.S.	Metric
½ ounce	15 g
1 ounce	25 g or 30 g
4 ounces (¼ pound)	115 g or 125 g
8 ounces (½ pound)	225 g or 250 g
16 ounces (1 pound)	450 g or 500 g
1¼ pounds	625 g
1½ pounds	750 g
2 pounds or 2¼ pounds	1,000 g or 1 Kg

Oven Temperature Equivalents

Fahrenheit Setting	Celsius Setting*	Gas Setting
300°F	150°C	Gas Mark 2 (very low)
325°F	160°C	Gas Mark 3 (low)
350°F	180°C	Gas Mark 4 (moderate)
375°F	190°C	Gas Mark 5 (moderate)
400°F	200°C	Gas Mark 6 (hot)
425°F	220°C	Gas Mark 7 (hot)
450°F	230°C	Gas Mark 8 (very hot)
475°F	240°C	Gas Mark 9 (very hot)
500°F	260°C	Gas Mark 10 (extremely hot)
Broil	Broil	Grill

*Electric and gas ovens may be calibrated using celsius. However, for an electric oven, increase celsius setting 10 to 20 degrees when cooking above 160°C. For convection or forced air ovens (gas or electric), lower the temperature setting 25°F/10°C when cooking at all heat levels.

Baking Pan Sizes

Imperial / U.S.	Metric
9×1½-inch round cake pan	22- or 23×4-cm (1.5 L)
9×1½-inch pie plate	22- or 23×4-cm (1 L)
8×8×2-inch square cake pan	20×5-cm (2 L)
9×9×2-inch square cake pan	22- or 23×4.5-cm (2.5 L)
11×7×1½-inch baking pan	28×17×4-cm (2 L)
2-quart rectangular baking pan	30×19×4.5-cm (3 L)
13×9×2-inch baking pan	34×22×4.5-cm (3.5 L)
15×10×1-inch jelly roll pan	40×25×2-cm
9×5×3-inch loaf pan	23×13×8-cm (2 L)
2-quart casserole	2 L

U.S. / Standard Metric Equivalents

⅛ teaspoon = 0.5 ml	
¼ teaspoon = 1 ml	
½ teaspoon = 2 ml	
1 teaspoon = 5 ml	
1 tablespoon = 15 ml	
2 tablespoons = 25 ml	
¼ cup = 2 fluid ounces = 50 ml	
⅓ cup = 3 fluid ounces = 75 ml	
½ cup = 4 fluid ounces = 125 ml	
⅔ cup = 5 fluid ounces = 150 ml	
¾ cup = 6 fluid ounces = 175 ml	
1 cup = 8 fluid ounces = 250 ml	
2 cups = 1 pint = 500 ml	
1 quart = 1 litre	